Putting Resear[ch] to Work in Elementary Physical Education: Conversations in the Gym

Lawrence F. Locke
University of Massachusetts

Dolly Lambdin
University of Texas

Human Kinetics

Library of Congress Cataloging-in-Publication Data

Locke, Lawrence F.
    Putting research to work in elementary physical education :
conversations in the gym / Lawrence F. Locke, Dolly Lambdin.
        p. cm.
    ISBN 0-7360-4531-7 (softcover)
    1. Physical education and training--Study and teaching (Elementary)
2. Physical education and training--Research. I. Lambdin, Dolly, 1951-
II. Title.
    GV362 .L63 2003
    372.86--dc21   2002007808

ISBN: 0-7360-4531-7

The Web addresses cited in this text were current as of October 22, 2002, unless otherwise noted.

Acquisitions Editor: Scott Wikgren
Managing Editor: Susan C. Hagan
Copyeditor: Scott Jerard
Proofreader: Jim Burns
Graphic Designer: Nancy Rasmus
Graphic Artist: Yvonne Griffith
Cover Designer: Kristin A. Darling
Photographers (author photos): Michael Janeczek (p. 206, top) and Teresita Ramirez (p. 206, bottom)
Art Manager: Kelly Hendren
Illustrator: Kelly Hendren
Printer: Versa Press

10 9 8 7 6 5 4 3 2 1

Human Kinetics
Web site: www.HumanKinetics.com

United States: Human Kinetics, P.O. Box 5076, Champaign, IL 61825-5076
800-747-4457
e-mail: humank@hkusa.com

Canada: Human Kinetics, 475 Devonshire Road Unit 100, Windsor, ON N8Y 2L5
800-465-7301 (in Canada only)
e-mail: orders@hkcanada.com

Europe: Human Kinetics, 107 Bradford Road, Stanningley, Leeds LS28 6AT, United Kingdom
+44 (0) 113 255 5665
e-mail: hk@hkeurope.com

Australia: Human Kinetics, 57A Price Avenue, Lower Mitcham, South Australia 5062
08 8277 1555
e-mail: liahka@senet.com.au

New Zealand: Human Kinetics, P.O. Box 105-231, Auckland Central
09-523-3462
e-mail: hkp@ihug.co.nz

To
Andrew,
Becca,
Christopher,
Jason,
Jonathan,
Joseph,
Katherine,
and
Matthew,
the next generations, with thanks, high hopes, and all our love.

CONTENTS

PART I
The Basics—Numbers, Time, Space, Equipment, and Behaviors

PART II
Managing the Class

PART III
Interactions Among Students

PART IV
Strategies for Teaching and Learning

PART V
The Voices of Students

PART VI
Teachers in the Workplace—Training, Experience, and Context

PART VII
Assessment As Part of Teaching

PREFACE

This book is written for physical educators. As we wrote it, we included in our imagined reading audience schoolteachers, teacher educators, preservice students, graduate students, school and program administrators, and (perhaps surprisingly) researchers doing work in teaching and curriculum. The contents of our book include the exchanged comments between a researcher and a teacher (our "conversations") as together we considered 30 studies that concerned topics such as instruction, class management, program design, and workplace conditions in elementary school physical education.

How Each Chapter Is Organized

Each study is briefly described, then commented on from a researcher's perspective, a teacher's perspective, and finally, a shared perspective. Although Locke wrote the first draft of the researcher's perspective, and Lambdin did likewise for the teacher's perspective, both sections were exchanged in draft, discussed, and subsequently revised. It is in that sense, then, that the final product reflects a conversational exchange between professional colleagues.

An Invitation to Readers

We invite you to join us on a journey through the research products of 69 scholars (many of the selected studies involved several investigators), all of whom have used their inquiry skills to achieve a better understanding of physical education. In each of these accounts, presented here in the abbreviated form of annotations, you will have a window into the minds of the investigators as they puzzled about teachers, students, and programs. What you see as you peer through those openings may seem surprising or expected, simple or elaborate, certain or tentative, or even unsettling or reassuring. But on this journey, we can guarantee one thing—the view will never be boring.

Reading the reports of the selected studies for this book gave us great pleasure. The task rarely felt like work, and it never failed to connect with our own experiences, both past and present. Best of all, however, what we found was often valuable to us. Today, in our various roles as teachers, advisors, and scholars, we regularly use some of the information, ideas, and questions acquired in the course of preparing this book. Our hope is that you will make similar discoveries that prove valuable for your own work.

The Scope of This Book

To avoid any possibility that you will be disappointed by the content of the following chapters, we want to be explicit about what we have not addressed. This is not a book about how to do research on teaching nor is it a compendium of pedagogy in the gym or a textbook on teaching skills supported by research-based knowledge (for the latter, see appendix E). Neither is this a guide to the improvement of instruction or program design in the public schools. This book simply offers an invitation for you to eavesdrop on a career-long conversation between a researcher and a teacher—a professional dialogue that emerged from the distinct vantage points of formal inquiry and practical application, no more and no less.

We would like to have you join in this ongoing conversation, but, of course, that must be your own decision. You can decide to read and reflect in solitude, or you can read and share your thoughts with others. Naturally, we would enjoy hearing your reactions to the studies and to our conversations. Consider us extended members of your discussion group, and, if inclined, feel free to contact us through e-mail or postal mail. We are readily available, and we certainly would welcome your comments. Our contact information can be found on page 206.

Authors and Readers: Who Are "We" and "You"?

We are two physical educators who have taught in schools, worked in teacher education, and conducted research. Our collective time of service in education totals more than 75 years, and our continuing dialogue about physical education dates back to 1970. Throughout all of that time, we have never failed to be delighted by what we could teach each other. Simple longevity, of course, gives us no right to claim great expertise. However, what we do have is substantial practice in conversing about the work of teaching and the ways in which research can inform that practice.

We can also claim the special advantage of a perfectly matched set of vantage points. Although much in our careers overlap, one of us (Lambdin) has maintained deep and active roots in the crafts of teaching and program development as a teacher with specialization in elementary school physical education. The other, Locke, has focused his efforts on exploring the planning and uses of research as a professor and research consultant.

When we have the opportunity to talk together about a study, what we bring to bear is at once the same and yet, distinctly different. Where our dialogue cuts across the vantage points determined by our careers, we can produce the sort of hybrid vigor often observed in multidisciplinary collaborations. Of course (lest you wonder), we sometimes find that we just have to agree to disagree on some point of understanding, but such an occurrence has only served to lend a kind of zesty unpredictability to spice the conversation.

Finally, in case you have not already noticed, this book is a distinctly personal product. It reflects the beliefs and experiences of two authors whose careers have happily engaged them in the work of physical education to this very day. We intend to be fully present in these pages as commentators on research and practice, and as advisors to your own efforts. In consequence, you will find the words *we* and *you* on almost every page.

We know that you the reader will have various motives for reading this text—some readers, for example, may be conscripts rather than volunteers (and for the former, we do hope to provide a mostly painless experience). Further, each reader brings a unique set of experiences, dispositions, and needs to this encounter. Accordingly, we expect a variety of responses, particularly in terms of what is—

or what is not—found to be meaningful, useful, or satisfying. We have accepted such reactions as inevitable, and we have responded to that inevitability by simply doing our best to design a book that can be used by different people in different ways.

Having introduced ourselves, we now can turn our attention to you, the reader. So, who actually reads research on teaching physical education anyway? Perhaps you will be tempted to respond with: "Mostly other researchers and a few of their unlucky graduate students!" Despite the evident cynicism, that response actually does contain more than just a grain of truth—and about that point, we want to be both clear and frank.

Research reports published in scholarly journals indeed are written with the intention that they will be read by other investigators working in the same field of inquiry. Outside readers (in educational research most particularly, teachers) are not the author's imagined audience—which of course accounts for the arcane style and format employed in most reports, as well as the highly specialized books, journals, and electronic outlets selected for their publication. In writing reports that are inaccessible to most outside readers, researchers intend neither disrespect nor a display of intellectual superiority. They simply are doing what is practical in terms of the nature of their work as scholars.

The formal writing style used by researchers reflects the need to be precise and absolutely clear about what was done. That requirement has roots that lie deeper than just the motive for writing lucid prose. It is through the use of correct and careful procedures that researchers can argue for the credibility of their findings, and telling that exacting story requires a systematic (rather than casual) use of words. As a consequence, the text you find in reports is subject to discipline and rules we do not apply to everyday conversation or to other forms of writing. Research prose can be at times graceful, but it always is dense, restrained, exact, and packed with the special terminology shared by other researchers. All of which makes for reliable communication among the inside readers and for difficult comprehension by the outside readers.

Fortunately, we were not so constrained by the exacting demands for communication among scholarly peers. Because most of you are likely to be among the many outside readers who find the task of reading research challenging (at best) or impossible (at worst), we elected to provide "translations" in the form of brief, nontechnical annotations. Once the problem of reading technical material has been eliminated or at least reduced (we make no claim to being perfect translators), you may be surprised at how valuable the content can be to your thinking and teaching.

The Purposes for This Book

In writing this book, we were guided by just three main purposes, all of them quite straightforward:

1. To present research in an understandable way
2. To illustrate how ideas found in research can be helpful to physical educators
3. To demonstrate the value of sharing perspectives

In the following sections, we will individually address and elaborate on each guiding purpose.

To Present Research in an Understandable Way

First, we want to present research questions, procedures, and findings in a way that teachers and other nonresearchers can understand and come to value. By making a diverse group of studies accessible, we hope to enrich how physical educators think about their work, and of course, we hope to encourage the practical application of research-based information to teaching methods and program designs.

All of the studies annotated here have been previously published, and with sufficient time and adequate retrieval skills, they can all be accessed by any interested reader. All of that required legwork, however, has already been done in this book. In addition, we have provided the value of annotations, which extract the essential elements of each study and present them in economical and user-friendly terms. That no similar resource is available for students, teachers, and others interested in elementary school physical education makes this text truly unique within the literature of our field.

The task of making research reports more accessible turned out to have much less to do with simplification than it did with contextualization. Simplification is just leaving out detail that was not required for our present purpose. Contextualization, on the other hand, is helping the reader understand how a particular question fits into the wider frameworks of other questions, how its answers serve the different purposes for education, where the question resides in the range of challenges

in the practice of teaching, and how knowledge accumulated from other studies supplements the question at hand. In that sense, the challenging part of translating the research was not decoding the reports. We had to figure out how to situate the studies in ways that allowed the readers to connect the process and products of inquiry with their own experiences. For us, conversation between teacher and researcher seemed to be a perfect vehicle for finding that location.

To Illustrate How Ideas Found in Research Can Be Helpful to Physical Educators

Our second guiding purpose was to argue the following: When given commonsense advice about how to read our annotations (or even the original published reports), physical educators of all kinds can find research far less mysterious and a lot more useful. Our ideas about this assertion were formed by a combination of our own experience as educators and by a review of what we regarded as relevant research—that is, studies of how teachers actually read and respond to research. If you are interested in learning more about that topic, see appendix C, where we have included a brief survey of what we found in those reports. In addition, we placed our own annotations for a representative collection of such studies in appendix D.

From our review of that material, we extracted information that proved to be valuable in establishing criteria for the studies to be included, as well as in deciding on the general format for the book. In some of the reports, we found information about teachers as readers of research that was completely new to us. In some cases, that information involved ideas that we never would have hit upon if we just had sat around thinking and talking about what sort of book would truly be user-friendly for our audience. Put simply, we found valuable assistance through doing the very thing we are suggesting for our readers—paying attention to research as a source of valuable insights, ideas, facts, and possibilities.

We found one particular finding that appeared several times in the items reviewed. To help teachers be more successful when attacking the task of reading research, investigators found that it requires no more than a simple set of reading guidelines—basic, nontechnical advice on how to do it. That fact served to remind us that most teachers are competent readers and skilled learners . . . which is probably one reason why they became teachers in the first place. Our presentation of information, therefore, needed only to be clear and well organized, rather than crafted to meet some imagined set of limitations.

Another impact on our preparation of this book was the fact that most teachers require only some clear instructions to begin improving how they consume research. It was precisely for that reason that we devised a relatively simple and straightforward set of guidelines for reading research (see pp. xx–xxv). We urge you to read and consider them before beginning to immerse yourself in the studies and our accompanying comments. Even if you later find yourself returning to the guidelines for additional assistance, some initial preparation will serve you well.

To Demonstrate the Value of Sharing Perspectives

The third and final purpose that guided our writing was to demostrate the following: Interesting things happen when you bring the knowledge and vantage points of researchers and practitioners around a single study. We believe such exchanges (when they are respectful and open) have been much more rare than commonly is assumed. The 30 examples in the following chapters are intended to give an explicit demonstration of how stimulating and potentially fruitful such dialogues can be—and why they should become far more commonplace.

There was a deeper agenda, of course, behind the immediate intentions that shaped the book. We wanted to persuade you to try our approach to reading and thinking about research, and we wanted to encourage you to have meaningful exchanges with professional colleagues concerning the uses of research in application to everyday practice.

Our agenda imposed constraints on both content and style—that is, not much would be accomplished if we made demands for specialized knowledge that some of our readers might not possess. Accordingly, you will find that you do not need a highly technical vocabulary, advanced scientific and mathematical knowledge (including statistics), or a detailed background concerning research methods. The only requirements to navigate the journey ahead are careful reading and serious reflection.

Even more important than our desire to encourage reflection and conversation was the need to make doing so relevant to the concerns of teachers and those who care about elementary school physi-

cal education. Our agenda for making the relevance of research too obvious to miss led us to employ two simple standards for deciding which studies to use in this book. First, they had to be understandable, and second, they had to offer practical implications. Put in functional terms, the 30 research reports discussed here were selected for their intelligibility and for their obvious relevance to problems and issues easily recognized by anyone familiar with what happens in a physical education class.

Reading the Original Research Reports

It is inevitable that one question will occur to many of you: Was it our hidden agenda to lure you into reading the original reports from which the 30 summaries were drawn? Our response is simple: No. Some of you might find it interesting or useful to do so, but probably most of you will not. Do so at your own discretion and leisure, but it is certainly not required.

The primary motive for consulting the journal versions would simply be to get the rest of the story. We tried to accurately represent what was in the original report, and we tried to be fair in our paraphrasing of the authors' own commentaries; however, our coverage of each study was far from comprehensive. For obvious reasons, we simply omitted a great deal of detail and in some reports, even entire subsections. If a particular study appears to contain information that might be valuable in your work (or just be plain interesting), then you might profit from perusing the original. Otherwise, our summaries should be entirely sufficient for the present purpose.

A Note of Encouragement

Finally, we are perfectly aware that even carefully crafted research annotations can present some significant problems of comprehension for the beginner. The process of consuming research, though, is in large measure a skill that can be developed through simple practice, particularly if you have some initial assistance of the kind we have tried to offer here. In short, you do not have to be trained as a researcher to read annotations of research reports with reasonable comprehension. If your purposes are those of a teacher or student looking for useful ideas and provocative questions, we think you will find this book to be a wise place to begin.

Additional Resources

In addition to the help we have included here, there are excellent supplementary guides that can provide beginners with assistance in reading and understanding research. For reasons that should be self-evident, we think that one of those, *Reading and Understanding Research* by Locke, Silverman, and Spirduso (1998), would make a particularly fine companion to this book. If you would like to examine a range of such support tools, we have provided in appendix A an annotated bibliography of introductory-level books that deal with reading and understanding research.

A Final Word

We hope that you now have a clear picture of who we are, why and how the book was written, and what it contains. In the introduction that follows, we will explain how to use this text for both fun and profit.

ACKNOWLEDGMENTS

Between the two of us, we have been the beneficiaries collectively of nearly 8 decades of informative dialogues, fruitful collaborations, and vigorous debates with a truly remarkable array of mentors, colleagues, and students. If, at the outset of our professional careers, we had set out to locate the best possible people from whom to learn about the work of teaching physical education, it is doubtful that we could have found better than those we encountered. Much of this book constitutes our gatherings from them.

Some groups and individuals, of course, stand out in memory, and we will acknowledge their contributions here as worthy proxies for the whole. Our first note of appreciation must go to our faculty colleagues as well as our undergraduate and graduate students at the University of Texas, Mitchell College, University of Massachusetts, University of New Mexico, and Columbia University Teachers College. In addition, there were invaluable contributions from colleagues and students at the Town School, Cathedral School, St. Andrew's Episcopal School, St. Mark's School, and Blanton Elementary School, as well as the public schools of Austin, Texas and West Hartford, Connecticut. Across the years, those people provided lively human context for the development of our ideas about the uses of research in physical education. We extend our deepest appreciation for all they have taught us.

More directly with regard to preparation of this book, our gratitude goes to our technical readers, Kim C. Graber and Katherine I. Locke, who patiently and perceptively sorted through the tangles of our first drafts. Subsequently, our professional colleagues Jim DeLine, Linda Griffin, Mary Henninger, Alisa James, Karen Pagnano, Kevin Patton, Teresita Rameriz, and Fran Rush all gave us feedback on significant portions of this book and through their helpful comments and suggestions contributed directly to the final product.

As always, the primary support in the process of producing a book had to come from the professionals. Susan C. Hagan was our editor at Human Kinetics, and in that role she managed to guide us through the development process with just the perfect blend of firmness and flexibility. Scott Jerard copyedited every line of every page, and in doing so he provided a level of economy, clarity, and precision for our prose that we never could have achieved with our own less-than-modest writing abilities. Whatever is homely or obscure in what follows can be attributed to our perverse stubbornness because we did not always have the wit to take the sound advice of the pros.

If you already have glanced through the following chapters, you will understand the extent of our debt to the authors of the 30 research reports that served as the objects of our dialogue. This book belongs to each of those investigators as well as to the two of us. Every one of them has our respect as a scholar and our appreciation for providing us with an opportunity to use their ideas, creative insights, and hard work for our own ends.

We have two other author-scholars to thank for the initial inspiration to undertake the project, as well as for the general format in which it has been cast. In 1993, David Berliner and Ursala Casanova combined their years of experience as teachers, professors, administrators, and scholars to produce the elegant paperbound volume *Putting Research to Work in Your School*. Designed with a format similar to the present text, their book was intended to stimulate reflection and discussion among classroom teachers. It will be obvious that both our intended readership and the details of our conversations about research differ substantially from their earlier effort. Nevertheless, there is no doubt that we here have offered Berliner and Casanova the most sincere form of all flattery—a close imitation of their original idea.

In addition, there also is much within the following pages that reflects invaluable guidance by the staff at Human Kinetics. Foremost among those contributions, however, was the invitation of its CEO, Rainer Martens, who said, simply, "You should write it, and then we will publish it." Among many other laudable characteristics, he is a man of his word.

Finally, our deepest appreciation must be reserved for our respective spouses whose patience, encouragement, and understanding sustained the entire effort. Because they are both teachers and scholars, it is certain that our dialogues with them (over hundreds of hurried breakfasts and endless hours of pillow talk) are extensively represented in these pages. Larry and Lorraine, as for so much else in our lives, we stand always in your debt.

INTRODUCTION

Reading Research—
A Commonsense View

In this introduction, we explain several things about our book: how it is organized; how to put it to best use; and how to interpret the definition, characteristics, and scope of the research it contains. We then discuss educational research as applied social science, and we explore whether research on teaching can even be done. We conclude our introduction with a short personal story about research.

How This Book Is Organized

As you can see from an examination of the table of contents, this book is divided into 10 sections. Those divisions serve to cluster related studies that either attend to a particular set of topics, such as class management, assessment, and student interaction, or employ a particular research strategy, such as student interviews or longitudinal follow-up.

Each chapter contains an annotation for a single study. That summary is followed by individual commentaries from a researcher's and a practitioner's perspectives, as well as a closing statement of our shared perspective.

We have also devised 12 guidelines that should help you to enjoy the process of reading the research annotations—and they should also make it much easier for you to identify ideas that might inform your work as a physical educator. Those guidelines appear following this introduction.

How to Use This Book

With the exception of completing (and digesting) your reading of this introduction as the first order of business, there is no particular sequence of sections or chapters that are more advantageous than any other. You can start and finish wherever you

wish, following your personal interests and professional needs (or, of course, following the order prescribed by an instructor). We do, however, urge you to consider the rest of the introduction before moving on to the chapters that follow.

We also urge you not to skip over the section following this introduction, our "Guidelines for Reading Research." There truly are some tricks of the trade that can be helpful in trying to understand what the investigators did and what the findings suggest. Their application will come in the process of actually reading and interpreting the research annotations. With the assistance of our guidelines, we think you will find that reading and thinking about research requires the use of an ability you already have in good supply—common sense.

We will now finish setting the scene by defining some of the terms and constructs you will encounter. We will also share some of our own enthusiasm for exploring what research has had to say about physical education in the elementary school.

Here, Today, in This Book, What Is Research?

The word *research* has both common-use and technical definitions. We might say, for example, "I'm going to the library to do some research for my term paper." Or, "Before purchasing our car, we researched all of the new models by using the Internet." Those are perfectly proper uses of the word in its generic sense.

As a technical word within the language of science, however, *research* is restricted to designate only a narrowly defined set of activities. This latter definition is the case for scholars in general and for this book in particular. Although we might use the general sense of the word *research* in everyday conversation, as authors, we have not done so here.

Therefore, for the purposes of this book, we have used the term *research* to designate one particular process within the discipline of science; all other general meanings have been excluded.

Characteristics of Research Included in This Book

To be included as research in this book, each study required all of the following procedural steps:

1. Development of a question, which may have been as narrow as "How frequently does that happen?" or as broad as "What's going on here?"

2. Explanation of how the question fit into what we already knew (literature review) and why it was worth asking (rationale)

3. Design of a carefully specified method for collecting accurate information (data) bearing on the question—information that may have been collected as numbers or words

4. Recording and preserving of data in a careful and systematic way

5. Analyzing of the data in a manner that maintained its integrity while clarifying its meanings

6. Specification of exactly how the data related to the original question (findings)

7. Presentation of the investigator's interpretation of what the findings may have meant when considered in the light of the entire study (discussion and conclusions)

8. Preparation and submission for review by other researchers (a procedure commonly called *peer review*) and subsequent publication of a reasonably complete account of each of the steps above (the research report)

If all that sounds like a large order—it is. But for a study to be designated as research for the purposes of this book, each of those steps is unequivocally required. If some of the procedures seem foreign or confusing, don't be concerned. With the examples and opportunities for practice provided in the chapters that follow, the criteria for what constitutes research should become perfectly clear.

In addition, it is important to note that researchers may perform other activities in some of the studies, such as the development and calibration of the instruments used in the research. They may create a set of recommendations for an extension of the conclusions into practical applications, or they may even include a discussion of alternative interpretations of the findings. Those, however, vary from study to study and are not considered essential hallmarks of research.

You should also understand that the actual process of doing a research study rarely moves along in the tidy and linear fashion as displayed in the sequence of activities laid out in our definition. Neither does the reality of many investigations perfectly mirror the logical development portrayed in the published report. Research, like any other enterprise involving human beings, often becomes a distinctly messy business. Thus, because readers cannot always simply assume that everything in a study followed a perfectly predictable path, they must depend on the researcher to tell it like it truly was. This faith in the integrity of a researcher is one reason why honesty, precision, and thoroughness are so important in writing up the story of a study.

Publications That Were Included or Excluded

It should be clear, then, that we have included here only published research—though of many kinds. By extension, it also should be evident that we have excluded the writing of journalists (even those who are knowledgeable about our field), the published opinions of scholars concerning the nature of teaching (no matter how authoritative the source), and articles in which practitioners describe teaching strategies or program designs that have proven successful for them. Each of those is valuable and when well executed, should have an honored place in our professional literature. In this book, however, they are not included because they do not constitute research by our working definition.

For our purpose, within this book, we focus entirely on assertions about teaching physical education that are supported by evidence from research. We made that choice precisely for the following reason: What researchers have to say in their reports differs substantially from the assertions of practicing teachers, authors, journalists, philosophers, and theoreticians. Unlike teachers, researchers are trained "outsiders" who can step back from the buzzing confusion of a busy classroom, sometimes catching a clear glimpse of the whole forest, rather than the nearby trees. Unlike novelists, researchers are not constrained to tell a good yarn at the expense of describing the sometimes tedious nature of school life. Unlike journalists, researchers do not have to meet deadlines and thereby rush past a part of the whole story. Unlike philosophers, researchers have to ground their descriptions in the hard stuff of actual observations, rather than on the foundations of persuasive logic. And, unlike theoreticians, researchers must deal with how things did happen, rather than with predictions of how they are likely to happen.

Above all, the researcher uses investigative strategies that help to answer the ultimate question of any reader, "Why should I believe you?" All of that does not make researchers either inevitably right about anything or all-knowing about everything. It simply gives readers sound reason to listen to their voices—just as we may attend to other sources of knowledge.

We have imposed one other arbitrary restriction on what was selected for our dialogues. There is a vigorous and growing movement in physical education to encourage and support teachers in the design and conduct of research on their own teaching. Sometimes called *action research,* this form of inquiry allows teachers to be the architects of their own studies and producers of their own research-based knowledge. Each of us has advocated teacher-initiated research as a natural response to positive encounters with research on teaching (and we urge you to try some of your own action inquiry as part of reading this book). Nevertheless, although such studies offer substantial value to the teachers or preservice students involved, few reach publication in journals served by peer review. Thus, they have not been included here.

An entire book populated exclusively by reports of action research produced by "insiders" might someday be possible. For the present, however, we have limited ourselves to research conducted by people who were playing the role of professional outsiders. Of course, in physical education, many researchers spent significant portions of their professional careers as public school teachers and thereby are not complete strangers in any gymnasium.

Educational Research As Applied Social Science

It is important to remember that investigations directed at questions in education are substantively different from those conducted in other fields. Most notably, research in the field of education differs from research in the natural sciences (astronomy, biology, chemistry) by being "soft" rather than "hard." Used in this context, the word *soft* is only a descriptor and not a pejorative. In other words, the findings of educational research generally are not cumulative within a theoretical structure, and they often cannot be verified by simple replication since holding the conditions for inquiry constant is rarely possible in living social settings. This scenario is often the case with research in the social sciences (sociology, psychology, history) as well as the humanities (philosophy, literature, the fine arts).

Each social setting, such as a classroom, is different, dynamic, and enormously complicated. Unlike studies of tangible objects under controlled conditions (hard research), investigations of structures and events in social settings (soft research) require penetrating their idiosyncratic nature in search of regularities and commonalities that often lie hidden below the surface.

In consequence, the knowledge claims derived from such soft studies are never regarded as definitive in the sense of providing universal descriptions of what we "know" about all schools or every instance of teaching. These limitations are inherent because all soft sciences deal with people, who by their nature possess intentions, beliefs, values, and purposes that serve to make them unpredictable.

Educational researchers, of course, have been compelled to be creative and energetic in finding ways to accommodate and limit the problems imposed by the social nature of their science. For example, in the present collection of studies, several represent steps in a logical sequence of inquiries directed at one aspect of teaching. Such cumulative studies are powerful instruments for dissecting the anatomy of education. In yet other studies, the investigator has identified variables that appear to be sufficiently powerful to offer some hope of replication across other study settings—if not other populations. In the main, however, you must remember that these are social science studies, each of which bears at least some natural and inevitable limitations.

Educational research is predominantly applied in nature. The investigators are moved by a desire to improve the practice of teaching, which is distinct from the motive to simply understand how things work, as in pure (or "basic") research studies. Education is also a profoundly political process, and so too is educational research. Researchers in physical education, for example, invariably feel under pressure (real or perceived) to focus their inquiry on practical issues that arise from specific contexts. Several of the studies here, however, do come close to breaking away from the tradition of applied study by seeking general patterns—regularities of behavior that might lie within all teaching of physical skills. In the summaries of those studies, you may sense that the investigators were following their own interests and curiosity concerning how things work, rather than striving for immediate practicality or attending to the latest crisis for physical education in the elementary schools.

In all of this, it is important to remember that the categories of applied and basic study are not discrete. They sometimes overlap in such messy ways as to make the terms almost useless in describing actual research. Most of the studies used here, though, would fit comfortably into the genre of applied research.

Properly characterized, then, as both soft and applied, the studies we have selected are examples of educational research that deal with pedagogy and programs in physical education. All of them represent reasonable levels of adherence to standards for careful planning, sound data collection, thoughtful analysis, and appropriately cautious conclusions. That assertion, however, raises a question about our judgment of quality in the studies selected for this book. Allow us to address this issue in-depth.

The Question of Quality

All of the studies presented in this book were drawn from journals that employed peer review by other qualified researchers before publication. Beyond that, however, there remains the following question: Do all of the studies abstracted here meet the highest technical standards for research design, sampling, and data analysis? Our answer may surprise you: "We doubt it." But, for the purposes of this book, it is important to consider what we have to say about the quality of the research before you discredit the value of these 30 studies.

First, the adequacy of research methods is indeed a crucial matter, at least to the extent that the research method is precisely what supports the credibility of a study's findings. Holding absolute standards for quality, however, can be a self-defeating posture. By their very nature, almost all studies in education have some limitations—and that is exactly the case with the studies we selected for this book. None are perfect, and some even have limitations that the investigators themselves draw to the attention of readers. We made the judgment, though, that each of them was done carefully; each of them gave a reasonably thorough account of what transpired; and each of them presented an appropriately conservative assessment of the conclusions.

One standard for screening research, therefore, is the dependability of the findings, as supported by the research methods employed. But it is not the only possible standard. For example, some studies have methodological characteristics that limit the extent to which findings can safely be generalized to other settings or populations. Nevertheless, such studies may raise excellent questions, utilize innovative methods of data collection, involve interventions that have a strong theoretical foundation, and present thoughtful interpretations of the data. Findings may matter to a reader, but one should understand that there is much more to learn from a report or annotation than just the results produced by a study.

Accordingly, we did not impose stringent tests for adequacy of method beyond those used by the peer reviewers who screened the original reports before publication. Instead, we put our emphasis on finding studies that would teach our readers about many things. The result was elimination of some perfectly sound studies that were either redundant or too narrow in focus for our purpose. Only rarely did we have to set aside studies for reasons of inadequate conceptualization or defective research procedure.

The final selection of 30 studies contained a wide range of valuable ideas, including some with designs and methods that would pass muster in the most rigorous qualitative review. From that simple account of our procedures, then, you can understand that we employed standards of quality that seemed appropriate for our purpose in this book. Necessarily, those standards were relative and not absolute.

Research on Teaching: Can It Be Done?

As a final note concerning the nature of the research used in this book, we want to acknowledge an old and sometimes troubling dispute. You still can encounter people who deny that it is possible to study teaching—at least not with the tools of systematic inquiry. They hold that teaching is an art, or at most, a moral craft. It can be discussed, as can philosophy or morality, but it cannot be studied directly by empirical methods—that is, by observation of events and collection of data. Many other people argue that even if you could use research tools in the classroom, the level of complexity represented in teaching makes it impossible to identify causal elements with any degree of certainty.

From the pessimistic view that there is no body of reliable knowledge about teaching and learning (what's to study?) come a number of corollaries.

Those include the following propositions: First, good teachers are born and not made (you either have it, or you don't); second, the best way to prepare teachers is through apprenticeships in the classrooms of veteran practitioners (teacher preparation programs are no more than trade-unionism); and third, the only way to improve teacher performance or program quality is through imitation of successful models (just practice the proven model and don't waste time trying to create a model for the practice).

We think every one of those conclusions is a dangerous half-truth. In respective order, consider our counterarguments. Some teachers indeed are born, but most are not. Experience in real schools and classrooms is an essential part of teacher training, but it is a wholly inadequate substitute for a systematic program that uses many resources and instructional formats. In addition, the remarkable skills demonstrated by a master teacher can be a source of inspiration and valuable insights, but variables such as classroom context, individual teacher characteristics, and stage of professional development make simple imitation of experienced practitioners an unreliable way to transmit expertise to others. Finally, educational research has not produced a comprehensive set of universal and absolute laws about teaching, but there is robust evidence to support much that we have learned.

Time and the accumulation of evidence have worked to undercut both the proposition that teaching cannot be studied and the notion that teachers cannot learn about their work from people who have systematically examined it. The key to appreciating that evidence is looking to research for what it is designed to do—not what it can never accomplish.

Teaching indeed calls upon human qualities that may be forever beyond the ken of science—creative art and swift intuition, moral force and deep wellsprings of empathy—gifts that are neither defined nor captured by our best descriptors. But teaching is more than those human mysteries. Teaching also consists of explicit behaviors, conscious decisions, concrete plans, repeated sequences, and detectable rhythms, all of which present regularities to the close and patient observer. Those patterns can be recorded, analyzed, and ultimately understood.

Within the limits imposed by findings that always must be contingent on their context, and probabilities that never can be perfect, teaching actions have consequences for learning that can be discovered by research. In this book, we assert that learning more about those consequences by reading and contemplating research can (and should) be used as a valuable resource for improving both teaching

and program design. How best to access the lessons from research, however, is a very different matter. Before attempting to give you advice about how to read and profit from the studies annotated in this book, we want you to consider a general rule that we think is applicable to any encounter with research, whether here or elsewhere: *It is wise to make a conscious attempt to keep an open mind about what you are going to learn from reading research.*

Perhaps because they are so intellectually rich, so packed with ideas, decisions, clues, and questions, studies of physical education offer wonderfully complex possibilities for learning. Some of the lessons will be unexpected, or, at least, they will not be obvious at first glance. For that reason, it will be the watchful reader, the one whose mind is prepared to wonder about any aspect of the story, who is most likely to come away with new understanding or useful information. The most valuable result from a study may be the one you didn't expect—and one that the investigator didn't even intend. What follows here is intended to demonstrate that very point.

A Short Story About Research

The following story about reading research is both true and directly relevant to the present chapter. Once upon a time, long, long ago, one of the authors (Locke) was an undergraduate major in physical education. He encountered a study of warm-up procedures for sprint swimming (50 meters). Because it had been conducted by one of his much admired mentors, he set out to read it—and thereby hangs this tale.

The two kinds of pretest preparation consisted of what were called "formal warm-up" (actually swimming a number of brief sprints) and "informal warm-up" (performing swimming-like movements against moderate resistance in a training room near the pool). The design involved carefully specified sequences of trials, monitoring heart rate after warm-up, and a number of checks on accuracy that were considered advanced for that day.

In terms of tested sprint times, one warm-up method proved to be significantly superior to the other. That method and result seemed mildly interesting, and it certainly appeared to certify the warm-up of choice for use in competitive sprint swimming. A casual perusal of the table that contained the raw data for each subject (the swim times), however, presented an unexpected surprise. The grouped and averaged performance scores used to detect the main finding had, on the first reading, obscured another fact within the data. Times for a few performers did not follow the main trend for the majority of subjects. Several participants persistently swam their best times when using the method identified as inferior, and several swam their worst times after warming up with the activity that had been significantly superior for the average participant. Their individual scores could not exert enough influence to change the overall results, but those atypical performance times were right there in the middle of the data—insistent little contradictions to the main trend.

It took some time, but the meaning of those deviant scores slowly filtered through. Some people really are different, even when most people are the same. Averages tell you where to place your bets if you have no other information. Knowing how individuals respond, however, allows you to make even better choices. One size rarely fits all.

That small encounter with research had four aspects that may interest you. First, Locke never taught or coached swimming (or any sprint activity), so there was no occasion to make application of the results. Second, because his memory never was very good, within a year or so, he had completely forgotten which warm-up was superior. Third, by modern standards, the study design and physiological controls probably would be judged wholly inadequate. Whatever the conclusions of the study may have been, Locke would regard them today as unsubstantiated—interesting, but no more

than suggestive. Fourth, despite all of that, no other study was to have so much impact on his teaching and research careers.

Effective teachers have to learn the difference between what is effective with most students and what is appropriate (even essential) for others. Locke learned that lesson from a less than perfect study with findings he never used and conclusions he couldn't remember! None of that mattered, however, because reading about that investigation presented him with an unforgettable example of how necessary it is for a teacher or coach to consider individual differences. It also provided the perfect reminder of how easily such valuable points can be lost amidst the busy detail of a report.

With that brief excerpt from real life, our introduction is completed. We hope you now have a clear sense of what to expect in terms of content, as well as an overview of how the book is organized. There is, however, one remaining step in your preparation for tackling our 30 annotations of research on elementary physical education. In the guidelines section that follows, we have tried to provide some commonsense advice about reading research. There is nothing complicated in that counsel because it is based on the problems that people commonly encounter—and those problems mostly involve simple mistakes, such as trying to read too fast, getting hung up on technical points that don't really matter, and holding unreasonable expectations for perfection. Equip yourself with some simple skills and a good attitude—and then let the games begin!

GUIDELINES FOR READING RESEARCH

The following 12 guidelines are intended to help you get started with the task of reading the annotated research reports that form the 30-chapter core of this book. They include simple advice about how to do it, what to look for, and how to think about what you discover. There is no instruction about technical matters (none will be needed), and much that we have to say should closely match your own commonsense ideas about how to approach the task. The guidelines do, however, reflect a particular set of assumptions on our part, which in turn reflect our understanding of who our readers are likely to be and why they might find value in research.

We have assumed that our advice should be directed specifically to people who are seeking information and ideas that might illuminate the work of teaching elementary physical education. As you will see when reviewing the guidelines, our choice of the word *illuminate*, rather than *improve*, was deliberate, and it reflects one of the perspectives we urge you to adopt. Also, to the extent that the guidelines were devised to serve the needs and interests of a particular audience, the advice they contain differs in content and emphasis from what we might counsel for people with other backgrounds and needs.

We have tried to think about what you might find helpful. Please give the guidelines your close attention, read a few chapters, then make your own judgment about how well they have served your needs.

Guideline Number 1: Take Your Time

Notice the small things, and wonder about the unexpected. Pause to reflect on your own experiences, then compare them to the observations and assertions of the investigators. What is valuable in a study may lie as much in the thoughts it provokes as in the conclusions it asserts. We can't guarantee that you will encounter a career-altering revelation within the 30 annotations that follow, but an open mind is prepared ground. Who knows what amazing ideas might take root? None of that will be possible, however, if you turn the reading task into a race.

When you think you understand the contents of a chapter, you will more likely find those contents useful and retained in memory if you take the time to reflect on what you learned, how it fits with your experiences, and where it might serve your own purposes. If it is possible to do so, give your new insight an informal trial run in one of your classes and by all means, share the study with others.

The same general caution applies to the pace at which you proceed through a series of studies. Try to limit yourself to one study per sitting. Plowing through four or five chapters at a time will overload your memory, dull your sense of adventure, and mush many important details and distinctions into a single amorphous heap. Like any substantial meal, a good research study requires time to consume—and digest.

Guideline Number 2: Use the Headings and Proceed Step by Step

As arcane as they may seem at first, research reports are nothing more than elaborate stories—or, to be more precise, histories. As such, they must address a familiar set of questions: what, why, who, where, how, and with what result? The headings we have inserted into each chapter mark the locations where you will find the authors' answers: The Study (what and why?), Participants and Context (who and where?), Design and Method (how?), and Results (with what result?). The remaining sections of each chapter consist of our individual and joint comments on the story laid out in the annotation: The Researcher's Perspective (Locke), The Teacher's Perspective (Lambdin), and Common Ground: Our Shared Perspective (Locke and Lambdin).

The headings used in the annotation actually represent an abbreviated version of a longer checklist that was designed for use in reading full reports in their original published form. If you are interested, that tool for reading and studying can be found in *Reading and Understanding Research* by Locke, Silverman, and Spirduso (1998). As you will be reading only brief annotations here, however, the smaller set of basic headings should be sufficient to keep the unfolding story organized in your mind—provided you take things one step at a time and resist the temptation to try to comprehend too much, too quickly.

One by one, you can accumulate each part of the study's history. You need not be concerned about grasping the whole picture; it will become clear at the end. This is an instance in which part/whole learning is an effective strategy. After you have concluded a first tour through the annotation, if you sense that something is missing, just go back to the heading where it should be found. In most cases you can quickly track down what you missed. In some instances, however, you may not find the fugitive fact because we made an editorial decision that the particular bit of information was not essential to the story—that is, we simply left it out (remember that annotations are by nature much abbreviated versions of longer stories).

Finally, please note that when we prepared the annotations for this text, we emphasized the storylike qualities of the original reports. There was no attempt to write equal amounts of prose under each heading—some are paragraphs long and others consist only of a single sentence. Also, what we chose to write about often reflects what we thought you would find interesting or useful, rather than what the researchers had elected to emphasize. Accordingly, we freely edited the original in an attempt to maintain clarity and a good story.

Guideline Number 3: Use Your Study Skills

Whether in the form of an abstract, an annotation, or a full report, most accounts of research have to be studied, not just read. Perhaps one in a hundred readers can start at the title of an investigation and read straight through to the end—and really finish with a clear picture of the entire story. If you are not one of those lucky few, then you must be like the rest of us. You will actually have to study research, which means doing things like initial skimming to get an overview of the study; skipping forward and back in the text to puzzle through difficult points; underscoring, highlighting, and writing in margins

to give emphasis to key points; and creating mental summaries as you go along. Most beginning readers quickly identify a number of such personal study strategies that improve efficiency and maximize comprehension. Those processes represent active studying, not just passive reading.

Reading research is often interesting, frequently provocative, sometimes satisfying, and on memorable occasions, even exhilarating. To be completely truthful, though, much of it is work—wholesome, respectable, and productive—but work nonetheless. Even with our carefully devised research summaries, nobody here is promising you a stroll in the park. With a modest investment of time and effort, however, this is work you can learn how to do (and do probably far better than you expect).

Guideline Number 4: Don't Panic If You Can't Understand Everything

It has been our experience that published research reports rarely contain defects that are absolutely fatal to the reader's understanding. That said, it also is true that failures to achieve complete clarity in the explanation of an investigation are fairly commonplace. Such problems are not surprising, given the complexity of a task that requires crafting a report that will be fully transparent with regard to every detail (to the eyes of every potential reader). The question here is, How are you going to feel when one of the annotations is not transparent to you? We have some firm advice on that matter.

When you find yourself confused, you will need to exercise some good mental hygiene. That healthy response begins with one simple rule—*Don't panic!*

Two valid reasons exist for not getting into a panic that will ultimately undermine your confidence. First, the problem may not be yours; it may be the authors' (or the annotator's). Key bits of a story do get lost, writers do make unfortunate word choices that mislead the reader, and complexity itself sometimes obscures prose that seemed perfectly lucid to authors, editors, and annotators. What you have to remember is that *the person who is out of step may not be you!* Sometimes a report may be unintelligible for the simple reason that *it is unintelligible*—and would be so to any reader. That is the way things are, and no matter how hard we try to make it otherwise, sometimes we truly do have to just live with it.

The second reason not to get into a panic is that you simply may lack some particular bit of background that is critical to understanding the material, or maybe you simply find this kind of reading more difficult than other intellectual tasks. It would be a surprise, in fact, if any of us failed to have problems when navigating in unfamiliar waters. If any of these are the case, believe us, it is neither the end of the world nor is it an indication that you will fail to glean something valuable out of what you have read. And it most certainly is not an indication that nobody can help you (they usually can) or that you won't be able to understand the next chapter perfectly well, even without assistance. Through all of this, our advice remains constant: *Don't panic!*

We have sound reason for persisting with such an injunction, and it comes from years of our own reading experiences in the research literature, as well as those of our students. The rule is simple. *Missing a specific piece of a study almost never prevents grasping the more general whole.* Just be careful to identify what you don't understand, then set it aside and proceed. You will be surprised by how often the problematic point turns out not to have been essential to getting the main message. In sum, a valuable asset when practitioners read research is a capacity for ignoring troublesome details—technical jargon and statistical analysis included. So relax, give it your best shot, jot down a note about what puzzles you (the next guideline explains how to use that note), and move on.

Guideline Number 5: Get Help by Having Your Own Conversations

One of the best ways to get through (or around) unclear accounts of a research study is to share the confusion! Whether you put caution flags in the margins or make notecards to record points that puzzle you, don't keep them to yourself. The popular image of the lonely scholar sweating away in solitude over a giant stack of books and research journals is mostly fantasy. People who keep up with the research in their specialty do read, of course, but most of them also spend as much or more time talking about what they have read with others (such poor souls include hapless students, entrapped office mates, and innocent secretaries).

Whether in doctoral-level seminars, research courses for undergraduates, in-service workshops, or our roles as consultants and research advisors, we have found that conversation is the single most efficient agent for clarifying and enriching the consumption of research. Accordingly, our advice to you is to find a friend, form a club, corner a colleague, or post an invitation on the Internet. In other words, somehow start a dialogue about the research you read—whether here or elsewhere. Sharing the confusion is an effective way of reducing confusion, and it is a lot more fun than struggling alone!

Guideline Number 6: The Main Purpose of Reading Research Is to Help You Understand Your Work

The primary purpose for reading research should be to help you think about your work in more sophisticated ways. We do not mean to disparage the idea of finding practical applications that change and improve what you do. This is simply a matter of what should be first priority when you read. In the end, beneficial changes may be inspired by ideas from research, but they have to come from you, from your understanding of your world. If you are looking for things that can help you get a better handle on what is happening in your classes and your program (things that we call *valuables*), you will have the right priority when you read research.

Given that broad definition of what to look for in research, useful items will not always consist of specific instructions for how to teach. For example, you can collect valuables such as the following: new ways of thinking about particular problems, explanations that never occurred to you, clarification of complex relationships, precise language for describing things, potentially useful questions that you had never thought to ask, and lines of argument to support requests for change. Those are the sorts of particulars that add up to better understanding.

In the course of explaining what they did in their study, researchers can often complicate what you think and believe about your teaching. That is exactly the effect you should expect and welcome because teaching physical education is complicated work and demands complex thinking to match. No matter what the findings of the study were, all of those complicating ideas are there in the annotation or the full report, just for the taking. Snap them up, add to your fund of professional knowledge, then look at your work in more sophisticated ways. If you deal with your own understandings first, concrete applications will come in their own time.

Guideline Number 7: For Many Readers, the Results Are Not the Most Useful Product of Research

The formal account of "results" produced by a study may turn out to be the least important item in the study for physical education teachers who want to learn more about their work. Such a rule applies just as much to the annotations in this book as to the original published reports. Studies are designed to find answers, but that singular purpose is only rarely achieved in any absolute sense. As in other areas of life, it is the journey, rather than the destination, that has the greater value.

Studies that are less than perfect as research or that fail in some respect to completely match your initial expectations may contain all manner of valuable materials. As you read your way toward the investigators' conclusions, pay attention to everything else you encounter. You can come out the winner even when the unfortunate researchers clearly lose their struggle to find a completely satisfactory result.

Sometimes, of course, the results from a study truly are exciting, provocative, or useful. When reading, however, resist skipping to the Results heading in our annotations and then quitting (in full reports, results often are located in the section called "Findings"). If you scan or even ignore the body of the study, you may miss some or all of what would have been valuable: provocative questions, identification of alternative explanations for student learning problems, leads to new ideas (and even to other studies), better ways to describe one of your teaching objectives, and improved tools for evaluating student progress—all of which can be scattered throughout the study and not mentioned at all in the concluding sections. When you read about an investigation in the gym, you have to keep your eyes and your mind open. For your purposes, the results may not be the only useful product of a study.

Guideline Number 8: Expect to Find Valuables, Not Easy Answers

The notion that you can just read about a study and then immediately apply the results in your classes is naive. At the worst, a quest for prescriptions in research puts blinders on your eyes. At the best, however, you can adapt (not adopt) whatever findings and conclusions there are to the particular circumstances of your workplace—to your students, your program, your gym, your school, your skills, and your personal style. You can expect that it will require hard work, creative effort, and at least some risk of failure. But have some fun with it. An attempt to implement a new application that results in failure is always more valuable than no attempt at all.

We all want to find things that make our programs better and our teaching more effective. Most researchers sincerely want to discover things that help us accomplish exactly those objectives. It would be useful, however, if everybody could manage not to hold unreasonable expectations for what can be accomplished at a single stroke. Not all perfectly sound studies can generate explicit instructions for improving practice. You should always find new things to consider, but remember that the perfect prescription for all of your professional headaches is a rare and improbable find.

Guideline Number 9: Remember That Context Controls, and It Is Your Context That Matters

Findings from educational research are always influenced by the context within which they were derived. What appeared to work with one teacher, class of students, school, measure of achievement, or subject matter may not function perfectly at another place and time. Universally applicable truths are mighty hard to come by in physical education.

The familiar teacher complaint "You just don't know my students (or school, principal, gym, or teaching schedule)" is right on the money when it comes to research. The researcher does not (and cannot) know all of those things and thereby cannot possibly write a report that lays out every conceivable adaptation of the findings to fit every imaginable setting. In any case, figuring out exactly how to make use of a research finding in your gym is not the researcher's job. It is yours.

It is you, the reader, who must play the key role here. You have to stand between each study and the realities of your own workplace. You have to be there with all of your craft wisdom, creative skill, professional training, and common sense. You must then think, "What is here that might be useful to me, and how could I put it to work?" No researcher in the world can do that for you. There is no substitution in this game. If you want to play, you have to stand and deliver.

Guideline Number 10: Skepticism Is Wise, but Cynicism Wastes Your Time

You already know that you can't believe everything you are told (and that you should only believe half of what you see). That rule of caution applies to research with equal cogency. As we all sometimes do, researchers do make mistakes and fall into embarrassing traps for the unwary. That is why a degree of skepticism is a healthy thing to have when you settle down to read about a study of teaching physical education.

That does not mean that you need to get all hung up over questions such as "Is this good research?" and "Was that the correct way to analyze the data?" Few experts can make those qualitative judgments with perfect reliability, and even with some training and practice, you might find yourself unable to decide. Instead, we urge you to simply post a yellow flag next to anything that sets off your commonsense alarm, then press on to the end and store the results under "perhaps" in your mental file. Checking out those caution flags with someone who can evaluate the problem may later allay your suspicions—or it may not. Just keep those grains of skeptical salt handy, and remember that you can learn a great deal without believing everything you read.

Cynicism, on the other hand, is destructive for everyone! Healthy disbelief is one thing, but disrespect is quite another. If you truly believe that most researchers are pursuing only their own self-interest, promoting their pet notions about physical education, or just using their craft to recruit you to their personal ideology, then reading research certainly

is not for you. Our view of the research enterprise in physical education and the people who work within it is far more positive.

We have known literally hundreds of physical educators who have made research a regular part of their professional careers, and the number we would suspect of serious and intentional academic sins is close to zero. The vast majority of research workers in physical education, as in other fields of inquiry, are honest scholars who receive scant reward other than personal satisfaction for their labors.

They also are people who hold their public reputations dear. Aside from personal integrity, there are truly draconian mechanisms within the research community that exert discipline by putting reputation at risk with every published report. A researcher gets caught cheating only once. There are no second chances.

As for bias, of course researchers root for certain outcomes as the study proceeds. Only a fool would not know the difference between findings that are congenial or hostile to a line of inquiry, and only the brain-dead would not care. All the scholars we have known, however, could be counted on to let the chips fall where they might (however painful) and in their report to tell you exactly how it happened. Anyone who tries to do that deserves your respect—not necessarily your agreement but always your respect. A wary reader is a smart reader, but cynical and disrespectful readers are only wasting their own time.

Guideline Number 11: Don't Toss Out Studies That Produce Conflicting Results

It is understandable when newcomers to research make the assumption that if several different studies find conflicting results, the investigations must have been defective and should thereby be disregarded. That appealing logic, however, does not fit the realities of research and leads to the false conclusion that nothing can be learned when findings diverge. While the goal always is to achieve congruent and replicable findings across studies, divergent findings often represent valuable steps toward that objective.

It is a fact that such conflicts are not at all uncommon, particularly in the early stages of inquiry into a complex problem. Once you begin to read research, it will not take long to discover instances where the findings of two or more studies appear to be at least partly, if not wholly, discrepant. That, in turn, can lead to concerns about the truthfulness and dependability of research. How can two studies involving the same question produce different results and still make legitimate claims to validity?

In the majority of cases, the answer is disarmingly simple. The divergent results were produced by differences between or among the studies in terms of circumstances, procedures, or participants. The research may have been perfectly competent, but the results reflected the study of apples in one case and oranges in the other.

Close inspection of reports with apparently conflicting results often reveals likely suspects for the source of divergence, and such comparisons can serve to further understanding of the variables involved. A learning curve exists for the design of research in any complex area of inquiry, but as studies accumulate so does sophistication. It is then that findings begin to converge.

Guideline Number 12: Don't Wait for the Perfect Study

Searching for the perfect study can be like Captain Ahab and the great white whale—long on waiting and short on satisfaction! As with the redoubtable Captain in *Moby Dick,* even if you do find your quarry, it may not make you all that happy. Think about this matter in terms of what makes perfection so difficult to achieve.

Even a modest study can be expensive in time, money, and human resources; thus, getting a study done frequently involves tradeoffs. The researcher often has to give up some ideal aspect of design or method here to reinforce something over there. Virtually all studies involve limitations resulting from imperfect conditions and the difficult choices they demand. Investigators have to work around the limitations as well as they can, then scrupulously plant caution flags in the report to warn the reader about consequent weak points in the evidence.

Those hard realities lead to an inescapable conclusion. If you insist on waiting for the perfect study before you invest any reading time, you may end up with a very long wait. Of course, there is a theoretical continuum of qualitative perfection on which every study must find its place. What we can tell you with certainty, however, is that the number of published studies falling at the extreme ends of that mythical line will be only a tiny fraction of the whole. So, don't insist on playing Captain Ahab! Do your best to find valuables in the studies we have annotated here and (if you go beyond them) from the thousands of solid, if sometimes imperfect, studies that are right at hand. White whales and perfect studies may not be extinct, but they certainly are on the list of rare creatures.

PART I
The Basics—Numbers, Time, Space, Equipment, and Behaviors

THE STUDY

RESEARCHER

TEACHER

COMMON GROUND

How Equipment and Class Size Make a Difference

Hastie, P.A., & Saunders, J.E. (1991). Effects of class size and equipment availability on student involvement in physical education. *The Journal of Experimental Education, 59,* 212-224.

"Too many students and too little equipment." If that is not the universal complaint of physical education teachers everywhere, it must be nearly so. The research dealing with such factors in academic classrooms is voluminous and hence decisive on many points. The gymnasium, however, is quite a different case. It is difficult to find more than a handful of studies that apply to the context of physical education—and those found often raise more questions than they answer. The authors of this study challenged that problem head-on with an ambitious effort that employed an elaborate and creative design for investigation.

 ## The Study

This study was designed to allow examination of the influence of class size and equipment on what students actually did during a period of instruction. By manipulating both the number of students and how much equipment was available, the investigators created classes with distinctly different conditions for teaching and learning. The impact of each set of conditions was then measured by recording how much of the students' time was spent in various kinds of activity.

As much as the goal of the study sounds like an exercise in simple common sense, the design for accomplishing that goal was both sophisticated and unusual for a study conducted in physical education. The classes were selected at random (i.e., by procedures governed only by chance) from the full population of all those available, students in each class were randomly assigned to groups within the study, and lesson conditions for each group were also randomly determined. Therefore, the design for this investigation meets the primary requirements for a "true" experiment—a powerful and reliable way to explore complex questions, such as those raised here.

Participants and Context

Three experienced physical education specialists in three elementary schools participated in this experiment, in addition to 480 of their fifth- and sixth-grade students (160 at each school).

Design and Method

There were three class sizes—24 students (normal), 12 (half-sized) and 44 (double-sized)—and two conditions of equipment availability—unlimited and restricted, the latter with only two balls and four marker cones. Combining the variables of class size and equipment thus produced six possible conditions for instruction. Each of the 3 teachers taught 30-minute soccer skill lessons under conditions representing each of the six possible permutations (half-sized with unlimited equipment, half-sized with restricted equipment, and so on)—each teacher rotated through the conditions in a different order. The purpose of these procedures was to counterbalance and reduce (if not eliminate) the impact of individual teachers and particular groupings of students, leaving the variables of class size and equipment as the primary sources of influence.

But influence on what? There were many possible places to look for the consequences of class size and equipment availability: learning, student attitudes, discipline problems, average time on task, total number of practice trials, instructional strategies selected by the teachers, and so on. The investigators decided they wanted a broad picture of student involvement and lesson context; thus, they selected an observation and recording instrument popularly referred to as the Academic Learning Time—Physical Education (ALT-PE). It uses time as the measure of student activity—such as waiting, doing cognitive tasks, doing appropriate motor tasks, being off task—and of class contexts, such as warm-ups, management activities, transition between tasks, scrimmage, rule instruction, and so on. Each of the 18 classes was video- and audiotaped, and with stopwatches in hand, trained coders calculated how much time students spent in each activity and context.

Results

Given the complex nature of the design, it is not surprising that the report contains a long string of observations that concern the impact of student numbers and equipment. The investigators were careful, however, in clarifying and displaying the main results. Exactly as you would suspect, the number of students and how much equipment they had made a large and often predictable difference—and those factors did so for both students and teachers.

In the larger classes, students were relatively disadvantaged for a very simple reason. Organizational activities, particularly transitions between tasks, consumed more class time. It simply required more time to move the larger classes from one activity to another. For reasons you might easily guess, teachers with larger numbers of students devoted less time to practice drills and relatively more to scrimmages.

In contrast, students in the smaller, half-sized classes devoted more time to practice of skills and refinement of technique. It required much less time to move the half-sized class from one activity to another, preserving time that was then available for learning activities. If you have to guess what the results showed for the relative amounts of time spent by students in off-task behaviors in large and small classes, then you must have neither attended nor attempted to teach a physical education class! These were experienced teachers, so the amount of off-task time was never large in absolute terms, but it was significantly greater in the double-sized classes. Big classes are difficult even for the best teachers.

Similarly unequivocal results were found regarding the equipment variable. Limited equipment produced a substantial inflation of time spent by students simply waiting their turn. It also produced a similar reduction in the time actually spent on practice that could be recorded as *motor appropriate* in the ALT-PE category system. In contrast, when there were plenty of balls and markers, pupils engaged in skill practice for much greater periods of time—and spent almost no time in either scrimmage or full-scale games.

 **A Researcher's Perspective**

In this study, researchers used no measures of learning outcomes, such as skill in kicking at the end of the unit. The observations made, however, were of the activities that engaged students in the subject matter—opportunities for practice that constituted the necessary intermediate step between teaching and learning. In that equation, time spent on practice tasks is the spring that drives the machinery of learning, and opportunities to act are what dole out time for each student.

Within broad limits, the teachers in this study did have some control over student opportunities to practice. No doubt, some were better than others in extracting every possible second of active learning out of each class period. In the end, though, more students and fewer items of equipment were implacable burdens that produced predictable consequences. Such an impact may be larger or smaller in any given class, but you can be certain that there is a ceiling on learning in every double-sized class and in every class with restricted equipment. In this study, that limitation was imposed on teachers and students from the outset—by the simple logistics of numbers.

> **You can be certain that there is a ceiling on learning in every double-sized class and in every class with restricted equipment.**

Given the two variables involved (class size and equipment availability) and the dependent measures employed (student involvement and class activity context), it appears that the availability of equipment produces a somewhat larger and more persistent impact on what goes on in class. The amount of motor appropriate activity favored smaller classes as predicted, but not significantly so. Differences favoring unlimited equipment were both numerically large and statistically significant.

 ## A Teacher's Perspective

This study certainly confirms what common sense would dictate. With more equipment, students have less waiting and a lot more time to spend on appropriate practice tasks. If we ever needed encouragement to find ways to equip every child with a ball—here it is. I say, "Three cheers!" for the researchers who pose practical questions and publish such useful results.

What is not mentioned anywhere in the report, however, is the considerable jump in organizational complexity that a wealth of equipment can produce. For instance, this study used experienced teachers. For the less skillful (or less experienced) teachers, even such a seemingly happy condition as one ball (or other item of equipment) for each child sometimes produces chaos, and time spent trying to distribute, control, and collect the equipment is time lost, just as surely as any other form of organizational expenditure. It is for exactly that reason that some teachers leave 20 balls in the equipment closet and take only 2 out for class!

> **We need teachers who are prepared to manage equipment efficiently to obtain the most benefit from such conditions.**

Providing adequate equipment is shown here to be important for the "time on task" that is accumulated by children over the course of a class. Like the experienced teachers who participated in this study, we need teachers who are prepared to manage equipment efficiently to obtain the most benefit from such conditions.

The fact that ample equipment is usually associated with an increase in small-group formats for practice creates yet another potential management challenge for the teacher. Without adequate preparation of both students and class routines, too much of a good thing can overwhelm a teacher. Children who are unused to working independently with only one or two partners can respond poorly to the demands for cooperation, self-discipline, and task focus that characterize the small-group setting. To use the findings from this study wisely, teachers must first think clearly about the organizational patterns they employ in their classes.

The use of squads, for example, has long been an organizing format for physical education classes. Clearly defined and well-practiced routines allow squads to serve as the basis for managing large counts of equipment. Responsibilities can be spread among squad members to handle class materials quickly, reliably, and efficiently. By periodically rotating equipment-related roles (distribution, collection, marking areas) among squad members, teachers can equitably assign such chores to their students. Even though it does take a significant amount of class time to teach routines for handling large volumes of equipment, this study shows that the investment can be well repaid by the increase in student learning time.

Although this study focused on teaching problems that are high on my list of things that deserve more attention than they usually receive, it also presents some features that restrain my enthusiasm. The summary of this study contains no definition of the various ALT-PE categories (nor did the original report), and I find this frustrating. While it is reasonable to omit some technical information on the grounds that readers will be familiar with an instrument that is in common use in the research community, it seems clear that the main utility for this study rests with practitioners. (In fact, the investigators say that they selected the variables of class size and equipment availability because they were of particular interest to teachers.)

Without knowing how data were gathered for an ALT-PE category, such as *motor appropriate*, the numbers given in the report are meaningless to the average teacher. A brief footnote would have clarified the matter, and the effort expended in making the report more user-friendly would express respect for the teachers who constitute a large part of the intended audience.

Those concerns aside, however, this small study establishes what can serve as a kind of benchmark for the economics of public school physical education. Adequate conditions for class size and instructional equipment are among the elements that control the learning outcomes produced for children. Experienced teachers can often compensate when those conditions are less than optimal, but there is a point at which skill and hard work can no longer sustain a reasonable level of educational profit. "Too many students and too little equipment" is more than just a complaint. It is a formula for educational bankruptcy.

Here, as elsewhere in the school, if we solve the problems of underfunding and growing student numbers by crowding classrooms and asking teachers to invent creative substitutes for needed equipment, then we do so at the peril of opportunities to learn.

Common Ground: Our Shared Perspective

In their report, the investigators put it succinctly (if modestly): "The results support the contention that changes in class size and the amount of available equipment will affect student lesson involvement"

(p. 221). One might add that those changes seem likely to be consistent, predictable, and substantial in magnitude. If you care about student achievement in physical education, it is not difficult to draw the most straightforward conclusion. Here, as elsewhere in the school, if we solve the problems of underfunding and growing student numbers by crowding classrooms and asking teachers to invent creative substitutes for needed equipment, then we do so at the peril of opportunities to learn.

A second conclusion comes to mind, however, that might be missed by readers whose concerns are primarily with immediate and practical problems in the gymnasium. What was true in this experiment is likely to be true in any other experiment where groups of students are exposed to some kind of treatment. One can only wonder how many studies of physical education have reported results that were driven as much by class size and available equipment as by the variable that was (supposedly) under investigation. Hastie and Saunders have reminded us about the critical significance of context (including all the varied aspects of class environment) when any of us try to think carefully about the processes of physical education.

Who Gets
the Teacher's Attention?

DeVoe, D.E. (1991). Teacher behavior directed toward individual students in elementary physical education. *Journal of Classroom Interaction, 26*(1), 9-14.

As early as 1974, educational researchers Jere Brophy and Thomas Good had produced unambiguous evidence that teachers have differential interactions with individual students in their classes. That teachers treat particular students differently than others in the same class would come as no surprise to veteran practitioners. At the least, we have always encouraged teachers to individualize some of their instruction and that alone would produce such a result. What was a surprise, however, was that those differences often appeared to be patterned by groups of students (students who shared particular characteristics) rather than simply by individual students. Moreover, it was what characterized those groups that caused educators to begin raising questions about what was happening—first in classrooms, then in the gymnasium.

Few people were surprised to learn that elementary school boys received teacher interactions that were different in number and kind from those that girls received. Folklore has it that boys are more salient (noisy, assertive, inattentive, noncompliant) than girls are. If the folklore were true, such teacher behavior would certainly be expected. Boys would naturally receive higher levels of teacher attention although it would be in a form loaded with criticism and requests to "Cut it out!" That sort of attention, of course, represents neither prudent pedagogy nor gender equity. As research accumulated, however, it became clear that there were many other distributions of individual teacher attention that were neither benign nor neutral.

For example, children who were more physically attractive received more positive comments and task feedback interactions than children who were less physically attractive. Students who were bright or particularly compliant likewise received more teacher interaction and supportive forms of individual attention. Not only did such findings raise questions of teacher equity, but they also led researchers to wonder about the origins and impact of such asymmetrical distributions of teacher attention. Were they, for example, simply the result of the teacher's reaction to preexisting student characteristics, or were characteristics such as compliance or attentiveness promoted, or in a sense created, by initial patterns of teacher attention?

The Study

This was a descriptive study. Its purpose was to capture and display the rates and kinds of teacher behavior directed toward individual students in elementary physical education classes.

Participants and Context

Six experienced elementary physical education teachers (3 male and 3 female) and 310 of their fourth-grade students participated in the study.

Design and Method

Two of each teacher's regular classes were used, and information was recorded 3 times from each of those classes, producing a total of 36 occasions for class observation and recording. It is interesting to note that the investigator was careful to be present in each class for at least three classes before any formal recording work was done, just to be sure the teacher and class were accustomed to the presence of an outsider.

The study employed a widely used instrument (the *Individual Teacher Behavior and Analysis System*) that allowed on-the-spot recording of each time the teacher verbally interacted with a specific pupil and the categorization of that communication into one of seven categories: criticize, praise, ask question, give directions, lecture, accept or use idea, and accept feeling. Each student wore a coded vest so that individuals could be reliably identified. Two observers coded each class, and their records were frequently cross-checked to be sure that they were consistent in how they categorized each teacher behavior. They tried to be unobtrusive, remaining close enough to hear accurately but far enough away to attract little attention. Finally, in advance of the observed classes, teachers were asked to categorize students in each class according to how much they participated in the typical class. They had to select 7 who were high participators and 7 who were low, with the remainder being assigned to a middle category.

Results

In all, 4,632 individualized teacher behaviors were recorded and categorized. Using a computer, the investigators searched for regularities within this large body of information, seeking patterns that were so clear and pervasive that they were unlikely to have appeared by accident. The results were clear-cut and substantial. Students who had been preclassified as high participators received much more praise and encouragement. Their ideas were accepted by the teacher almost twice as often as those offered by low participators. In terms of how often interactions occurred, the teachers' perceptions of participation levels was associated with attention. The average high participant received 18 instances of attention, the medium (middle level) participant 15, and the low participant only 12.

Male students received more individual attention than female, but those interactions more often consisted of criticism of the student's behavior or justifications of the teacher's authority. Again, differences were substantial: boys were three times more likely to be criticized than girls.

A Researcher's Perspective

Hypotheses are readily available that offer explanations for some of these results. Many elementary school boys, for example, are more aggressive and less compliant than their female counterparts. It would be easy to account for their higher rates of teacher interaction simply in terms of the frequency with which they act out in class. But is that logical connection correct, and does it really account for the rather large gender disparity? Could it not be that girls are as much ignored or less closely monitored by the teacher as they are compliant with teacher instructions and rules for class behavior?

An alternative explanation might rest in the old "rich getting richer" problem. Sometimes it is the pupils who already are doing well who receive disproportionate shares of teacher approval and support when in fact those teacher interactions might be better directed to slower students who need them more. Whatever the circumstances may have been in the classes used for this study, there is no scarcity of possible causes for the observed disproportions in who received the teachers' attention.

> **Sometimes it is the pupils who already are doing well who receive disproportionate shares of teacher approval and support.**

A Teacher's Perspective

With studies such as this one, it is probably inevitable that the first response of most teachers will be defensive. Certainly that was my own reflex. I immediately said, "But not in my classes!" After some cooling off, however, I thought about the findings and found several things to say that I hope are not as defensive.

First, fairness is taken to be a serious issue by both students and teachers, which probably explains much of our sensitivity to what this research suggests. Most teachers truly want to provide equitable opportunities to every student, but the range of behaviors presented by students sometimes makes that difficult indeed. The teachers who I see doing the best job of equalizing their class interactions do so through systematizing their distribution of attention, particularly during such instructional activities as practice with individual feedback, turn-taking, and question and answer sessions.

Second, I have to admit that how you divide your attention among 30 pupils over a half hour or so of rapid and complex interactions is hard to self-monitor and probably difficult to recall with much accuracy. My guess is that there could be some fairly large discrepancies in the kind and amount of attention I give to individuals, without my being aware that it is even happening. If letting that go on in my classes can have a bad effect on some students or can give others an unfair advantage, then surely I need to do something about it.

My third response to that concern is that as a teacher, once I am aware of this discrepancy, I am obliged to take corrective action! It takes no great effort, cost, or scientific skill to check and see exactly how your teaching looks with regard to passing out individual attention because I have done it for both myself and with preservice students. All you need to do is audiotape a few classes by wearing a lightweight recorder—or, better still, videotape them. Video captures the personal attention with eyes or gestures that we often use in teaching. With videotape, you also get to see exactly what preceded your interaction with a student. A cordless microphone works best as the sound source, but just setting the camera up in a corner and letting it run without audio catches a lot of the action as well. Taping is not likely to be something you will have time to do every week, but even once a year can provide fascinating feedback about the patterns in your own teaching behavior.

However you record your actions (audio or video), just sit down for the playback with a class list in hand. You can mark tics for each time you give individual attention to a student. Consider even doing some coding by using such things as a plus (+) for positive words, a zero (0) for neutral ones, and a letter *N* for nags and criticisms. As an alternative, you can draw lines to form columns for those types of interaction opposite the names. Just put a tic in the column that matches the kind of attention you gave. If there are patterns on the list of student names, you won't need statistics and a graduate degree to spot them! If you are like me, things such as a completely missed student will jump right off the page.

To be completely honest about this, I have to admit that feedback of that sort can be disturbing. It is perfectly natural to have some strong reactions. My own first response was to invent rationalizations for explaining my interaction patterns as things I had to do—usually in the name of class management, individualizing instruction, or responding to special needs. My advice here is to remember that it takes a while to let go of such defense mechanisms and face what you are seeing with a hard and honest eye. Don't rush to judgments, just live with it for a few days and when there are those rare moments to spare, simply think about it.

For me, the really neat thing about this kind of problem is that it is one of those teaching behaviors that you can change promptly, permanently, and without a lot of heavy lifting. For example, consider following a plan for alternating your attention between two groups—boy/girl, high-skill/low-skill, tall/short, shy/assertive, and so on. It takes a little effort the first few times but by itself can produce noticeable shifts in the pattern of your class interactions. You may be surprised by how quickly such protocols become habit.

Jim DeLine, an elementary physical education teacher in my own school district in Austin, Texas, does two things with regard to individual attention. He teaches a class protocol in which every student should expect to be called on at any time. He presents this not as a "caught you" system, but as a part of student responsibility and as an opportunity for good performance. Students have to be focused on the lesson if they are to be ready because the call may come to anyone at any time. He then works hard at systematizing his public interactions with students. He often uses the boy/girl protocol, but sometimes invents new ways of spreading the call around, perhaps selecting every third student in a circle, just so he doesn't get in the rut of calling repeatedly on either the eager beavers or the daydreamers.

> **Most teachers truly want to provide equitable opportunities to every student, but the range of behaviors presented by students sometimes makes that difficult indeed.**

If you were to watch his classes, you would see high levels of students' paying attention and an impressive degree of quality in what students have to say when they are called on because they all are expecting that call, all the time. By working out a plan to eliminate much of the annoying hand-waving and the tendency to call on a few students over and over, he achieved much more than just greater equity for distributing his own attention across students. He achieved higher and more uniform attention among the students and a consequent improvement in their ability to reflect on the day's learning.

Did that very practical strategy evolve out of his response to the findings from a research study such as this one? You bet it did! He read the study; he examined his own classes; he created a better environment in which children could learn.

 ## Common Ground: A Shared Perspective

Differential teacher-student interactions are a fact of life in many physical education classes. Some of those differences should be disturbing to us. If we ask whether or not teachers are typically aware of what they are doing with regard to those differentials, the answer probably will be that some are,

many more are not, and some would deny it vociferously. Whatever may be true, it appears likely that teachers are reacting to certain student characteristics in ways that would be difficult to interpret as consciously planned for the benefit of the pupils.

Teacher actions such as these form part of the environment within which students learn. In a physical education class, it is quite possible that they are important factors in how much students learn and how well they learn it. More important, the interactions themselves contain messages that *are* learned. For example, students whose ideas are often accepted and praised probably learn to attend closely to instruction so that they can have more and even better ideas. A reading of this modest study leads us to conclude that all teachers, ourselves included, could profit from knowing what their typical patterns of interaction are like. With that knowledge in hand, it would be possible to correct inequities or plan even more effective ways of interacting with students.

> **Students whose ideas are often accepted and praised probably learn to attend closely to instruction so that they can have more and even better ideas.**

More Days per Week Equals More Learning

Treanor, L.J., Vanin, S.K., Nolan, C., Housner, L.D., Wiegand, R.L., & Hawkins, A. (1997). The effects of 3-day-a-week and 1-day-a-week physical education on the development of children's motor skills and knowledge in the United States. *Pedagogy in Practice, 3*(2), 3-18.

The familiar research format suggested in the title for this small study obscures the fact that it was more than a routine reexamination of a variable that is already well understood—time to learn. The authors make perfectly clear that the investigation was designed to have a political utility that was just as important to them as the research purpose. In short, they wanted findings that teachers and parents could use to convince school administrators that more frequent class meetings would yield important improvements in what pupils learned in physical education. To that end, they needed not only sound methodology and clear-cut results but also a report that was sufficiently clear to be understood by most laypersons. You can judge how close they came to that ideal by retrieving their end product in its full form. Our intention here, however, is to tell you enough to make that task seem worthwhile.

 ## The Study

The proximal purpose of this study was to investigate the relative effects of participation in a 1-day-a-week program versus a 3-day-a-week program on the development of children's motor skills and knowledge. The more distal purpose, however, was to inquire into the effects of typical curricular policy decisions (in North America) that determine the time allotted for elementary school physical education.

As with many of the studies selected for this text, this investigation would be classified as a *quasi experiment*. The label is not intended to suggest an inferior status or inherent defect in design. Quasi experiments are employed when circumstances dictate that the researcher is not able to exercise control over every variable in the study (certainly a condition that would be present in most public schools) or able to assign students and treatments by random procedures.

The Participants and Context

Investigators compared the outcomes of 3-day-a-week and 1-day-a-week physical education programs using 76 fourth- and fifth-graders from four intact classes at one elementary school. With two fifth-grade and two sixth-grade classes, the programs could be assigned so that each level had a 3-day-a-week and a 1-day-a-week class. The same physical education specialist taught all four classes over the 8-week span of the study. The teacher's limited objective for both programs was to improve pupil performance of and knowledge about three fundamental skills: throwing, kicking, and catching.

Design and Method

The potential for differences in the teaching for the two programs was controlled by review of lesson plans and an analysis of the systematic observations of the teacher and student behaviors. Both the teacher and the students were found to be doing just about the same things in both programs, but total class time in the 1-day-a-week program was just a lot less.

Student performance in the three skills was tested before the study began and tested at its conclusion for quantitative measures of outcome (how far, how fast, how accurate) and qualitative measures of form. Among the innovative measures employed was radar measurement of velocity for both thrown and kicked balls. Assessment of form was based on students' performance of critical elements in each of the three skills (lists of these key components are included in the report and by themselves may justify an effort to retrieve the study). Students' knowledge of concepts associated with the skills was measured with a short written examination.

Results

Although scores for the boys were uniformly higher than those for the girls, the four classes appeared to be similar in performance levels before the study began. At the end, however, after 8 weeks of instruction at the specified frequency for each group, students in the two 3-day-a-week classes were ahead on all measures. The margin of difference was sufficiently large to indicate truly practical significance, with the largest margins being seen in knowledge, kicking, and catching. In addition, analysis indicated the presence of what researchers call a *main effect for gender*. In this case, the main effect for gender means that the gains over the 8 weeks were largest for the girls.

A Researcher's Perspective

Children learn more when they receive more instruction and more opportunities to practice—granted that the instruction is competent, well-planned, and appropriate to their stage of development and that the practice is supplemented with accurate feedback. Exactly how much of these two factors contributed to the findings is beyond the scope of this study. That question, however, does not really matter, given the purposes of the investigators. There is convincing evidence that time in the form of class meetings per week makes a difference. Here the difference is clear, dramatic, and unambiguous. Perhaps most important of all, the difference is greatest for the girls, who, if they are typical of fourth- and fifth-grade girls, are already being left behind in their development of important movement skills.

> **There is convincing evidence that time in the form of class meetings per week makes a difference.**

A Teacher's Perspective

It's always satisfying when there is some research to support what we know intuitively. Of course, students make more progress when they are given more opportunities to learn. The amount of practice time really does affect the quality of children's motor skills, and given sufficient opportunity, all girls and boys can learn to throw, catch, and kick. The findings here constitute powerful and important information, and the investigators deserve our appreciation for paying attention to the topic.

As comforting as these concrete findings are, however, they are not going to serve the political ends that motivated the investigators in the first place. To make this study truly influential, we first would have to be dealing with policy makers who care about children's development of physical skill.

If what I have seen of policy concerning the scheduling of physical education in the school districts of my state is close to the norm for the nation, then that essential condition is not commonly in place. The findings of this study, however powerful they may seem to us, would be irrelevant to most of the school boards that I know. Developing motor skills simply has not been seen as a significant educational outcome—except in the case of elite athletes. Until we can help the general public connect the impact of children feeling competent in motor skills with the likelihood of their adopting a physically active lifestyle, most makers of public policy will continue to be an impediment to progress.

New evidence concerning physical skills and cognitive development has received some positive attention in both educational literature and, more significantly, the public press. An impact at the level of local school policy, however, appears to be unlikely in the near term. Potentially more powerful has been the growing attention given to the relationship between daily physical activity and personal health. Publications from the surgeon general and the Centers for Disease Control and Prevention have stimulated wide concern about the epidemic of obesity and related conditions such as diabetes. With that as a background in the public consciousness, recent congressional passage of the bill *Physical Education for Progress* (PEP) may provide growing support for maintaining a segment of time devoted to physical education in the public schools. Unfortunately, however, the apportioning of time in the school day is a zero-sum game— that is, more time for one subject means less time for another. Fierce competition is the inevitable result, and while having life and death issues on our side would appear to be rather convincing artillery, it is certainly not a guarantee of success.

The findings of this study, however powerful they may seem to us, would be irrelevant to most of the school boards that I know. Developing motor skills simply has not been seen as a significant educational outcome—except in the case of elite athletes.

My own sense is that we will escape this catch-22 situation only by creating small class-sized experimental programs within schools or districts. Although limited in scope, such programs within programs allow direct examination of the consequences (academic, physical, psychological, and social) produced by a commitment to physical education that lasts for several years, rather than several weeks or months. When findings of that kind are then placed before parents and the community at large, it is easier to get attention and ultimately support for larger initiatives. In other words, statistically significant results based on longitudinal study will always yield more action from the general public than recommendations sent up the administrative ladder to the superintendent's office or reports cited at a school board meeting as a means of fending off budget cuts.

Such strategy almost certainly would require outside grant funding, and the cooperation of a building principal would be absolutely essential (at the very least). All of that would be difficult—but none of it is impossible. Indeed, the new federal PEP legislation already is providing the support needed to get such small pilot programs started. If positive findings from the evaluation of those time-enriched programs are then replicated, we may at last have the attention of policy makers. Beyond the bounds of such practical strategies, however, there is a more important source of persuasion—parents. Parents who see children who are healthier, happier, and more skillful can exert the kind of genuine political power that research reports will never be able to apply.

As excited as I am about the evidence here that girls, given the opportunity, can improve greatly in their motor skills, this is the sort of study that makes me want to slice the data in a different way. If we could look at before-and-after measures for high- and low-skilled students, would they break as cleanly by gender as the authors and their mean statistics imply, or would we find both boys and girls in both ability groups? Were most of the girls at the bottom of the distribution when they started, and is that the reason for their significant improvement? Were most of the boys close to the ceiling for performance, and is that the reason for their much smaller gains?

My own experience as a teacher tells me that this is unlikely . . . but that the point is not trivial. It is all too easy to fall into the habit of stereotyping gender differences ("Boys are like this and girls are like that") when important exceptions make those much less than valid characterizations. My own bet is that the lower-skilled students, both boys and girls, registered significant gains. Social factors could easily be misinterpreted as a biologically based gender difference. For example, pervasive support for physical activity by boys would almost surely mean fewer boys in the lower-skilled portion of each class.

As a postscript for my reaction to this study, I want to share one highly personal response. Is anyone else made uncomfortable by the fact that we struggle so hard to maintain physical education time while at the same time we accept the cutting of students from school athletic teams? And let there be no equivocating about it, those cuts not only deprive students of opportunity—they erode desire for participation as well!

I know all of the traditional justifications concerning budget, space, and scheduling complexities. But, if participation in sports genuinely teaches students the value of effort and teamwork, shouldn't sports be made available to all students who want to invest the effort? If the surgeon general's report, and all of the powerful arguments it contains about the value of physical activity for health, applies to physical education, then why does it not apply to interscholastic sports? Don't school teams serve as important routes to active lifestyles as our students become adults? I wonder what contradictory patterns of physical activity might be found if we tracked the consequences over time for those students who got to play and those who were cut from a school's athletic teams?

Common Ground: Our Shared Perspective

Of course there were differences among students. Certainly some aspects of skill learning were more promptly influenced by the opportunity for two extra sessions of practice and instruction each week. None of that, however, alters the bottom line. In physical education as in any classroom subject, more time to learn means more learning for more students. We will dare to extract one more conclusion from this study. At least through the upper-elementary grades, the disastrous decline in girls' performance of skills needed for participation in physical activity might be delayed or substantially reduced if they had daily physical education taught by a qualified practitioner.

> **In physical education as in any classroom subject, more time to learn means more learning for more students.**

This statement is a considerable leap if we were to make it only on the basis of this single, modest investigation. If this study were combined with all the accumulated evidence that now is available, the result would be far more persuasive. The critical question, of course, is whether policy makers are prepared to assign sufficient value to what physical education can provide for both boys and girls. Once they arrive at such a conclusion, perhaps then they can give physical education an adequate portion of the most valuable school resource of all—time. That question, however, is for another day. First things first, this study can be used to urge that if learning is the game, 3 days per week handily beats 1 day per week!

Modifying Equipment to Fit the Students

Chase, M.A., Ewing, M.E., Lirgg, C.D., & George, T.R. (1994). The effects of equipment modification on children's self-efficacy and basketball shooting performance. *Research Quarterly for Exercise and Sport, 65,* 159-168.

A significant portion of the adult world is inaccessible to children—because key components of that world are structured to match the size and strength of an adult body. Bicycles, kitchen cupboards, piano keyboards, and even carnival rides can present physical barriers to a child's ability to sample the activities of grown-ups (at least to do so safely and comfortably). With volleyball nets (too high), golf clubs (too long), baseball bats (too heavy), and basketballs (too big), the domains of sport and physical recreation provide many familiar examples of the mismatches that deny access to children.

The commercial marketplace, of course, is replete with implements that have been scaled down to fit smaller hands, shorter statures, and limited physical abilities. But what about the typical elementary school gymnasium—and equipment closet—what modifications would we find there? What real account do physical education teachers there take of the fact that their pupils are neither adult in stature nor mature in physical capacities? More to the point of the present study, we might wonder about the consequences when teachers do modify equipment (or the formal rules and dimensions of an adult game) so as to admit their charges into the mysteries and pleasures of full participation. The following study offers an example of how the tools of research can be employed to explore just such questions and concerns.

The Study

The investigators here have brought the tools of sophisticated research design and modern data-analysis to bear on an old question, one familiar to any elementary school physical educator: What is the effect of modifying ball size and basket height on children's shooting performance? Readers should note that with only 10 attempts per shooting test, this was not a study of learning over an extended period of practice. The results show only the effect of equipment changes on whatever shooting skills the participating children already had acquired.

The study involved two variables: first, shooting performance with different-sized balls and basket heights, and second, children's sense of self-efficacy as influenced by their shooting performance (that is, the degree of confidence in their ability to perform a skill). In this annotation, however, we focus on the variable of equipment modification, making only brief mention of the self-efficacy measures.

Participants and Context

Investigators recruited 74 children for participation in this investigation. Unlike most of the research included in this text, the study was not performed in physical education classes in a public school. The venue was a community recreation program, and the study participants were volunteers from teams playing in its basketball league.

Nonetheless, by age (9-12 years, $M = 10.10$) and gender (34 girls and 40 boys), the children were not unlike those who appear in elementary school physical education classes in grades 3 through 6. Only in terms of playing experience (girls 2.0 years, and boys 2.3) did they appear to be exceptional, and even then their abilities spanned a substantial range. Finally, the activity itself—shooting baskets from a set point on the floor, 12 feet from the basket in the center of the foul lane—was identical to something included in virtually every basketball unit taught in physical education. We make those points specifically because we think it is reasonable for readers to assume that the results can apply to other settings, most notably in elementary school physical education classes.

Design and Method

The basketballs used were the official women's ball and the official men's ball, weighing and measuring 19 ounces with a 29-inch circumference and 21 ounces with a 30-inch circumference (respectively). Basket height was adjusted so that the rim was either 8 or 10 feet from the floor (the league used the women's ball and baskets set at 9 feet).

Rather than the official foul-shot distance of 15 feet, investigators used a distance of 12 feet. Pilot tests had showed that with the full-sized ball at a distance of 15 feet, the shots of most children would not reach a rim set at 10 feet. This set of variables produced four shooting conditions: the smaller ball at each of the two basket heights, and the larger ball at each height.

Demographic information such as age, gender, and experience was gathered by questionnaire, and a set of simple anatomical measurements recorded height and hand size. The participants' sense of self-efficacy was measured with a standardized paper-and-pencil form, completed before and after shooting, at each condition. The shooting test consisted of 10 shots under each of the four conditions, the first 2 shots serving as warm-up and the remaining 8 shots being scored on a 4-point scale: zero for an air ball, 1 for hitting backboard or net, 2 for hitting the rim, and 3 for a basket. Children were not made aware of the scoring system except for the recording of baskets made, which served as a second measure of shooting performance.

Participants were randomly assigned to groups of 3 or 4 that then rotated through the four conditions, each in a different randomly assigned order. Shooting performance was tested in a small-group setting to make the task appear more gamelike, as well as to provide efficiency in ball retrieval. Investigators completed all testing in the same gymnasium within a single day.

Results

As a preliminary to the main analysis, the investigators first examined the relationship between anatomical measures and shooting performance. For both boys and girls, height and hand-size correlations were positive but low—in the range between .12 and .26. Likewise, the number of years of playing experience showed only a small correlational relationship to shooting scores: .22 for girls and .17 for boys. It is thus clear that most of the variance in shooting was accounted for by factors other than physical size and experience (strength, however, was not tested). Finally, there were no significant differences attributable to the order in which students performed the tests (i.e., the four conditions).

The full set of results occupied three double-columned pages of the report, including four data tables and one figure. For present purpose, however, they can be boiled down to a small number of primary findings. First, boys performed significantly better than girls did for both basket heights—and this applied to both the 4-point scoring system and the number of baskets made. This advantage was modest at 8 feet (4 points) but became large at 10 feet (9 points). Second, girls achieved significantly better shooting scores at the 8-foot basket as opposed to the 10-foot basket (14 points versus 8 points, respectively). Third, the boys' performance under the scoring system was not significantly different at the two rim heights. Fourth, both boys and girls made significantly more baskets at the 8-foot rim versus the 10-foot rim. Fifth, and finally, the 9- and 10-year-olds had significantly better shooting scores at the 8-foot height, but for 11- and 12-year-olds, basket height was not a factor. No significant differences were found for the factor of ball size on any test for either gender or grade level.

As with shooting performance, the results for measures of self-efficacy were complex but could be reduced to a small set of findings. First, children had higher expectations and greater confidence before shooting than after shooting. Second, boys generally had a higher sense of self-efficacy than did girls. Third, and finally, children produced higher scores on the self-efficacy tests when shooting at the 8-foot rim and when using the smaller ball. Grade-level analyses of self-efficacy scores revealed no significant differences for either boys or girls.

A Researcher's Perspective

It seems clear that although the two distributions of shooting performance must have overlapped substantially for boys and girls, modification of rim height would be especially important for girls. The fact that the data show 40% of the attempts by girls at the 10-foot rim produced air balls (scored as zero) suggests that their disadvantage could have been related to strength. In other words, some of the children may have been attempting an impossible task.

On the other hand, the researchers point out some interesting alternative explanations for the gender difference. Boys and girls both averaged about two years of playing experience, but a factor that might have been influential in producing a gender difference was the amount of practice. On average, boys reported practicing 2 more days each week than did girls. The consequence of that difference would be cumulative, perhaps beginning earlier and surely exerting an increasingly pronounced effect as the children grew older. This variable suggests an interesting alternative to gender as the basis for analysis of the data—that is, divide the participants by the estimated number of practice sessions they had previously attended.

Another provocative explanation for gender differences might be found in the quality of basketball instruction available to boys and girls, both in the recreation league and elsewhere. The authors note the fact that the boys' shooting scores were much less variable than the girls' scores. These scores suggest a greater degree of homogeneous ability among the boys—a pattern that often emerges when one group is exposed to strong instruction and frequent opportunities for practice that are not available to a comparison group.

Whatever the set of conditions that determined the girls' scores, one thing seems certain. Children who continue to fail during shooting attempts will choose not to practice shooting, will exert less effort when they do practice, and will persist in basketball for a shorter period of time than those who are more often successful. In those terms, it may well be that equality of opportunity to develop their abilities may depend on the simple stratagem of having an 8-foot basket available for instruction, practice, and games. Beyond that, however, there truly are unanswered questions about the relative quality of instruction and coaching available to girls—in gymnasiums with baskets of any height.

> **Children who continue to fail during shooting attempts will choose not to practice shooting, will exert less effort when they do practice, and will persist in basketball for a shorter period of time than those who are more often successful.**

The failure of ball size to exert a significant effect on performance was both a surprise for the investigators and a finding that runs contrary to previous research. The best hypothesis seems to be that the differences in size and weight between men's and women's official balls simply were too small to be of much consequence for the participants (1 inch and 2 ounces). The authors speculated after the fact that the use of an intermediate, or junior, ball with a circumference of 27.25 inches might have provided a more functional contrast. The authors correctly caution readers not to extend the nonsignificant findings for ball size in shooting to other basketball skills, such as dribbling and passing. There is some reason to believe that such findings are highly task-specific.

A Teacher's Perspective

I am so glad that adjustable baskets now are more commonly found in elementary school facilities. I gather from this annotation that they now are appearing in the recreation centers of public and private agencies as well. The review of literature provided in the original report of this study offers some valid reasons for making such equipment the standard for new school construction. Higher rates of success, more rapid acquisition of skill, and all kinds of positive responses from children are among the benefits that have regularly appeared.

With regard to educational practice, studies such as this one that offer information bearing directly on decisions teachers have to make always deserve special acknowledgement. Evidence about the impact of basket height on success as well as sense of efficacy is directly helpful—even if it only lends support to a commonsense belief that equipment should fit children. For that we owe the authors a vote of thanks.

From my vantage point, this study contains two points of special interest. The first point is immediately practical and rests in the central finding itself—that adjustable heights are valuable. I suspect that I am not the only veteran teacher who has argued with parents who didn't want their child to be disadvantaged in competitive play because they had practiced at an 8-foot basket in physical education class. Data such as these won't win over all of those skeptical parents; however, they do give me even greater confidence as I try to explain why my own decision has always been to modify any dimension of the learning environment that serves to promote learning.

The second point of interest that attracted my close attention was the analysis of scores by gender and the resulting collection of findings. That initial step, analyzing the data by using the construct of gender, provided an important conceptual frame for the study. The authors were obviously interested in finding explanations for why there was a substantial score disparity favoring boys. Their various analyses provide several plausible and thoughtful explanations as well as a number of cautions that should guide our understanding of the situation.

All well and good, but I am just not sure that gender is the most appropriate and fruitful variable for analysis in such a study. It is at least possible that the researchers selected gender simply because it was easy. The gender variable quickly provides two groups based on a simple and highly reliable indicator, but this variable is not always the most revealing or most powerful option. The authors themselves emphasize that there were all kinds of gender correlates at work in producing scores, not least of them strength, experience, quality of instruction, and motivation. And all of those factors are

modifiable variables, rather than the inevitable consequences of biology.

If you consider how the scores were distributed in the actual published report, you will see immediately that there were some girls who scored exactly as the boys did—and the reverse was true for boys. A substantial number of them performed at or below the average level for girls. Now just for speculation, suppose that we did the analysis on the basis of prescores for self-efficacy. What would you conclude if the same sort of score difference appeared for the self-efficacy factor, with more confident students shooting better than the less confident, irrespective of gender, height, hand size, and so on? For me, the implication would be to locate and provide special help for students with a poor sense of optimism about what they could learn and do with a basketball. I would not conclude, however, that I needed to take special care to support girls. Sometimes such special care provides a strong message that girls always need extra help, and thus it may actually serve to erode their sense of self-efficacy.

That there would be some girls in the less confident group goes without saying, but by selecting a variable other than gender for our analysis we would have to let go of what might be a false and limiting assumption. In a like fashion, the real factor that produced score differentials might be strength (a point noted by the authors). While strength is a correlate of gender, it also is a physical characteristic that can be improved for both boys and girls, even within the restrictive confines of many physical education programs.

The same thing is true of experience in the form of opportunity to practice. As we all know how powerful that is, why not make it the variable of first choice when inspecting the data for important relationships? For example, compare the scores of children who had experienced more than 60 practice sessions with children who had experienced fewer than 20 practice sessions. It seems to me that the cause of doing good research ought to be a sufficient rationale for considering a richer array of possibilities other than gender.

What does this study say to me as a teacher? I think it suggests the following. First, we should provide adjustable baskets and instruct at various

> The gender variable quickly provides two groups based on a simple and highly reliable indicator, but this variable is not always the most revealing or most powerful option.

shooting distances for children of all ages and skill levels. That is, for those who are younger, smaller, or less experienced, we should lower the rims and shorten the shooting distances. Second, we should make sure the magnitude of equipment modification is big enough to make a real difference for the learners. Third, and finally, we should not jump to the conclusion that gender is the best explanation for why some girls may not be as successful as some boys at shooting the basketball. At best, that assumption is no more than the automatic reflex of a mind that has become closed to other really interesting and useful possibilities. At worst, when such an assumption is communicated to girls, it carries a destructive message: Boys are inherently better at this activity than girls, so it must be a boys' activity!

Common Ground: Our Shared Perspective

We will not attempt to summarize the authors' lengthy discussion of findings for self-efficacy. It is sufficient here to note that previous research suggests that there may be a positive relationship between children's sense of efficacy and their performance. If that is the case and if one result of persisting failure is the downward adjustment of efficacy expectations, then modifications of equipment may be a far more important factor in learning than has generally been understood. At the very least, once basketball is introduced in the elementary school program, the fun of "swishing one" ought to be available to all children—irrespective of gender, grade level, or physical size and strength. It is clear that an appropriate way to achieve that end is by modifications of equipment, and in some cases, the required changes would be substantially greater than those employed in the present study.

> Once basketball is introduced in the elementary school program, the fun of "swishing one" ought to be available to all children—irrespective of gender, grade level, or physical size and strength.

PART II
Managing the Class

THE STUDY

RESEARCHER

TEACHER

COMMON GROUND

Reducing Disruptive Student Behaviors

White, A.G., & Bailey, J.S. (1990). Reducing disruptive behaviors of elementary physical education students with sit and watch. *Journal of Applied Behavior Analysis, 23,* 353-359.

If it is to be conducive to instruction, practice, and learning, a physical education class requires a degree of structure, predictability, and security for both teacher and pupils. When those qualities are undermined by disruptive student behaviors, the possibilities for learning are reduced and the work of teaching becomes far more demanding and invariably less pleasant. That much is obvious to anyone who has spent time in school. Insiders also know that one key element in the transition from novice teacher to expert practitioner is the acquisition of a repertoire of methods for preventing disruptions and dealing with students who persist in misbehaving.

Not all of those methods are equally effective, however, and not all are appropriate to the contexts in which they are used. There is a great deal of sometimes-useful lore about various strategies that teachers have used in attempting to prevent or manage disruptions in physical education. Surprisingly, though, only a few systematic attempts have been made to raise questions about any of those tools. This modest investigation provides an exception to that unhappy tradition.

The Study

For this study, you are returned to one of the most venerable and widely used methods of class man-

agement at the elementary school level, the *time-out*—or, for the purposes of this annotation, the *sit-and-watch*. Here, the researchers asked a number of simple questions: Does it really work? Does it work consistently over time? Will it work with really difficult students? As a teaching skill, is it difficult to master? Is it acceptable in the views of colleagues, administrators, and parents? Can it be used in ways that do not interrupt ongoing class activities? Can it be operated in a manner that encourages a degree of student responsibility?

This small-scale investigation used two classes and one teacher with simple definitions of what constitutes disruptive behavior and with commonsense procedures for recording what was observed. This particular approach is called *behavior analysis,* and more elaborate examples of such designs can be found in chapters 7 and 11. Understanding the results requires no knowledge of statistics or other research conventions. In short, this is commonsense science, not rocket science. The design of the study and the graphic presentation of results are easy to understand and yield a surprising degree of persuasive power.

Participants and Context

Two elementary-level physical education classes met three times a week for 30 minutes: a regular fourth-grade class composed of 30 students and a special class of 14 fourth- and fifth-grade boys who had displayed severe behavior problems in school. The regular teacher (female) first learned then implemented a simple procedure for suppressing the frequency of disruptive incidents. The investigators initially had been directed to the special class because the teacher had reported serious concerns and had requested help with frequent student disruptions and dangerously aggressive behavior. The study context, then, involved the researchers in the role of teaching consultants.

Design and Method

Plastic juice bottles, tape, and fine sand were used to construct primitive but durable and relatively indestructible hourglass timers. A set of three simple rules were then explained to the students. First, respond promptly and appropriately to teacher requests (give compliance); second, do not touch or interfere with other students in any way (no aggression); and third, do not treat equipment in inappropriate ways (use correctly). The consequences of transgression were made equally clear. Once identified as engaging in disruptive behavior, the pupil immediately had to go to a designated area on the sidelines, place one of the inverted hourglasses directly in front of him- or herself and watch silently until the sand had run through (about 3 minutes). The student then was responsible for stowing the timer and quietly returning to the ongoing activity of the class.

Teacher training took only 30 minutes, including the reading of an instruction sheet, demonstrations, some role-playing, and discussion of the rationale for sit-and-watch. Emphasis was on prompt and consistent use of the sanction. Throughout the study, the teacher received and was encouraged to seek advice concerning appropriate use of the special class management procedures.

Three specially trained observers watched each class meeting from different vantage points spaced around the instructional area. They then recorded the total number of disruptive pupil behaviors observed, whether they were noticed or sanctioned by the teacher, or not. A cordless microphone worn by the teacher ensured that each observer could hear all verbal interactions with perfect clarity.

Before the implementation of the management program, observers obtained a clear and accurate impression of each of the two classes by recording frequency counts of total disruptions for at least 4 weeks. As you would expect, there was consider-able variation from day to day, but generally the level of student misbehaviors was quite high. Per 10-minute block of observation time, number of misbehaviors averaged 219 in the special physical education class and 53 in the regular fourth-grade class. This level of disruption had persisted despite the teacher's efforts to suppress misbehavior through use of her own class management techniques, which the observers noted were used infrequently and inconsistently.

Results

The sit-and-watch timers were put to use at the 18th meeting of the regular fourth grade, during which the average rate of disruptions per class immediately fell to 4, where it remained without much change for the remaining 4 weeks of program use. The timers appeared in the special physical education class one week later, with precisely the same result, slightly more than 4 disruptions per class for the remaining 10 class meetings. The largest number of students sitting out at any one time was 4, and the typical situation was 1 or 2 removed from active participation. Repeat offenders in any one class period also lost access to other desirable activities, such as time available for free play and computer use, which appeared to restrain any inclination to experiment with deliberate misbehavior.

Students appeared to accept responsibility for use of the timers and usually managed a self-governed return to class activity. The sanctioning of pupils offered only brief interruptions to ongoing instruction, and indeed, the reduction in disruptions appeared to allow smoother lessons and greater opportunity for learning. The teacher indicated that she liked the system, and a careful check confirmed that a sample of other teachers, parents, and school administrators saw nothing inappropriate about its use.

 **A Researcher's Perspective**

One has to wonder whether the apparent magic produced by sand in a bottle would persist over a longer period of time as novelty can be a powerful factor and whether eventual phasing out of the system would leave behind students who had internalized a greater level of self-control. Unfortunately, simple, short-term experiments such as this one often prohibit answers about the long-term persistence of effects. On the other hand, many teachers, especially beginners who are struggling to master the mysteries of classroom control, would be delighted to have a little magic in a bottle, even if it could not be counted on as a permanent feature of class management.

In this consideration, it is important to remember that factors other than just the timing mechanism were involved in the system. For instance, the sanction was prompt, rather than delayed. It was predictable rather than capricious; the pupils knew precisely what would happen. The punishment logically related to the crime, rather than being purely arbitrary: "If you interfere with others in the class, then you must leave the class!" Sit-and-watch is reasonable, rather than excessive in measure—although 3 minutes must have dragged when exciting things were happening on the floor. Finally, it was intentionally designed to engage the student in responsible application of the process. That is, the culprit had to act as both the prisoner and executioner by manually turning over his or her fate in the form of a homemade hourglass. Across many studies of this topic, those features appear to be characteristic of successful class management systems.

> Many teachers, especially beginners who are struggling to master the mysteries of classroom control, would be delighted to have a little magic in a bottle . . .

A Teacher's Perspective

Three cheers for this teacher who recognized the problem and was willing to seek and use help. Reaching out is never easy to do, and truly effective assistance is not always available. Obviously, though, 50 or more disruptions in 10 minutes would drive anyone crazy rather quickly! Rather than bailing out or becoming a tyrant and punishing the entire class, this teacher sought assistance and got it. Sometimes the system actually can work as it should.

What a relief it must have been for her when the average number of daily disruptions in the regular class fell from 53 to 4. What a blessing also for the children who had not been disruptive in the first place; at last they could have a safe and uninterrupted chance to participate and learn. I suspect that the new regimen was a blessing also for the pupils who had for whatever reason felt it necessary to engage in disruptive behaviors every day, rather than just relaxing and getting into whatever the lesson was about. The original report shows that only

1 student in the fourth-grade class and only 4 in the alternative class ever went to sit-and-watch for a second time during a single class period. For me, that is evidence that the intervention truly was powerful stuff!

Can you imagine the frustration created by 657 disruptive episodes in one 30-minute class (219 disruptions per 10 minutes times 3), which would be the average number of observed incidents prior to application of the procedure? Does it happen? Sure it does. Do the teachers it happens to find it painful? Of course they do. Do they try to solve the problem? Certainly they do. Can they struggle without success? Obviously! Almost invisible in that litany of frustration, however, is a valuable lesson that this study drove home for me.

The authors state that the baseline observations revealed disruptions that seemed to result from the teacher's inconsistent application of disciplinary consequences for students' inappropriate behavior. In other words, there the teacher was, trying to deal with a serious problem, but at the same time oblivious to her own part in creating that problem. That scenario fits my own experience with situations where my own behavior is tangled up in a teaching situation gone sour. It invariably took another pair of eyes to untangle things by spotting my role in the problem. That is, it's hard for teachers to see their situation without bias when they themselves are the cause of their own difficulty. If you think of it that way, sit-and-watch in this study may have served as a modification strategy for teacher behavior, as well as a means for suppressing student misbehavior. If that is the case, then all the more reason to think that the teacher's courage in accepting outside observers was a critical element in the happy outcome.

If consistent responses to misbehavior are a key part of successful class management, then the teacher must be sufficiently comfortable to apply the sanction regularly. Because the response technique used in this study was neither complicated nor unreasonably tough, the teacher apparently did not hesitate to apply it when needed. That response is the kind of personal comfort that allows consistency to develop.

One of the questions I have with regard to the sit-and-watch technique as used in this study is, How does it actually work to help students become more responsible? I think there are some obvious answers, but I also suspect that there may be others that are less apparent.

For example, in general, knowing that there are logical consequences that follow certain actions serves to guide what we as humans do in many situations. We say to ourselves: If I do this, then that will happen. When that result seems to us to be fair, certain, logical, and unpleasant, we often are inclined to say: And because I don't want that consequence to happen again, I won't do the thing that triggers it. That sort of reflection is one of the ways children learn to be responsible for their actions. When consequences are clear and relatively certain, children can and will pay attention to them. That logic has to be part of what made sit-and-watch so effective.

> **When consequences are clear and relatively certain, children can and will pay attention to them.**

Most teachers are aware of another fairly obvious bit of machinery in the sit-and-watch strategy. Children often act out their frustration when they are bored, and one source of boredom is the class chaos that can result from the disruptions created by other children. In other words, student misbehavior feeds on itself. When the teacher interrupts that cycle by promptly and efficiently dealing with the initial outbreak, it serves to pour water on the spontaneous fires that ordinarily follow. Order feeds on itself as well. But are those completely adequate explanations for what we saw in the results of this study? I doubt it.

Let me suggest another scenario to account for sit-and-watch, one that is more complicated but for some students, a lot closer to the truth. I think children feel better about themselves when they are required to pay their debts and be responsible for themselves. Students who misbehave, for example, often get down on themselves for their actions. Without an available form of restitution, they become more and more frustrated, and ultimately, they start to consider themselves "bad." The negative thought then serves as a precursor to behavior that is consistent with that negative belief!

Therefore, I think it is entirely possible that in addition to motivating students to behave appropriately (to avoid a negative consequence), sit-and-watch allowed misbehaving students to feel that they had paid their dues—and were then free to act appropriately. We should not underestimate either the power of restitution in building self-esteem or the value of a few minutes of sitting and watching to calm things down, thereby promoting reflection on inappropriate behaviors.

Finally, something caught my attention because it was not reported in the study. Given the novelty of the sand timers, I was amazed that there wasn't initial misbehavior by some students to get an opportunity to have the cool new equipment in their hands. The excitement of the class activities coupled with the management explanation may have produced a truly compelling environment. Nevertheless, I suspect that experienced teachers would be alert to just such an outbreak!

Common Ground: Our Shared Perspective

The success of any method for managing disruptive students will be responsive to the context in which it is used. Many factors are powerful determiners of success: grade level, subject matter, class size, teacher experience, school atmosphere, presence of students with severe behavior problems, administrative backup, parental support, and time of year . . . to name just a few. No single method works everywhere, for everyone, all of the time. What we can safely conclude is that this system did work effectively—even in the open spaces of a physical education class, even with students identified as persistently disruptive, and even in the hands of a teacher who clearly had been having serious problems with pupil misbehavior.

> **The success of any method for managing disruptive students will be responsive to the context in which it is used.**

Our second conclusion really requires that you look at an actual report of the study; the journal in which it appeared is in most college libraries. What that reading will demonstrate is that the particular design used in research of this type (the technical term is *multiple baseline*) lends itself to reports that are easy to follow and very persuasive. The sudden downward deflection of the graphed lines for frequency of misbehaviors occurs exactly at the points where the system was introduced into the two classes. The graphs also convincingly illustrate the substantial and persisting difference between average levels of misbehavior before and after the intervention as well as confirming that classes were not going well on a typical day before sit-and-watch arrived. The results of this study simply cannot be missed. For a modest study with limited goals, that is a considerable achievement, and we believe that it is one that might well have important practical implications.

Active Supervision and Student Learning

van der Mars, H., Vogler, B., Darst, P., & Cusimano, B. (1994). Active supervision patterns of physical education teachers and their relationship with student behaviors. *Journal of Teaching in Physical Education, 14,* 99-112.

Textbooks on the teaching of elementary school physical education have long included the recommendation that supervision of student learning activities include a number of active teacher tasks. Among those commonly suggested are monitoring student compliance with appropriate behavior, providing students with specific verbal and nonverbal feedback about behavior and performance, and communicating a general state of attentiveness to individuals and events (what has been termed *teacher with-it-ness*).

To accomplish those tasks, teachers are enjoined to avoid spending extended time with any one individual or group. They are also strongly encouraged to keep the majority of students in view by supervising with their backs to the wall and to move about the activity space in a steady but unpredictable pattern. None of that is rocket science. When such active supervision is considered a management strategy, the reasoning is both transparent and commonsensical. A deeper concern, however, rests in the less commonly heard proposition that teachers do not—indeed, cannot—produce student learning. It is what students do that produces learning. All teachers can do is establish conditions for students to engage in learning behaviors, keep them engaged with those tasks, and provide feedback when appropriate. Thus, the truly valuable outcome of active supervision ought to be more student time

spent on learning tasks such as attending, practicing, and thinking.

 ## The Study

Following the logic of that analysis produced two simple questions for the team of investigators who undertook this study. First, how do experienced teachers in real schools actually supervise their students? Second, are those supervisory behaviors related to their students' learning behaviors? Although there is a scattering of provocative clues concerning the answers, there is surprisingly little empirical evidence in the form of research. Given the obvious importance of supervising student work and given all of the assumptions we have made about how to do it effectively, a study seemed well justified.

Participants and Context

Eighteen certified elementary school physical education teachers from three school districts volunteered to participate in this study. The group included 8 females and 10 males, with experience ranging from 1 to 16 years. The study included classes from the first through the sixth grade, with sizes ranging from 24 to 31 students. All teachers used the same curriculum, a standardized multiactivity introduction to a variety of physical education content. In terms of space, their indoor facilities were roughly equivalent multipurpose rooms of about 5,400 square feet.

Design and Method

The behavior of each teacher and his or her students was videotaped during one regular class (averaging 30-minute periods). Each teacher's verbal behavior was recorded through use of a wireless microphone. Before each lesson, the floor of the teaching area was divided into nine equal sectors by means of unobtrusive taped crosses and small cone markers. Video- and audiotapes were then analyzed to extract information concerning the following: where the teachers were located at all times during the lesson, how frequently they moved from one sector to another, how long they remained in any one area, what they said to students, and what the students were doing.

Results

The patterns of the teachers' locations revealed how they positioned themselves in and around the activity area, as expressed in the distribution of time spent in each sector and the frequency of visits to each sector. What the teachers did can be expressed in what on first encounter sounds like a paradoxical result. They spent 88% of their time on the periphery of the class, but they visited the center of the floor more often than any other sector. In other words, when they moved closer to pupils in the center, it tended to be only briefly, often in crossing from one side to the other. They did indeed teach most of the time with their backs to the wall where they could be aware of the entire class while interacting with particular students. Furthermore, they were constantly on the move, making an average of six sector changes each minute. Finally, they were anything but silent spectators, giving verbal feedback at rates averaging more than three each minute, much of it positive and specific to both pupil motor performance and class behavior.

The patterns of student behavior included only 8% off-task behavior, and a substantial 32% of the time spent in the critical category of correct and successful practice, a measure commonly called Academic Learning Time—Physical Education (ALT-PE). In the context of findings from other studies, these would be considered busy and well-organized classes. The deeper question, however, still remains. Was there any evidence that the teachers'

active supervisory behaviors were related in any way to students' active learning behaviors?

The answer is a firm yes. The results indicate that the more a teacher was located on the periphery, the more students were engaged in actual movement tasks. The more a teacher moved from sector to sector, the more the students' practice was characterized by successful trials. And finally, the more positive feedback a teacher provided, the more inclined students were to stay on task. Other results confirmed these relationships by revealing reverse associations. When the average time spent by a teacher in any one sector rose, the average time tended to decline for students engaged in motor activity and particularly in successful learning trials.

 ## A Researcher's Perspective

For this group of teachers, skills in active supervision were related to students' successful engagement in learning tasks. To that finding can be added the observation that the degree of association was rather substantial. In other words, no single teacher action is ever likely to account for a great deal in the broad arena of student learning activities; however, the variable of active supervision appears to have been more powerful than I would have anticipated.

> **The variable of active supervision appears to have been more powerful than I would have anticipated.**

There are some cautions to keep in mind, as there always are in educational research. First, to find a relationship between two events in a class does not establish that one causes the other. Scores for active teacher supervision may be correlated with scores for desirable student behaviors (that is, they may operate in parallel), but both sets of activity may be caused by a third factor. In this case, such a candidate for causation might be a strong schoolwide expectation for high levels of hard work by teachers and students alike. Also, as you might have suspected, these teacher volunteers may not have been exactly like elementary physical educators in general. For example, their overall rates for giving specific feedback were higher than what has been found in other studies. Those, however, are cautions that simply remind you of the importance of always remaining aware of just how complicated everything is in the work of teaching.

A Teacher's Perspective

When I read this study, the first thing that came into my mind had nothing to do with supervision or student learning. I was reminded of how much energy it takes to get through a school day and how exhausted I can be at the end. Teaching physical education is sometimes like running a marathon every day, 5 days a week. Much of the energy cost is just the result of constantly moving around in classes and working to stay completely focused on what is going on.

Teaching is far more physical than any outsider would ever expect. The pedometer I wear often registers 2 miles at the end of a 75-minute university class in children's movement. And that is just a small sample of the real thing. My deepest admiration goes to my colleagues who on every school day must trek so many of those long miles to do the work of teaching.

The study also reminded me of a favorite metaphor I use: "the zone of good behavior." It is like the zone of good driving behavior that surrounds a state police car moving down the highway. For 10 cars in front and 10 in back, there is nobody breaking any rules! I suspect that is what explains at least some of the findings here. I can just feel the same little cloud of on-task behaviors, about 20 feet across, that floats along with me as I move among the students in some classes. The more I move, the more students get caught under the shadow of my cloud.

It might be interesting to figure out why my sense of that effect is not equally distinct in every class. Have more of the students in some classes developed a greater degree of responsibility for their own behavior and thus become less obviously responsive to my immediate presence? More important, I wonder what kind of teaching might create classes that have, or don't have, sharply defined zones that move around when the teacher supervises learning activities? I have long been interested in discovering successful strategies for actually teaching attending and practicing behaviors to students,

> **Teaching physical education is sometimes like running a marathon every day, 5 days a week.**

which would allow them to monitor themselves. Achieving that might actually make the zone of good behavior fade or disappear completely, thereby increasing productive learning time for all.

I also sometimes wonder whether all the things we do when we are moving about really contribute all that much over and above the impact of just being close to students and showing interest and concern. The teachers in this study apparently were giving lots of feedback, repeating instructions, or giving new challenges while they were traveling around the class. For some class activities, however, it seems to make sense just to move and watch. When using a reciprocal teaching format, for example, I feel like my talking often distracts or interrupts. I wonder if it would be useful to study the effects of just moving and watching intently, perhaps with only nonverbal signals? Certainly that seems like something you could experiment with, perhaps getting a friend to come in who could help you watch how the students respond.

Reading a study makes me more aware of individual aspects of my teaching, like keeping my back to the wall most of the time during a class. Probably, the result is that for a few days it is in the back of my mind and really acts to guide what I do. I am absolutely sure, for example, that this process works when I teach my morning class at the university. For instance, on a morning when I am working with preservice students on maintaining smooth transitions between instructional segments, that very same idea is right in my mental queue when I start teaching my own classes at a school in the afternoon.

I imagine that the same thing is true for what a teacher reads in the morning. It might be fun to check the influence of reading one of the abstracts in this book on how you teach the next day—and on how long any effect lasts. I suspect that the focusing effect on your attention would be even stronger for rereading a study several times!

Common Ground: Our Shared Perspective

There still is much to learn about the most effective forms of active supervision. For example, do the results here apply with equal strength across different kinds of student activities, such as fitness exercises, sport skill instruction, and so on? What are the roles played by active visual scanning or by nonverbal signals projected across longer distances? It is nonetheless clear what we can legitimately conclude from this modest study: These teachers were not standing around for extended periods of time passively watching their pupils. For them, teaching meant moving, monitoring, and interacting. Those activities were directly related to their students' successful engagement in activities that are known to lead to learning. If you are a new recruit preparing for employment as a physical education teacher or if you are a veteran teacher seeking ways to become a more effective practitioner, we think this constitutes sufficient evidence to pay close attention to what you are doing while your students are learning.

> These teachers were not standing around for extended periods of time passively watching their pupils. For them, teaching meant moving, monitoring, and interacting.

Teaching Social Behaviors

Patrick, C.A., Ward, P., & Crouch, D.W. (1998). Effects of holding students accountable for social behaviors during volleyball games in elementary physical education. *Journal of Teaching in Physical Education, 17,* 143-156.

Like other studies in this book (chapters 5 and 11), this investigation utilizes *behavior analysis,* in which instances of individual student behaviors are the unit of analysis. The behavior of interest here is "socially responsible behavior," long promoted as an educational objective in physical education—and frequently claimed as an outcome. In fact, educators have created quite a number of curricula to address the need for children to develop social skills in the sport and physical activity environment: *Fair Play for Kids* (Commission for Fair Play, 1990), *Teaching Responsibility Through Physical Activity* (Hellison, 1995), and *Sport Education* (Siedentop, 1994).

Claims, good intentions, and available models all aside, it is also true that only rarely does one encounter an elementary school physical education teacher who (a) utilizes a planned and systematic approach to teaching appropriate social skills and (b) discourages or extinguishes undesirable student behaviors, other than those that directly interfere with instruction. One consequence of this neglect is the persistence of destructive social interactions within the class context and the inevitable alienation of students who are victims of verbal or physical abuse by their peers. One might expect that such an important issue in physical education would have drawn the attention of researchers, with a resulting accumulation of knowledge, theory, and practices verified as effective. For complex and obscure reasons, such has not been the case—a fact that makes this study both unusual and of particular importance.

The Study

In the design for this investigation researchers utilized what is called an *intervention,* something done to students or teachers that would not occur in the normal course of events in their physical education classes. Such actions are referred to in some reports as the *experimental treatment.* Here, the intervention involved holding students accountable for their verbal and physical actions (social behaviors) directed at each other in a volleyball game. Accountability, in this instance, meant that there were immediate consequences for what students said or did to each other while playing the game: desirable consequences for appropriate behaviors (positive, friendly, mutually supportive) and unhappy outcomes for inappropriate behaviors (negative, discouraging, offensive).

Researchers who do behavior analysis studies often call such consequences *contingencies* because a desirable or undesirable outcome is caused by (is contingent upon) a behavior. It is a simple matter of establishing a system in which, "If you do this, then that will happen to you!" In this study, the primary purpose was to ascertain whether the treatment conditions had detectable effect on the verbal interactions of students in the predicted and desirable directions.

Participants and Context

Participants in the study were the teacher and his three intact physical education classes at a suburban elementary school: a fourth-grade class (21 students), a fifth-grade (25), and a sixth-grade (21). The total sample contained 34 boys and 33 girls. Fifth- and sixth-grade classes were held daily for 30 minutes, and the fourth-grade class was held for 20 minutes. The study involved a 20-lesson volleyball unit. Students in each class were grouped into four teams of 5 or 6 students, where they remained for the duration of the unit. Following a rotated schedule, teams typically played each other for half of each period.

Design and Method

Each game was videotaped for 5 minutes, and all data were subsequently extracted from replays of those tapes. Two kinds of data were collected to represent appropriate social behavior during game play: nonverbal, a pat on the back or a gesture such as thumbs-up; and verbal, statements that were supportive in nature such as "good play!" The same procedure was followed for inappropriate social actions: nonverbal, such as fighting, pushing, or dismissive gestures; and verbal, such as ridicule, laughing at others' mistakes, or making discouraging comments.

In addition, researchers presumed that a more positive social environment would encourage more students to participate actively and try hard to perform well. They therefore decided to count successful instances of two volleyball skills. The forearm pass and overhead pass were selected because they were emphasized in the instruction that preceded the games and are the most frequently used skills in volleyball. All criteria for successful performance were established by the teacher.

Two previously trained researchers collected all data by viewing the tapes independently (one was not involved in the study's implementation at the school site). Samples of their work indicated that they maintained a level of interobserver agreement ranging between 85% and 96% across the two categories of social behavior (positive and negative) and the two of volleyball skills (the forearm and overhead pass).

The intervention (the accountability system that imposed consequences for social behavior) consisted of five parts: first, the awarding or removing of points to or from the team's score during the game as immediate consequences of an individual player's behavior; second, public posting by a student on a nearby wall poster (during a break in each game) of points lost or gained as a consequence of player behavior; third, establishment of a daily behavior points goal for each team, based on the

team's previous behavior performance; fourth, a daily special activity reward for teams that met their good behavior goal (e.g., extra game time); and fifth, a special end-of-unit activity for the teams that met their good behavior goals most often during the unit.

Baseline data were collected from each grade level to establish what was typical of social behavior before implementing the accountability conditions. The intervention was initiated for each grade in sequence: for grade 5 at the 5th lesson, grade 4 at the 10th, and grade 6 at the 14th. This design is called a *multiple baseline,* and it is used in place of control groups (untreated groups) to establish evidence that an intervention appears to be related to an observed change in behavior.

Results

As sometimes is the case with multiple baseline studies, the graphs showing the number of desirable and undesirable behaviors at each class offer a powerful argument to the effect that the intervention worked as intended. During baseline conditions at the outset, the number of negative social interactions in each class was greater than the number of positive behaviors. Then, for all three grades, on exactly the day when the accountability treatment began, the number of good behaviors rose dramatically and negative player actions fell to near zero.

Two specific examples will suffice to make the point. In grade 4, instances of desirable social interactions during the 11 days of treatment rose from an average of 10 per class period to an average of 121. In grade 5, during the 17 days of the treatment, instances of undesirable social interactions fell from an average of 25 to an average of 3. In general, across the days of treatment for each class, the number of desirable interactions tended to increase with successive lessons while the number of undesirable events in each lesson remained low, showing no tendency to drift upward over time. In contrast, with implementation of the treatment in each class, the number of successful skill attempts showed no deflection up or down, remaining roughly at the same level over the course of the study.

The teacher reported one additional observation. It was his subjective judgment that with application of the good behavior contingencies, students appeared to relax, play more freely, and have more fun during the game portion of each lesson. This was interpreted as possible evidence that removing or lowering the likelihood of ridicule for a bad play created conditions that favored enjoyment. As students were not interviewed, there are no corroborating data for that conjecture.

A Researcher's Perspective

Results such as these often raise several concerns. Some people worry that individual students within the group may be unfairly punished by team members for their inappropriate behavior. No instances of this were observed during the study although this might have been related to the fact that most teams reached their behavior goals. Another concern is that students will invent "false" good behaviors to inflate their behavior scores. The authors report that such social acts (unrelated to actual incidents of successful play) rarely occurred (10 for the entire study).

Beyond those concerns, however, efforts to teach appropriate social skills must confront two challenges that are difficult to meet within the confines of any single study. The first is the question of persistence. As the year wound along and as the novelty of the intervention possibly began to wear thin, would the dramatic improvements in pupil behavior be sustained? All we know from this study is that the intervention effects persisted in one case across 17 lessons without any indication of decline (the fifth-grade class). More than that would require a different and more demanding design, with a longer period of treatment and, perhaps, observations following withdrawal of the intervention.

> **The intervention effects persisted in one case across 17 lessons without any indication of decline . . .**

The second question for social skills instruction is equally difficult to confront within a simple study design. Will the skills generalize to student behaviors outside the setting where they were acquired? Would the students in this study show more positive interactions with peers in the classroom or in out-of-school sport activities? No effort was made to collect data concerning generalization effects in this study, and the results of such behavior transfer in other studies have been mixed. The best we can say is that within the same context of volleyball games in physical education classes, most students

continued to improve their ability to engage in appropriate social interactions—obviously transferring what they had learned from one day to the next. Day-to-day transfer in the same context is obviously not the same as transferring the same behavior to another setting. It does, however, encourage a degree of optimism about what might be found if some of those settings were examined.

What is puzzling, though, is the absence of any apparent impact on the number of successful instances of forearm and overhead passing. Perhaps the level of negative interaction had not been high enough to depress skill performance, although a baseline mean of 135 per lesson in the sixth-grade sounds grim enough to us! Perhaps the criteria for successful performance were not sufficiently sensitive to change. More likely, however, is the possibility that the logic for expecting an immediate improvement in skill performance is itself somehow defective.

A Teacher's Perspective

My first reaction is one of absolute delight. If something so simple could have such a powerful impact, it gives me great hope for improvements in what goes on in physical education classes! Not only do I want to try some similar activities, but the study also stimulates me to think again about other areas where a simple and straightforward intervention might work. After all, what the researchers did here is really just a direct approach to creating the class environment every teacher desires.

The report immediately reminded me of what I have experienced in many in-service workshops for teachers. An invisible tension often exists between teachers on one side and administrators, curriculum development consultants, or program coordinators on the other. The latter are inclined to provide theoretical models, general guidelines, and frameworks that teachers could use to guide the decisions they have to make as educators. The former usually want a workshop to provide things of more immediate value, such as workable tactics for next Monday, rather than wider frames for thinking about next week, the next unit, or next year. The report for this study avoided that tug-of-war by providing both an idea to try next Monday and a theoretical framework to think about—and test.

The general behavior modification model is fleshed out with details about something that could be tried immediately: identify a problem, choose a behavior that is related to the problem, gather some baseline behavioral data, select something specific to do that might influence the behavior, do it, then gather more behavioral data to see if there was a change. Even without developing a full plan or taking several weeks to gather baseline data, a teacher could start the next class by taking time to carefully distinguish the difference between acceptable and unacceptable behaviors during practice or game play. Finding a way to include that aspect of participation in the scoring system for the game is also an exciting concept that is open to immediate exploration. These are ideas that have instantaneous utility, yet they come within a framework for further refinement—and thought.

Some obvious questions about the study are not touched on in the summary. For example, it would be helpful to clarify how the teacher taught the difference between positive and negative behaviors. In the original report, the authors indicate that the teacher took 10 to 15 minutes to explain the good-behavior game and the difference between inappropriate and appropriate behaviors. Ten minutes is not very much time to teach anything. One possibility is that the teacher had devised a very powerful instructional module. Another, however, is the more likely explanation that the students were already pretty clear about which were positive and negative behaviors, and they only needed a situation that provided the motivation to demonstrate one and avoid the other.

My own experience suggests that the biggest barrier to positive interactions in a game setting is the discomfort individual students feel in praising and receiving praise. Often, positive behaviors are not employed, because students fear ridicule for being "mushy." In addition, "cool" students sometimes gain a certain power by putting others down. Other students just find kidding each other about mistakes is easier than praising and encouraging, particularly when no one else is making positive comments.

Whatever the case, the importance of the teacher providing clear expectations for appropriate behavior is immense. I have seen the simple act of specifying which things are acceptable and which are not produce an immediately noticeable change in what is going on in a class. Then, adding the motivation

of reward points that make positive social behaviors as important as skillful play can form an even more powerful combination. My experience, however, leads to a warning about how such tactics are designed.

Anything that undermines the challenge of playing the game can make it fall apart. While it sometimes is possible to add behavior points right into the game score, with other activities or grade levels, it may be better to keep behavior rewards as a separate but equally important tally of accountability.

In all of these decisions, it is important to remember that you are working with a powerful paradigm. If you don't get the behavior changes you expected, pause to reflect on how you have set up the situation and what exactly is being reinforced. When working with young children, it is not unusual to find that you have inadvertently created conditions that encourage the wrong behaviors. Don't let that discourage you, however. Your ability to create contingencies that target the right behaviors will improve rapidly with practice.

If you decide to try an intervention like the one described in this report, I urge you to spend some time thinking it through with care and particularly with attention to how you will blend it into the specifics of your teaching situation. Then watch carefully, being sure to note instances in which it appears not to work, as well as those in which your intentions were achieved.

> My own experience suggests that the biggest barrier to positive interactions in a game setting is the discomfort individual students feel in praising and receiving praise.

Also, it will be wise not to expect too much in the short run. Being clear about what is acceptable and what isn't gives children permission to act appropriately, but it does not necessarily change their basic values. The results you get can range from acceptance without commitment, "We're not allowed to rag on other kids in Ms. Fairplay's class," and various displays of, "I'm not really being 'uncool,' I just have to do it this way," to a real buy-in for the importance of positive behaviors and making the class safe for everyone. The latter outcome usually requires some class time devoted to reflection in which the children identify and discuss instances that show the consequences of their behavior.

Which leads to a final caution about the application of things learned from this study. Not all of the kids I have known could make the switch after a 10-minute description of positive and negative behaviors. And the reason often was not so much a negative attitude toward the class or me, but the fact that they simply did not have positive behaviors in their social repertoire. They had not grown up experiencing others using them; they had seen a lot of negative verbal behaviors modeled; and they had deeply ingrained habits of interaction that made primary use of putting others down.

There still were conditions in the class environment, such as fear of public failure, that could trigger those old responses. It was unreasonable to expect them to get it on a single trial—or, for that matter, in a single month of trials. They really needed specific examples of what the desired behavior looked and sounded like. They also needed a lot of practice and a lot of positive reinforcement when they did attempt the appropriate behavior.

A teacher in my school district found that in one school, he literally couldn't teach because the students did not have the basic social skill of listening to anyone else—including the teacher. Most of them were too busy defending their own beings and countering constant verbal attacks from others to give the cooperation that is essential for teaching to begin.

Could they learn to listen, to stop the steady flow of verbal jousting, and to begin small acts of positive behavior? Of course they could! But it took a set of carefully planned lessons (and several 10-minute explanations) to help them change. And competitive game situations were among the instructional elements in which change came most slowly. Success in that situation required the development of scoring rubrics that could incorporate the desired social behaviors. If you want to learn more about that story, see DeLine (1991).

In the end, don't allow my cautions to dampen your interest in establishing clear behavior boundaries for your students. In a real sense, our class-room is our castle, and we have final authority for what is acceptable. We have to take the responsibility for exercising that authority and doing so in a way that supports positive behavior while also directly confronting behaviors that put any student down.

 ## Common Ground: Our Shared Perspective

The discussion of concerns, questions, and limitations that apply to this study ought not to distract you from a vital fact. The treatment worked to perfection, at least with regard to the primary target of social interactions. Certainly, the development of social skills does not require the rationale of improved skill learning. That would be desirable, but it is far from necessary. Questions about generalizability and maintenance are legitimate, but they do not in any way diminish the main outcome—students behaved much better toward one another during game play in those physical education classes. That is a considerable achievement and one to be valued for itself. If you doubt that, ask any group of elementary school teachers if they would like to have that quality of interactions during game play in their classes!

> **Students behaved much better toward one another during game play in those physical education classes. That is a considerable achievement and one to be valued for itself.**

Recording and Classifying Teacher Management Behaviors

Henkel, S.A. (1991). Teachers' conceptualization of pupil control in elementary school physical education. *Research Quarterly for Exercise and Sport, 62,* 52-60.

Ordinarily, details concerning the development of tests, observation systems, and classification schemes are technical matters that bear little interest for school practitioners. Only the end products of such projects, in the form of usable tools, have direct relevance to their work. For several reasons, however, we believe that this project represents an exception to that general rule. First, teachers and researchers in this instance worked together to build an instrument that was solidly grounded in how pupil behaviors actually were managed in real class situations. Following the steps in that process serves to explain the final product in a way that no written manual could accomplish. Second, we found that the accounts of how teachers thought about their methods of pupil control helped us achieve both a better understanding of class management and a new appreciation for the complexities of that teaching task.

A specific element of this study separated it from the standard instrument-related studies. There are a number of classification schemes designed to capture the interactions of high school pupils and their physical education teachers, particularly with regard to techniques for pupil control; however, we have reason to believe that the content of those relationships is quite different in elementary physi-

cal education. Thus, the researcher here argues that it is important to create an instrument that is specifically designed for collecting information on how physical education teachers control pupil behavior at the K-6 level. We find ourselves in agreement.

Finally, existing studies of "discipline" and "class management" in elementary physical education have involved application of prior theoretical systems. Rather than starting with pupil-control techniques (as actually employed by teachers), researchers have traditionally collected and placed data in categories that "ought to exist." In contrast, the investigator in this study set out to establish both a conceptual framework and an instrument that would be based on the full repertoire of control techniques actually displayed by a group of collaborating practitioners. In other words, the former studies say, "These are the categories that theory predicts should fit your behaviors," while the latter, present study is saying, "Here are your behaviors and the categories into which they can be sorted."

The Study

This report describes a project that had two broad purposes: first, to construct a classification system for techniques used by elementary school physical education teachers to control pupil behaviors, and second, to use that system in describing control techniques that are intended and not intended to foster pupil self-control. We have annotated here only the first of those purposes—the development of a classification system

Participants and Context

From the entire population of elementary school physical educators in a Midwestern town, 8 were selected at random for participation in the first phase of the study (5 men and 3 women). Average age was 42, and average teaching experience was 17 years. Each teacher was observed eight times across at least three grade levels and two content units. At the time of those observations, all of the teachers knew they were participating in the development of an observation instrument, but none were aware that the focus was on methods of pupil control.

Design and Method

In addition to audiotaping each lesson, the investigator took field notes describing each control technique observed. A total of 2,089 actions were so documented. The notes typically included a verbatim record of what the teacher said, a description of the teacher's concern (some actual or potential misconduct), a reminder of the general class context in which the control was exercised, and identification of the students targeted. Teachers' spontaneous comments about pupil control were also recorded throughout the series of observations.

The audiotapes were fully transcribed and together with the field notes formed the database used for the first stage of analysis. Three strategies were used to create categories for the observed teacher behaviors: analytic induction, constant comparison, and topological analysis. We will not attempt to describe those complicated operations, but we can characterize their final purpose. Taken together, all of the analytic operations were designed to produce the smallest possible set of categories that could be used to reliably sort all of the observed instances in which teachers acted to control pupil behavior.

A teacher's intention in using a particular control technique can only be discerned by reference to class context and previous interactions with students; therefore, the construction of categories required frequent comparisons between field notes and transcripts and in some instances, the use of

discussions with the teachers involved. At the end of the data analysis, the investigator had accumulated a preliminary set of carefully defined categories into which they could sort the observed 2,089 pupil-control actions from 64 classes (8 teachers in 8 classes). In turn, the categories formed clusters called *classifications* in the report that represented distinctly different kinds of teacher intentions with regard to pupil control.

Three broad classifications were evident within the specific categories for pupil-control actions. First, anticipation: Teachers tried to prevent undesirable pupil behaviors by using anticipatory control actions. Second, tutoring: Teachers responded to undesirable behavior by tutoring targeted pupils about acceptable and unacceptable behavior. Third, punitive: Teachers punished pupils for behaviors that were deemed dangerous or particularly flagrant violations of class rules.

Some categories of teacher behaviors easily fell into a single classification. For example, specifying exactly when an activity is to begin was always intended as an anticipatory control technique, as in, "Please wait for my whistle to begin!" Actions in other categories, however, could serve several possible ends. Instructing a pupil about how to put an item of equipment under control may be used either in anticipation of a problem, as in, "Everyone will place the ball between their feet and remain standing still with hands at their side," or as a tutorial response to misbehavior, as in, "Do you remember that I asked you to place the ball between your feet and remain standing still with hands at your side?" Likewise, removing a pupil from activity might have represented the exercise of control through anticipation, tutoring, or punishment—it all depended on the circumstance.

From the total of 2,089 observed instances of pupil control, the largest numbers were sorted into the following six categories. (Numbers indicate the frequency of the observed behavior.) (Letters indicate either anticipatory (a), tutorial (t), or punitive (p) purpose.)

1. Gaining attention: Requiring the pupil to remain silent while listening or watching (399) (a, t)

2. Gaining attention/stopping: Requiring a child to stop an activity to listen or watch (297) (a, t)

3. Positioning: Requiring the pupil to assume a designated or elected body position (205) (a, t)

4. Starting: Indicating exactly when an activity is to begin (160) (a)

5. Locating: Instructing a pupil to go to a designated or elected place to begin or resume activity (150) (a, t)

6. Stating rule: Establishing or repeating a rule for expected behavior (145) (a, t)

Categories that did not include techniques used by at least two of the observed teachers were:

- Exercising: Administering exercise as a consequence for misconduct (t, p)
- Referring: Contacting another authority or sending the child to another authority, such as the principal or parent (t, p)

Definitions for the remaining 15 categories not described here are included in the published report. They include the following: waiting, rewarding, removing, confiscation, relinquishing, reinstating, redirecting, praising, physically reprimanding, ignoring, gaining attention by immobilizing, gaining attention by calling name, correcting, warning, and amending.

In the next phase of the study, the participants reviewed the list of categories, operational definitions for each, and examples selected from the database to illustrate each form of pupil control. After reading those materials, each teacher was interviewed and asked to (a) confirm the accuracy and clarity of the preliminary categories, (b) improve the category labels and definitions, (c) add categories for control techniques represented in the data but not identified by the investigator, and (d) add categories not represented in the data.

Although they urged renaming several categories to more accurately reflect the way practitioners understand the intentions involved (for example, "corporal punishment" was changed to "physically reprimanding"), teachers generally confirmed the adequacy of the definitions for most items. They also described several categories of pupil-control behaviors that had not appeared in the original set of observations. Using the suggestions produced through teacher interviews, the investigator then revised and expanded the preliminary list.

The revised list of 23 categories of pupil-control actions was then given to both the original participants and an additional eight elementary physical education teachers from the same district. All were asked to indicate the frequency with which they believed they employed each technique, and responses were made on a Likert-type scale using the choices *never*, *seldom*, *sometimes*, *often*, and *very often*. Of the 16 teachers, 11 indicated that they used all but one of the techniques *sometimes* (that one method of control was "administering exercise as a consequence for misconduct," which was mentioned by only 1 teacher). Returns from the survey also indicated that all of the techniques were used by at least one of the teachers.

Results

With data from observations, interviews, and surveys in hand, the investigator produced a final instrument—the Physical Education Pupil Control Inventory (PEPCI), which can be used as either a paper-and-pencil survey instrument, a conceptual system for considering questions related to pupil control, or as a tool for systematic observation (in live field recording or in the laboratory with video- or audiotapes). The reliability of categorizations made with the use of PEPCI was determined with two videotaped lessons from each of the original participants. The investigator and two trained observers independently coded randomly selected segments from each tape. Overall interobserver agreement exceeded 80% in each case.

A Researcher's Perspective

The teachers who participated in this project exhibited wide variations in using particular control techniques. The frequency counts in various categories showed persistent and distinctive differences in the way teachers handled pupil control. Surely, some of those patterns arose from the influence of particular lesson content and from contextual matters such as class size, equipment, and facilities. Other differences, however, appeared to be reflections of what individual teachers believed about pupil control and about the educational goals of physical education.

> **Other differences, however, appeared to be reflections of what individual teachers believed about pupil control and about the educational goals of physical education.**

The instrument offers a range of possible applications in the capacity to discriminate patterns of pupil-control behavior that were characteristic of a teacher's style. Teachers, for example, could use PEPCI scores from their own classes to examine whether they were acting in ways that were consistent with goals, such as fostering self-discipline. Teacher educators could also use PEPCI categories to help trainees become sensitive to the range of possibilities available; that is, how choices among means for pupil control might support or undermine progress toward particular learning outcomes. Student teachers could use the PEPCI categories in planning control actions that might reduce confusion when new learning activities were introduced. Finally, researchers could examine the consequences for student dispositions toward physical activity when they are subjected to control methods that reflect distinctive ideologies about teacher authority (a point developed in a section of the report not annotated here).

A Teacher's Perspective

What an elegant and thorough way to go about understanding pupil-control strategies. Watch teachers and record what they actually do; ask them to talk about what they do; group common strategies together into functional categories; then ask teachers to inspect and comment on your list so as to revise and tighten it; and finally, have several people use the categories to code teacher actions to be sure that they can consistently assign the same code to what they see and hear.

Elegant design aside, however, my first response is "Hallelujah!" Only one teacher in this study admitted to using exercise as punishment. We are making progress at last. My second response is in the form of two points that jumped out at me from this report, and readers will have to pardon me if I describe them in terms of my own long struggle to master the tasks of teaching.

The first point related to the nest of issues revolving around my need to identify the most effective ways to manage a physical education class.

What I have always wanted for my managerial repertoire were techniques that allowed for high learning time and, simultaneously, the greatest possible enjoyment for students. The second point that drew my attention pertained to finding ways to promote student self-control and responsibility as a goal for teaching. For me, the twin objectives of helping students learn to consider the common good and to acquire the ability to keep impulsive behavior in check have to be primary goals in my classes. Given those priorities for learning, I have had to confront the question of what constitutes the most effective strategies for helping students develop that kind of control.

With regard to the first problem, identifying forms of effective management, my first impulse on reading the report was to check and see which strategies I use most often in my own classes. I know that some of them were acquired because I had reason to believe that they truly were effective in terms of the criteria I noted above; however, it seems almost certain that other control strategies have crept in unnoticed (or, at least, unacknowledged) for less valid reasons.

I try hard, for example, to do a lot of anticipating so that I can do things that make the use of reactive control actions unnecessary. Nevertheless, certain kinds of misbehavior do turn up more often than others. Those suggest failures of anticipation and, quite possibly, the continued use of inadequate teacher responses.

As you can guess from this discussion, my value perspective makes me want to tutor more and punish less. That intention is explicit in how I teach, but what would PEPCI actually show me about what I do? I may think that I know, but in every other area of life, we can anticipate some differences between our perceptions and our actual behavior—why not in my teaching?

> What would PEPCI actually show me about what I do? I may think that I know, but in every other area of life, we can anticipate some differences between our perceptions and our actual behavior—why not in my teaching?

The only way to know is to have someone code one or several of my classes, or I could try myself to code video- or audiorecordings of my teaching. Either way, the result would be the perfect starting place for some serious reflection on my list of how best to shape student behavior—as well as on my personal image of how I think I try to carry out that agenda.

Obtaining and using feedback about control strategies would not be all that easy, of course, because classes are different. What is possible and appropriate for one may not be for another, which raises an immediate question. What would PEPCI show me about my control efforts in classes that I categorize as most and least cooperative? Do I appear to adjust, or do I just plough ahead with my standard repertoire of tactics whether they are working or not?

From the long list of possible teacher control strategies, there has to be a theoretically perfect combination that includes the optimal number and ideal kind of prompts, reminders, warnings, and reactions. My own goal has always been to use the smallest possible number of control actions that can produce a productive, enjoyable class for both students and myself. PEPCI might be a means for pushing myself closer to that optimal point of kind and number—with the resulting savings for my energy and voice.

Finally, I think this is the sort of study that simply cries out for extension to new and fascinating questions. What about the relationship between PEPCI frequency scores and results from an instrument such as Academic Learning Time—Physical Education (ALT-PE)? What would we find if we examined the PEPCI patterns displayed by novice teachers and those who hold certification from the new National Board? And, exactly how easy is it to effect changes in teachers' control behaviors? Is it possible that simple awareness of PEPCI scores could be potent enough to instigate change in some areas of teacher behavior? Questions, questions, questions—perhaps all of us ought to be finding answers.

Common Ground: Our Shared Perspective

Before we lose sight of the forest for all the trees, the technical elements in this study should not be allowed to distract attention from the central fact that is on display. The PEPCI categories confirm for us the striking elegance of what effective teachers learn to do as they quietly but insistently guide pupils through the complexities of a lesson. What you see in the 23 categories is the stuff of highly specialized craft knowledge.

> The PEPCI categories confirm for us the striking elegance of what effective teachers learn to do as they quietly but insistently guide pupils through the complexities of a lesson.

On paper, these teaching tactics can seem innocent and even obvious. Through the actions of a veteran practitioner, however, they can be revealed as precision instruments, drawn from a reservoir of highly flexible and surprisingly subtle skills. Knowing when and how to use such tools is what separates the master teacher from the apprentice. PEPCI makes a small part of the complexity in teaching visible by holding up a mirror to the action.

Returning now to what we can conclude about the particular outcomes of this study, given the way that teachers conceptualize pupil-control tactics in an elementary school physical education class, it seems likely that PEPCI measures what it purports to measure. It captures the frequency with which a teacher employs particular teaching acts that are intended to shape the behavior of pupils.

For the participants in this study, the instrument provided categories for all of the instances the investigator had been able to identify in a substantial sample of their teaching behavior. All of the categories were used, and the resulting frequency scores discriminated among the teachers. For an instrument of this type, those are solid indications of validity.

Whether a testing of PEPCI on a much larger scale would produce similarly optimistic findings remains to be seen. Nonetheless, what this study makes certain is that in the process of developing tools for use in the analysis of teaching, it is possible to make use of how teachers understand their own work—and to do so in a variety of ways. There are benefits in that research strategy for teachers, researchers, and ultimately, for pupils. When an instrument is grounded in a practitioner's perspective, the data it produces are far more likely to be recognized by teachers as valid reflections of real events in their classes. It is simply a powerful form of feedback. Further, such tools open the door for future investigations that address the central questions of "why?" and "with what result?"

Teaching Fair Play
in the Gym and School

Gibbons, S.L., Ebbeck, V., & Weiss, M.R. (1995). *Fair Play for Kids*: Effects on the moral development of children in physical education. *Research Quarterly for Exercise and Sport, 66,* 247-255.

With the exception of several short technical sections, you would find the full report of this study just as understandable as the annotation you are about to read. That statement is particularly remarkable because this is a truly complex investigation. We make the point about complexity because space considerations do not allow us to fully explain three important components of the study: (a) the *Fair Play for Kids* curriculum, (b) the measuring instruments used to produce data that reflect the impact of the curriculum, and (c) the statistical procedures used to analyze the data and identify results. We make the point about the report's reasonable level of accessibility because you may wish to pursue one or more of those topics by consulting the original publication in its full form. Whatever your decision about follow-up, however, please be assured that our summary provides a sound general understanding of the study and its findings.

In 1990, the Commission for Fair Play in Canada published *Fair Play for Kids,* a curriculum guide that includes a series of educational activities for children in fourth through sixth grades (ages 8 to 11). The activities were designed to focus on the development of attitudes and behaviors that exemplify ideals of fair play, such as respect for rules, respect for officials and their decisions, respect for the opponent, maintaining self-control, and equal opportunity for participation. The curriculum was based

on moral development theory and research; however, at the time this study was designed, the effectiveness of the program in promoting moral growth and good-sport behaviors had not yet been examined.

Previous studies involving other programs for the development of moral judgment and behavior had shown generally positive results in sport camps, public school physical education, and after-school athletics. The present investigators set out to design a study that would extend previous research by using a much larger student sample, a longer period of intervention with the curriculum, and multiple indexes with which to measure outcomes (that is, the various aspects of moral development). Also integral to the study was an ecologically valid study environment in which regular physical education teachers were allowed to implement the curriculum in ways that were appropriate to their individual school and class settings.

The Study

This experiment was actually performed "in the field," the "field" in this instance being the natural setting of intact public school classes. Such research efforts are relatively rare in physical education because they require truly heroic efforts to retain even a modest degree of control over the many variables involved.

The investigators pursued a question that has long bedeviled exponents of teaching fair play and good sporting behavior in physical education. Can a teacher produce a real impact on student attitudes and behaviors regarding fair play if the program is implemented only in physical education classes? Is this the sort of social learning that requires the effort of the entire school community, or can the results justify the time and effort expended by a single teacher?

Participants and Context

The participants were 452 students (248 girls, 204 boys) in 18 fourth-, fifth-, and sixth-grade classrooms from suburban elementary schools in two Canadian provinces. Both teachers and student participants were volunteers.

Design and Method

Six intact classrooms at each grade level were randomly assigned to three experimental groups (number of participants in parentheses):

1. Control group—no *Fair Play for Kids* curriculum (140)
2. Physical-education-only group—*Fair Play* curriculum implemented by physical education teachers only (146)
3. All-classes group—*Fair Play* curriculum implemented in physical education and other subjects, including health, language arts, social studies, and fine arts (166)

The time allocated for all classes was 90 minutes per week. The experimental intervention extended for 7 months of the academic year (mid-October through mid-May), and measures of moral development and fair-play behavior were administered before and following the treatment phase of the study.

The particular teaching strategies used in this experiment were selected by the researchers from the *Fair Play for Kids* resource manual. They made choices based on the contribution to the ideals of fair play and the extent to which activities were consistent with a model of moral development. Those activities often required confronting authentic moral dilemmas, dialoguing as the basis for judgment and intentions, and use of cooperative problem solving as a structure for decisions. The same strategies were used in the physical-education-only group and the all-classes group.

Each teacher met individually with an investigator to receive an explanation of the study, the fair play curriculum and its learning activities, and procedures for random assignment of treatment conditions. Teachers in the two experimental groups also attended an in-service workshop on use of fair play activities; teachers assigned to the control group received no special preparation. Researchers also distributed printed resource materials related to fair play.

As a general guideline, teachers in the experimental groups were asked to use activities from the fair play curriculum at least once each week. Teachers also were encouraged to try all of the available activities. The selection and timing of those strategies, however, were left to each teacher. Implementation of the curriculum was confirmed by means of a log in which teachers recorded when and how they used each strategy. Treatments also were validated through direct observations made during three site visits by members of the research team.

The fair play behaviors of students were rated by their teachers through use of an inventory that listed 10 behaviors associated with morally desirable or undesirable actions in game and sport: arguing with teammates, showing off, complaining, teasing others, hogging the ball, disputing officials' decisions, not taking turns, disobeying rules of the game, not sharing equipment, and ignoring teammates' suggestions. The inventory has a long history of use and well-developed evidence of both validity and reliability. If you are interested, consult the brief description and full citation found in the published report for this study.

The fair play behavior inventory required teachers to mark a 4-point Likert-type scale ranging from *not at all like this child* to *very much like this child*. For the pretest, teachers had been working with the children for 6 weeks before rating their behavior.

Students themselves completed measures for moral development. These instruments used the same assumptions, language, and situations as the behavior inventory. Three paper-and-pencil tests provided data on students' ability to identify moral dilemmas, judge what ought to be done in the situation, and decide how one actually intends to act (specimen test items for each development scale are included in the report). It was the teachers' ratings on the behavior inventory, however, that assessed how often and how well students actually implemented their moral reasoning and intentions in the real world of their physical education classes.

Results

The statistical analysis was performed in two different ways. One analysis used the 18 classrooms as the unit of analysis while the other used individual student scores as the basis for calculating the results. Neither analysis revealed any significant differences among the groups at the start of the experiment.

Class-level analysis of the posttest data showed that the physical-education-only and all-classes groups were significantly superior to the six classes assigned as control groups on all three measures of moral development. Posttest data from the behavior inventory filled out by the teachers favored the same groups, though not by the margin required to establish statistical significance. Finally, analysis of posttest scores for both moral development and behavior showed no difference between the two treatment groups.

> **The growth of moral attitudes and cognitive skills for moral reasoning, as well as the display of fair play behaviors, are not an automatic consequence of participation in physical education.**

The individual student level of analysis generally confirmed the class-level results. In all cases, the actual score differences between the control and treatment conditions were quite large. The authors assert that the study demonstrated differences that were more than statistically significant; in fact, they were large enough and persistent enough to be meaningful in practice as well.

A Researcher's Perspective

It might be easy to overlook one finding from this study because it does not deal with the success of the experimental treatments. The fact that the control group did not improve supports the assertion that the growth of moral attitudes and cognitive skills for moral reasoning, as well as the display of fair play behaviors, are not an automatic consequence of participation in physical education. Given the continued currency of that idea among practitioners, it is important to underscore the failure of students in the six control classes to make any progress in the cognitive or behavioral aspects of their moral development. It appears that systematic and continual delivery of a prosocial curriculum is necessary if physical education is to make any difference in that area of children's learning.

What is also intriguing is the fact that the results on the outcome measures were no different for the all-classes students versus the physical-education-only students. While that does not settle all questions concerning the efficacy of schoolwide efforts, it certainly does make one point loud and clear. Given the tools provided by a carefully designed curriculum, a single teacher acting alone in physical education can make a substantial difference for what children know, believe, and are inclined to do about playing fair in the gym.

The authors themselves point out some of the limitations in this study. One difficulty is that the teacher who rated student behavior on the pretests and posttests was also the teacher who implemented the fair play curriculum. The possibility of an expectancy effect certainly was present for them; that is, when you work that hard, you really want those kids to improve. But such an effect was certainly not present for control group teachers when rating their students. The next study might well make use of external raters who were blind as to which group they were observing.

Limitations such as that one and others are inevitable, even in studies that make a great advance over the quality of their predecessors. It is important to keep such problems in perspective, however, by remembering where things stood before this study was published. Research can only build our understanding one step at a time.

A Teacher's Perspective

What an important area of study! For years we have claimed that students' participation in our elementary school physical education programs develops sporting values and fair play behaviors. Unfortunately, there is little evidence to show that anything of the sort actually occurs, making it disingenuous to use such claims in justifying our programs. What a boon it would be if every teacher could have hard figures to show parents and school officials that they were really moving students in the right direction.

Of particular interest to me is the fact that this study shows how a solid prosocial curriculum can move students in the right direction—even when we are the only teachers working at the task! I've seen this result in many of the local schools where we place student teachers with top-notch professionals. For example, at Bryker Woods Elementary School in the Austin (Texas) School District, Michele Rusnak not only teaches social skills, but she reinforces them daily with a reflection time at the end of each class when students compliment each other. Her students demonstrate remarkable abilities in that setting, and it is clear that they are far more aware of the behaviors of their peers than we often realize. That is, they certainly know positive actions when they see or hear them.

How exciting to have research findings that confirm our experiential data. Both kinds of evidence suggest that systematic teacher effort can make a difference in children's moral development. In addition, while I have always believed that a schoolwide effort would be the most desirable strategy, here is evidence that a one-subject push is sufficient to produce results.

How much (if any) of that progress might generalize to other environments within the school is a matter not addressed by the present study. Nevertheless, where is there a physical education teacher who would not count it worthwhile just to improve the behavior of children in their own classes?

Many of the studies in this book demonstrate that when we stop to assess behaviors, beliefs, and attitudes, some of the things we want to have happen in our classes are more wishful thinking than reality. Here, however, is research (on a social skills curriculum, no less) to reassure us that when we get clear and precise about what is to be accomplished, plan specific teaching strategies to move students in that direction, then actually check to confirm results—it can work!

> **Here is research (on a social skills curriculum, no less) to reassure us that when we get clear and precise about what is to be accomplished, plan specific teaching strategies to move students in that direction, then actually check to confirm results—it can work!**

I know that at this point more than a few readers, especially active practitioners, will be muttering, "Swell, and how do I do those three wonderful things all at the same time and still juggle a workload that already threatens to overwhelm me?" I should be the last person to claim that there is an easy answer for having too many things to do. But I can testify that there are practical ways to cut a trial run with something such as a prosocial curriculum down to digestible size.

First, work on only one aspect of your teaching at one time by selecting a single grade level, or even a single class, for the venue. Next, gradually collect materials for instruction and assessment in advance, and sketch out a little step-by-step plan. Wait a few weeks, then cut the plan roughly in half. For example, consider doing any of the following to trim your plan: evaluate results only at the end of the unit rather than weekly; cut the questionnaire from 25 questions to just the 5 questions that matter; recruit some parents to do observing and recording chores rather than trying to juggle it all yourself; and always use materials already developed by somebody else. In other words, stay as realistic as you are enthusiastic.

One of my concerns about the integrity of the study (a limitation also noted by the authors) is conveniently linked to one of the suggestions above. In the annotation, we note that the possible rating bias (the expectancy effect) of teachers assigned to the experimental groups might be resolved by using observers who not only were outsiders but were blind to the treatment conditions as well. From my point of view as a teacher, who better to perform such a task than volunteer parents?

Colleagues, teaching interns, high school students on service learning assignments, or draftees from the local senior center—there are endless possibilities for assistance with assessing student outcomes. Parental involvement, however, offers a dual payoff: It is a wonderful way to inform them about what is happening to their children in physical education as well as convince them about the effectiveness of the program in promoting valuable learning. Every time we include others in doable pieces of our program, we increase the number of potential supporters and spread the word about the importance of our work to the wider community.

Common Ground: Our Shared Perspective

In this instance, we share the final conclusion reached by the authors as they looked back upon all that they had learned from this study: "The proactive approach toward the development of positive attitudes and behaviors taken by *Fair Play for Kids* is surely a positive step toward encouraging moral development in physical education and sport" (pp. 254-255). To that we would add our own conclusion that the particular mix of teaching strategies and student learning activities selected by the authors—experiencing moral dilemmas, talking about them in a cooperative social setting, and designing a morally balanced intention to act—was in itself a singular contribution to the resources available to elementary school physical education teachers.

The evidence laid out in this report seems reasonably clear. The fair play program worked to produce the intended outcomes. It is reasonable to conclude that fair play behaviors are not the result of playing games or engaging in physical activities. They are the product of deliberately designed environments and teaching strategies.

> **The evidence laid out in this report seems reasonably clear. The fair play program worked to produce the intended outcomes.**

PART III
Interactions Among Students

THE STUDY

RESEARCHER

TEACHER

COMMON GROUND

Using Trained Peer Tutors

Houston-Wilson, C., Dunn, J.M., van der Mars, H., & McCubbin, J. (1997). The effect of peer tutors on motor performance in integrated physical education classes. *Adapted Physical Activity Quarterly, 14,* 298-313.

Whether you examine the research record or question experienced teachers, the use of pupils to teach or assist other pupils in physical education classes has a mixed record of success—and a mixed degree of acceptance among practitioners. The arguments, pro and con, are complex, and we will not examine them here. Instead, we ask you to consider the results from this single, rather straightforward, and very carefully executed study. No one investigation, of course, can settle anything in the complex world of elementary school physical education; this one, however, has characteristics that make it stand out as particularly informative.

 **The Study**

Here, the investigators borrowed a design that commonly is employed in behavior analysis research (see chapters 5, 7, and 11). Designated a *delayed multiple baseline design,* the study protocol allowed the researchers to examine the skill performance of students over a sequence of 35 class meetings as they were exposed to practice conditions that included the presence or absence of trained or untrained peer tutors. The starting and ending points for those conditions were so arranged that it allowed the assertion that any observed change in the students' performance was due to the accompanying change in practice conditions, rather than some other variable in the class environment.

To use this design in assessing the efficacy of assistance from peer tutors, the researchers identified a type of student who truly could profit from help while they practiced—students with mild mental retardation and the associated delays in development of motor skills. The investigators were also careful to train peers in exactly the helping skills that would be most likely to assist those special students. The helping assignment given to the peer tutors was limited to a particular set of motor skills; their tutoring behaviors were carefully monitored; and when the students with disabilities practiced, the resulting performances, with and without peer tutors, were carefully measured. All of this took place within regularly scheduled, inclusion-based physical education classes. In short, if peer tutoring was ever going to work in convincing fashion, these were the right kind of conditions.

Participants and Context

For this study, 6 elementary school students (ages 9 to 11) with developmental cognitive and motor delays were selected as participants in six different physical education classes, each of which included normally developing peers. None of the participants knew how to perform the five discrete motor skills used in the study: horizontal jump, catch, overhand throw, forehand strike, and sidearm strike. From six other classes, 6 normally developing students (ages 9 to 11), all of whom had mastered the five skills to the level of mature performance, were selected to serve as peer tutors. The 6 tutors received two 30-minute sessions of training during their regular physical education classes. They learned how to give verbal cues, model skills, use physical assistance, provide encouragement, and give both general and specific skill feedback. At the end of their second period of training, they could demonstrate correct use of the helping skills and could pass an examination on the knowledge concepts involved. Finally, 3 other students were selected to provide assistance without having received any training in tutorial skills.

Design and Method

Two sets of procedures were used in the study (Procedures A and B). In Procedure A, 3 of the students with special needs were engaged in their regular physical education classes to learn to master the five noted motor skills. All class periods were videotaped in their entirety, and after three class periods, a baseline was established by recording each of their practice attempts. The three untrained peer tutors were each then assigned to a participant with the simple instruction to be as helpful as possible; three classes were recorded under those conditions. Afterward, three trained tutors were assigned to the same students for four classes, and the results again were recorded on videotape with audiotapes of what the tutors said while helping. Procedure B used the 3 remaining special students, the same baseline protocol, and the remaining 3 trained tutors for five classes of peer assistance. The main difference was that Procedure B omitted the use of the untrained tutors, who had been observed in Procedure A.

Researchers reviewed videotapes from a total of 57 classes and scored the quality of each practice. Five key performance criteria for each of the five skills were used, and an average "motor appropriateness" score could be derived from each class for each of the students with disabilities.

The Results

First of all, the audiotapes revealed that the trained tutors did indeed use their training when helping special students. The untrained tutors, of course, used very few of the assisting skills; they mostly gave general encouragement. Second, graphs of the motor appropriateness displayed in the participants' average performances showed a sharp jump upward exactly at the point in the sequence of classes when the trained tutors appeared. No such improvement could be detected when untrained tutors attempted to be helpful.

These patterns revealed some instances of interesting individual variation. For example, one or more of the students with special needs would on several days simply not accept assistance from anyone, trained or untrained. Overall, however, the evidence was convincing to support the proposition that the peer-tutor training program had been successful. Peer tutoring was associated with marked improvements in the degree to which students with delayed development made progress toward mature performance of the five basic motor skills in their physical education classes.

A Researcher's Perspective

Teachers in every subject field assess new ideas for their teaching in terms of practicality (cost and workability) in their particular context. They question whether the ideas match their own values, whether they can easily master any needed skills, and finally, whether a new strategy would produce any truly worthwhile improvement. Peer tutoring for special students must be evaluated in the same way. The procedures used in this study were inexpensive in terms of the investment of student time and materials (training required only two 30-minute sessions, materials included only handout sheets and a one-page knowledge test). The peer tutors volunteered readily and seemed strongly motivated to do a good job; in fact, they wanted to continue in their helping role beyond the end of the study.

> **The procedures used in this study were inexpensive in terms of the investment of student time and materials . . .**

A Teacher's Perspective

This study reminded me of how often our attempts to find effective strategies for dealing with children who have special needs end up helping us become better teachers for all children. The procedures described for preparing peer tutors to help pupils with developmental delays, for example, represent steps that would be appropriate in preparing tutors for any form of peer-based teaching. This study offers such gifts not only for those struggling to meet the needs of diverse learners but for all teachers who work at the details of planning their lessons. Let me explain that point with a bit more detail.

In my experience, effective teachers almost universally hail peer tutoring as a positive strategy. What those teachers know, however, is that the crucial step in using the strategy is the preparation of the tutors. Beginners often miss that point and think that information about the skill or activity is the only important part of setting up peer assistance. Nothing could be further from the truth. If you just throw students into unfamiliar tutorial roles, they may truly want to be helpful but are rarely able to support learning in appropriate ways.

That is why I think this study is valuable for a lot more than simply illustrating how peer tutoring can help students with special needs or how more mature students can learn how to be effective tutors. It illustrates that the key to successful teaching strategies is preparing students for anything they are supposed to do. Even experienced teachers are reminded of this now and then when a lesson falls apart because they did not take enough time helping their pupils to understand and practice appropriate behaviors and attitudes for the learning activity.

Really outstanding teachers do a wonderful job of anticipating what students will need to know and helping them with that knowledge before the activity begins—for example, "Today we're going to play two-on-two soccer games. In your games, sometimes you'll have a disagreement about what happened, like whether the ball went through the goal or outside the cones. What are some of the ways we can deal with those disagreements that will keep the game going and help everyone enjoy the activity? What are some other disagreements that might come up?" Anticipation is just one small part of the instruction good teachers use to prepare their students for learning and enjoying themselves in a new situation.

I think that sometimes we teachers forget all of the things that students don't know how to do because we learned those things so long ago. Wise teachers do what the investigators apparently did in this experiment. They remembered, and they helped students master some of the really simple skills needed when helping another person learn.

> **If you just throw students into unfamiliar tutorial roles, they may truly want to be helpful but are rarely able to support learning in appropriate ways.**

Not only does this study confirm what good teachers have always known about the importance of preparing students for peer mentor relationships, it also underlines the fact that specific factors can make mentoring effective: good verbal cues, appropriate modeling, various kinds of physical assistance, encouragement, congruent feedback, and attending closely to the key elements in performance. Concentration on those elements of teaching and learning probably would be just as beneficial for the whole class as it is for those acting as mentors—including the students with special needs and the teachers themselves! Being aware of all those important ways of supporting practice creates a focus on learning, rather than just on participating. That is powerful stuff, and I can only wonder what might have happened if the same training had been given to the entire class?

Although it is not mentioned in the research report, peer mentoring of the kind employed in this study sends a strong signal to everyone: "These skills can be learned, and we are going to act in ways to ensure that everyone does in fact learn them." That message directly counters the sense that in physical education, some students can do the things and others just can't. It sends that message by making "This is how we go about learning a new skill," the central theme of everyday class experience.

It is impossible not to wonder why we don't teach a short module on becoming a better peer mentor to all of the students, in all of our classes. Then it would be possible to make wider use of reciprocal teaching and various forms of peer assistance in all subsequent units. What was used in this study as a special intervention for children with special needs could realistically become part of operating procedure in an entire program.

The fact that two 30-minute sessions were required for training the mentors may seem daunting to teachers who see their students only once or twice a week. Nevertheless, that fairly modest requirement should be encouraging when they consider the substantial payoff for learning—particularly if calculated for an entire school year and potentially for a whole class, rather than a small subset of pupils.

Another element not addressed in the study is the fact that students with special needs often have aides who accompany them to physical education classes. It would be ideal if such support staff could have the same training in mentoring skills. Although some are excellent, others display well-intentioned yet unhelpful behaviors, much like those of the untrained mentors in the study.

Any reader of this report is going to wonder whether the same mentoring behaviors are equally helpful with all students and all skills? Will the training have to be modified to meet the demands of other kinds of students, including those without (identified) special needs? Is this the same sort of training that would work in preparing students for reciprocal teaching, and can the training be accomplished just as effectively with a whole class as it was with individual peer mentors? All of which illustrates how an intelligent study can provoke as many questions as it answers.

 ## Common Ground: Our Shared Perspective

The results were clearly beneficial and substantial, especially considering that students with special needs typically have difficulty mastering motor skills. Such students need extra support, but in a class of typical size, the teacher can only devote a limited amount of time to each pupil. Peer tutors can give assistance when the teacher cannot, and the act of helping allows them to practice a kind of responsibility for which there are few opportunities in a typical elementary school day. To us, that sounds like a situation with potential for producing winners all around.

> **Peer tutors can give assistance when the teacher cannot, and the act of helping allows them to practice a kind of responsibility for which there are few opportunities in a typical elementary school day.**

Peer-Mediated Accountability and Successful Practice

Crouch, D.W., Ward, P., & Patrick, C.A. (1997). The effects of peer-mediated accountability on task accomplishment during volleyball drills in elementary physical education. *Journal of Teaching in Physical Education, 17,* 26-39.

This study is one of several *behavior analysis* investigations presented in this book (see chapters 5, 7, and 10 for other examples). In this form of research, aspects of a behavior are charted in a graphic display that allows easy inspection of changes over time. In this study, for example, researchers charted the number of successful volleyball hits in a one-minute test on a graph that spanned five consecutive lessons. The line formed by connecting scores for each day could rise, fall, stay the same, or show only random changes. If the teacher had implemented a new teaching strategy on the 6th day and continued it for five subsequent lessons, the track formed by the line of test scores might be deflected—indicating both the nature and the extent of the new strategy's impact on student performance.

Researchers who employ behavior analysis designs do not ordinarily use statistics to analyze their data. They depend instead on the persuasive power of graphic display and the logical power derived from various arrangements of interventions. One of the arrangements employed in this study is called a *withdrawal design.* Researchers introduce a particular condition in the class, then they collect behavioral data for several days. The condition is eventually withdrawn, and some other condition is introduced, with the results then being graphed again. Data graphs that show predicted deflections in direction and magnitude thus provide evidence

that one condition is superior to the other. The behavior analysis studies we have annotated in this text introduce you to several aspects of such designs, including withdrawal, reversal, and the use of multiple baselines.

As you might guess, behavior analysis graphs are an economical format for presenting data and a powerful source of credibility for what the researcher concludes from the study. Our brief summaries of these studies give you the general shape of the results they produce, but to get the full effect, you will need to look at the graphic figures in the original publication. You certainly do not need to read the full report if you do not wish to do so. With our annotation as a starting place, the behavior graphs in the original report will be perfectly intelligible.

This particular study is valuable not only for the results it produces but also for the introduction it provides to several useful constructs. The first is the idea of a *task*—something a teacher asks students to do. Ordinarily, such tasks have a beginning, an end, and specific performance characteristics: "Please walk quietly now, put the balls in the rack, then walk back and sit down here in front of me." Any physical education lesson comprises dozens of such managerial tasks. Each can be examined in its own terms—clarity, specificity, intelligibility—as well as in terms of the behaviors students produce in response—immediate, delayed, correct, modified. In a physical education lesson, related tasks can conveniently be clustered into the major *task systems* that deal with instruction, class management, or social aspects of student and teacher interaction.

A great deal of research has confirmed that student responses to tasks established by the teacher are shaped by the consequences of doing or not doing the task. Teachers control some of those consequences and in that sense can hold students accountable for correct execution of the task. For example, accountability may be informal, as when a teacher closely and obviously monitors what students do, or it may be formal, as when a behavior can affect a student's grade. In many instances, students perform just as well when the consequences are informal, as in such instances as receiving teacher approval, getting praise from peers, or earning extra time in a desirable activity.

 **The Study**

This study is one in a series of investigations conducted by the authors of this report (a college professor and two elementary school physical education teachers) as they explored various aspects of the task accountability systems found in public school classes. The present study employs a construct called *peer-mediated accountability*. This protocol required that the teacher establish the learning tasks but that the informal system of accountability for good performance be provided by the actions of other students. In other words, peers were the source of the consequences. More explicitly, the primary purpose was to assess the effect of a practice condition in which students evaluated and recorded each other's performance of volleyball skills. Researchers then compared those results with performances observed under other more typical conditions for skill practice.

Participants and Context

For this study, 67 students in three classes—fourth grade (14 boys and 10 girls), fifth grade (13 boys and 12 girls), and sixth grade (9 boys and 9 girls)—and their elementary school physical education teacher participated. Physical education classes were held daily, 20 minutes for fourth-graders and 30 minutes for fifth- and sixth-graders.

Design and Method

To measure student performance, researchers used two outcome measures for two separate skills: the number of trials performed and the number of correct trials performed during 1-minute tests of the volleyball bump (forearm pass) and the volleyball set. Researchers established simple form standards to judge the correctness of the two skills performed. Success was scored as any trial in which the objective was accomplished—bumping or setting the ball into a target area—while performing the skill with correct form.

All assessments used standardized targets and performance areas. During the lesson, all students moved through the two testing areas, which were part of a circuit of four stations (including serving and minigame stations not used in the study). Students spent one minute at each station before moving on to the next. The teacher used a countdown timer and blew a whistle to signal rotations from one station to the next. Twenty such lessons were videotaped on consecutive days, and data were collected from replays of those tapes.

Each class had three experimental conditions:

1. Condition A—group instruction: Students simply progressed through the stations, completing the one-minute trials with no scores being recorded. The teacher gave encouragement and, when necessary, correction to individual students.

2. Condition B—peer-dyads: Students completed the circuit in pairs with instructions to encourage and retrieve the ball for each other. Partners were self-selected and remained constant throughout the study. No scores were recorded.

3. Condition C—peer-mediated accountability: Partners judged success and recorded scores for total trials and successful trials. Records were then immediately posted by partners on the gym wall.

For all groups, the emphasis during testing was on the number of correct trials, not just on the total number attempted. For Condition C, however, students had previously been given instruction and practice in how to judge correct form for the bump and set, as well as how to record and post partner scores. In addition, each day the teacher set a performance goal for students in that group and awarded special daily and weekly activities to students who achieved their goal. As the goal usually was to meet or exceed their previous score, almost all of the students succeeded.

Scoring of the videotaped student performances by members of the research team produced relatively high interobserver reliabilities. Agreement across the two skills and the three grades ranged between 84% and 94%. In turn, the investigators' scores for the total trials and successful trials were compared to a sample of the scores produced by student partners. Mean levels of agreement from the two scoring sources ranged from 83% to 94%, and with that, the authors assert that students had produced scores that were reasonably close to their own assessments.

Using four 5-day blocks of consecutive lessons (20 lessons total), all students in grade 4 were assigned to practice conditions in the following order: A, B, A, C. Such a design allowed direct comparison between each of the three test conditions. In grade 5, the order was changed to B, A, C, A to check any possible effect from the serial order used in grade 4. In grade 6, the order for conditions was C, A, C, A, which was designed to give two opportunities to observe what happened when Condition C was withdrawn.

Results

At all three grade levels the results were essentially the same. There was little difference between groups in Conditions A and B (group instruction and peer-dyads) in either number of trials or number of correct trials. The group in Condition C (peer-mediated accountability) produced the highest number of trials and percentage of correct trials. Deflections of the graph lines often reflected large numeric differences that convincingly illustrate the effects of the variables. For example, the total scores in grade 4 for the bump test were as follows: Condition A, 277 hits with 25% correct; Condition B, 312 hits with 23% correct; and Condition C, 403 hits with 40% correct. Results for bumps and sets followed each other closely. They did, however, deviate from that pattern in grade 6 where all conditions were about equally successful in bump tests (50%).

Peer-mediated accountability (as defined in this study) produced highly consistent results. The shift in performance was immediate whenever Condition C was instituted—no matter what condition had preceded it. The change in test scores invariably was an increase in the number of total attempts and successful attempts. Moreover, the degree of positive change for peer-mediated accountability was typically larger than changes recorded for shifts to Conditions A and B. The authors report that no instances of inappropriate behavior were observed in relation to the public posting of results—that is, students never ridiculed each other after the results were posted. In fact, students appeared to enjoy the peer-mediated account-

ability condition, often asking if and when they could do it again.

A Researcher's Perspective

The findings support previous research indicating that informal accountability (not connected to grades) can produce high levels of student performance. Here, however, the results allow us to compare a wide variety of practice conditions and forms of accountability. Little in this study is completely novel in the elementary school. For example, classroom teachers and physical educators have long made use of public posting of students' performances as a means of sustaining motivation. It is unusual, though, to have the opportunity to watch the change in student performance of learning tasks as that particular consequence is instituted, then withdrawn.

It is true, of course, that multiple consequences were involved in all of the conditions—some systematic and highly visible, others serendipitous and hidden from public view. It will take more studies to sort out the relative influence of those variables. For example, it is possible that the contingencies attached to meeting the teacher-established daily performance goal would have worked just as well without the presence of public posting for scores. What we do know is that in the present combination, peer-mediated accountability worked much better than two other conditions.

> **What we do know is that in the present combination, peer-mediated accountability worked much better than two other conditions.**

It is almost certain that the results produced under the conditions of a one-minute test could not be sustained for a whole class period, nor would one wish them to be. This particular intervention is no panacea for developing movement skills in physical education, and the authors make no such claim. On the other hand, consider the following: Compare the average number of opportunities to hit the ball produced in Condition A (20 times for bumps and 16 for sets) with the typical class volleyball game (probably 1 hit per minute per student). The advantage of clearly established tasks that have strong account-ability features becomes perfectly obvious.

A Teacher's Perspective

I love the clarity of this type of study. The impact of the teaching strategy is easy to see in the form of observable student behavior and performance. In addition, it is so convincing to observe the immediate change in student behaviors when the strategy is withdrawn. As usual, a powerful study such as this one starts me thinking about how easy it would be to study aspects of my own classes. All I really would have to do is carefully record a variable that interests me while at the same time changing some aspect of my teaching.

An example (out of the millions of questions I could ask about my own classes) is one with which I have actually had some recent experience: Can I get students to persist longer in working on a learning task if I put on music during practice? I have made some informal observations, and my impression is that the answer is probably yes. It would, however, be so much better to have evidence of the convincing kind produced in this study.

All I would need is some simple system to record how many students are persisting on a practice task (a sample lasting about three minutes would seem reasonable). Then I could put music on for several weeks as a practice run, then stop doing so for an equal number of class sessions. Finally, I could reintroduce the music once again. I might even want to try several types of music to see if one has a stronger effect on student persistence. If I had to change practice tasks as students moved through the unit, the trick would be to invent tasks that were roughly equal in difficulty and intrinsic interest.

Another target for this kind of inquiry could be other auditory signals. For example, do students put equipment away as quickly when there is an electronic metronome loudly ticking as when there is not? If there were evidence of an accelerating effect, I wonder if it would become less marked over time? If so, perhaps I could borrow from the research strategy of temporary withdrawal (not using the metronome for a while and then adding it again) to give it a periodic boost.

> **A powerful study such as this one starts me thinking about how easy it would be to study aspects of my own classes.**

I am anxious to get a copy of the evaluation procedures used by the authors in obtaining a combined score for form and outcome (what they called a *success score*). The original report names the key points used for each skill, but I need more detail. Obviously, the procedures were simple enough to be taught to elementary school students because that is exactly what they did in the study. Such an easy-to-learn and reasonably reliable assessment tool would be a great addition to my collection.

I particularly like the idea that to be counted as successful in this study, an attempt had to include both good form and the accomplishment of a desired outcome, such as hitting the ball into the desired target area (what the authors call the *product*). To my mind, practicing the good form makes it more likely that future attempts will be successful, but displaying good form without achieving the goal is simply not enough. That is exactly why I was so impressed by the fact that peer scoring and posting, the accountability procedures, worked to produce significant improvements in student performance when the measure of success included both form and product.

The research design for this behavior analysis study was also helpful to me in another way. In other kinds of control group or multiple-treatment group studies, it is sometimes difficult for me to tell whether the results come from the alleged treatment or from some other aspect of the research procedure. For example, I found myself on the first reading of this study feeling suspicious that the improvements might just have been caused by teaching the students how to score form and product. Then I thought about the design for the study and looked at the results again—of course, my suspicion could not be true! All students were trained for peer assessment during Condition C. When grades 5 and 6, however, subsequently practiced under Condition A, such knowledge just did not have the same impact versus when they actually recorded and posted their partner's performance scores (as in Condition C). Knowing the assessment cues was therefore not enough; actually using them as a form of peer accountability was what made the difference. I like that kind of clarity.

For the main variable of the study, peer scoring and posting of success for partners, there is an obvious application to practice. For short, bounded practice tasks that students can quickly learn the observation cues needed to make simple judgments about success, this strategy is worth trying. The reservations are also clear enough. Less appropriate candidates for this technique are tasks that require longer periods of practice, involve complex sequences of movement, and lack simple cues for evaluation of good form and product.

For my own classes, I would want to begin using some kind of peer scoring and recording protocol in each unit I teach so that my students would become familiar with that sort of responsibility. I also would want to reflect with them on the power of the strategy, discussing how and why it seems to work. Certainly there is no reason to treat such ideas as a teacher's secret. I am sure that understanding the rationale for peer recording and posting would make students more open to using it in class when asked, but I also suspect that the same insight might encourage them to see applications in other areas of their lives.

Common Ground: Our Shared Perspective

Our first conclusion might surprise you. It is personal and arises from our own experiences, as physical education instructors and as mentors for beginning teachers. A reading of this study persuades us to believe that constructs such as *task, task system,* and *accountability* are potentially powerful elements in the thinking of a truly professional teacher.

> **Constructs such as *task, task system*, and *accountability* are potentially powerful elements in the thinking of a truly professional teacher.**

First, they are part of a technical language that allows us to talk to each other about what we do. They provide convenient and economical labels for complex aspects of our work. Second, an abstract construct such as *accountability* can serve as a guide for perception. It would allow us to become aware of events and relationships in a physical education lesson that would otherwise escape our attention. Teachers need a shared technical language just as do scientists, artists, and other professional practitioners. When new constructs are illustrated by vivid descriptions of the sort provided in this report, they quickly become a usable part of our pedagogical vocabulary.

We must also acknowledge the more obvious conclusion that is supported by the findings in this study. It appears that clearly established tasks accompanied by some form of consistent accountability are a foundational part of effective teaching and sound lessons. We might choose to argue with those who understand the world of teaching and learning exclusively in behavioral terms. There will be no argument from us, however, concerning the virtues of communicating tasks to students in a way that is clear and complete. Nor will we dispute that teachers must find ways to assure students that doing the task and doing it right is important, will be noticed, and will have direct, postive consequences.

PART IV
Strategies for Teaching and Learning

THE STUDY

RESEARCHER

TEACHER

COMMON GROUND

Can Learners Guide Their Own Practice With Self-Talk?

Anderson, A., Vogel, P., & Albrecht, R. (1999). The effect of instructional self-talk on the overhand throw. *The Physical Educator, 56,* 215-221.

A number of studies have confirmed the efficacy of an instructional tactic long used by teachers and coaches. Learners can use self-talk to rehearse or guide a motor performance. The verbalization can be overt (public) or silent (private), and the spoken cues may be phrases or single key words. The purpose is to help focus the learner's attention on the critical elements of a task, including serial ordering and both temporal and spatial characteristics of the desired movement.

The theoretical explanation for the success of instructional self-talk is not yet entirely clear, but it seems likely that assigning the learners an active role in shaping their own efforts is a critical part of the mechanism involved. Despite the promise of this tactic, no studies have described the effect of its use within the context of an elementary physical education program. Such an inquiry is potentially of great significance because younger children do not appear to spontaneously rehearse information or instructions as part of trial performances.

 ## The Study

This study was designed to answer two questions that flow directly from the preceding observations.

1. Is the use of instructional self-talk an effective strategy for teaching third-graders a mature overhand throwing form?

2. Is self-talk less effective, equally effective, or more effective than traditional instruction or demonstration-only approaches that do not include the use of self-talk?

Participants and Context

Participants were selected in each of three third-grade physical education classes. Every student's overhand throwing form was assessed before the start of the study (the performance rating scale is available from the senior author). Students whose pretest scores indicated that they already had achieved mature throwing form were eliminated from the study population. After return of parental permission forms, 46 eligible students remained (18 males and 28 females).

Design and Method

The study lasted 3 weeks, and during that time, each class met three times a week for 30 minutes. An instructional videotape was prepared in which a skilled 10-year-old female model demonstrated mature form for the overhand throw. The video was subdivided into three phases, emphasizing (a) body position and hip rotation, (b) weight transfer, and (c) arm action. The audio portion provided step-by-step verbal explanation for the key elements of the performances portrayed in each phase.

At the beginning of each lesson, each of the three classes viewed the portion of the tape pertaining to the throwing phase that they would be practicing in that lesson. Students then completed 10 minutes of throwing practice against the wall with bean bags, a procedure that produced 90 minutes of active practice over the 3 weeks of the study. Three treatment conditions were randomly assigned to the three classes (number of participants in parentheses): Class 1, self-talk (16); Class 2, traditional instruction (13); and Class 3, demonstration only (17).

In the self-talk class, the model herself provided the voice-over that explained the components of the throw. She used vivid, metaphoric language that was easy to remember, such as "spread the wings of the eagle" (extending the arms) and "navel attack" (rotating the body so the navel is pointing toward the target). The students were instructed to use the same language to talk to themselves about what to do as they practiced throwing. Teacher feedback during practice was focused on both technical aspects of performance and reinforcing the self-talk aspects of the task: "You're doing a good job remembering to tell yourself to keep your elbow up."

In the traditional instruction class, the group received the same exposure to the instructional video and class demonstrations, as well as identical opportunities for practice and feedback. All instruction, however, was given by the teacher who employed nonmetaphoric descriptive language: "Stand sideways, bring the arms up to shoulder-height, and turn your hips toward the target as you throw." Students were not encouraged to use self-talk of any kind during practice, and feedback utilized traditional nomenclature that focused on direct communication about the needed action.

In the demonstration-only class, students watched the same video with the sound turned off. No additional instruction about throwing form was offered. Class demonstrations of the mature throwing form and opportunities for practice were identical to those for the other treatment groups, but feedback was limited to general encouragement: "Good try, keep practicing." The intention was to create an instructional environment that made primary use of the "watch me, now you try it" style of teaching.

Student performance was tested at the end of each of the three weeks. Students standing 25 feet from the wall were given three trials to throw bean bags "from the outfield to second base." Individual videotapes were made of each trial, and each trial was subsequently scored for form. Interrater reliability for two trained scorers was maintained at an acceptable level.

Results

Statistical analysis of the data from the three testings showed a significant advantage for self-talk over traditional instruction, and for traditional instruction over demonstration only. Inspection of the group averages indicates that the differences were of practical as well as theoretical significance. On the 20-point rating scale for throwing form, from pretest to the end of the study, self-talk students gained an average of 8.4 points while the traditional instruction and demonstration-only students gained 5.1 and 2.2, respectively.

A Researcher's Perspective

The results here are consistent with those found in other studies involving older subjects in which verbal self-cueing appeared to enhance learning of motor skills. One is left to wonder whether the use of vivid, metaphorical performance cues in the videotape might have been associated with similar learning gains even without the use of self-talk? Or, conversely, would self-talk have yielded the same learning advantage if it were composed of the standard descriptions from the traditional instruction group?

Whatever the case, the differences among the three groups were substantial. Clearly, demonstration alone was not enough, and just as clearly, demonstration with self-talk using vivid cues was superior to either of the other two conditions for teaching and practice. Future research will have to further refine our understanding of exactly which variables are the most important.

> Clearly, demonstration alone was not enough, and just as clearly, demonstration with self-talk using vivid cues was superior . . .

A Teacher's Perspective

I love practical, useful studies like this one. Although they don't provide unequivocal information about how things work exactly, they do examine variables that are just like choices we really have to make every day. This study seems to be precisely the type of research that can be important for teaching in the elementary school. It gets right to the crux of the relationship between how you teach and what students actually do and learn in class.

There are three aspects of the study that immediately seemed to offer possibilities for my own teaching. One was the primary variable defined in the study, the use of self-talk. A second was the element not treated as a formal variable, the use of creative, verbal cues. As in the swimming warm-up study described in our introductory chapter, I think there is the possibility that something tucked away out of the limelight, in this case giving catchy names to the required movements, might turn out to be as important as the main variable in the study. Third, and finally, my attention was drawn to the basic format for the study—teaching several classes in ways that introduce one major difference, then carefully watching the result.

> Was it self-talk, or was it vivid verbal imagery that made learners change their behaviors in desirable directions? Or, were both required to produce the observed effect?

Let me comment first on self-talk, which I am particularly attracted to because it represents a way of encouraging learners to pay attention to what they actually are doing when they practice. Darrell Williams, an extraordinary movement skills teacher at the University of Texas, introduced me to the importance of helping students focus on specific aspects of movement, particularly when they are at the early stage of practice and have only a general image of what they are supposed to do.

As an example, he explained the distinction between the words *attend* and *intend*, warning me that even good students can appear to *attend* to instructions but not internalize enough of the specifics to *intend* anything. The simple result is that when they perform a practice trial, they don't actually try to do any part of the skill in a particular manner. He suggested, therefore, that beginners should give themselves specific instructions and explicit intentions, such as, "I am going to rotate my trunk, then finish the movement with my arm across my body."

I am convinced that getting students to intend to move in specific ways is half the battle. The other half, however, is getting them to attend to what they are doing when they move. I often find learners who can initiate the movement, then not pay any attention to what actually happens. It seems to me that the self-talk strategy described in this study might help learners think about how they intend to move and recognize how they are moving when they carry out that plan.

Certainly, the power demonstrated by the self-talk strategy in this study ought to encourage us to use it. In physical education classes, teaching students to use self-talk as a regular practice protocol would be the way to go. I want to warn our readers, however, that just getting students to recite the appropriate movement cues at the right time may not always be enough. My own experience has taught me that the next vital link is getting students to tie what they are saying to what they actually do. For most students, that connection is more-or-less automatic, but it is not so for all. Learners who have marked difficulty in acquiring new skills often say one thing, then do something that has no relation whatever to the verbalization. I even see this phenomenon happen in college students as well as in elementary school children. Let me give you an example.

When teaching juggling, I often use lightweight scarves that actually float in the air, giving the performer time to think and move. The initial sequence for practice with two scarves is to throw one, then the other, catch the first, then the second. The verbal cues are "toss, toss, catch, catch." I usually spot at least one student reciting the cues correctly but executing the movement as "toss, catch, toss, catch," not even being aware of the obvious and crucial difference between words and action. Others will say "throw," but they will never let go of the scarf. They know the cues, perhaps even can visualize the action, but they can't produce matching body movements.

It sometimes takes a surprising amount of attention and feedback to get the two elements to match. I have a hunch that with a protocol for self-talk that also puts special emphasis on matching movement to the cue, the number of such out-of-sync movements might be reduced. If that turns out to be true, then this study will have made a really useful contribution to successful teaching—even though it was not the central point in the researchers' minds.

The second lesson I drew from this study is that we cannot be sure of the role played by assigning catchy cue words and phrases to movement components—as distinct from the act of actually reciting those cues. Was it self-talk, or was it vivid verbal imagery that made learners change their behaviors in desirable directions? Or, were both required to produce the observed effect?

63

My own guess is that learners are more likely to pay attention when there is an interesting connection between words and action. I can just imagine the kids laughing and demonstrating their "naval attack" in this study. It probably is significant that over the years I have noticed that outstanding teachers seem to be masters of that particular bit of pedagogy. They not only know the key performance elements in a skill, but they also have a facility for thinking up neat images or funny rhymes that make for memorable verbal cues.

Carole Smith who teaches at the Hill Elementary School in Austin, Texas always creates a rhyme to help children remember the cues or steps in progression for a skill. When I was much younger, I thought teachers like Carole just happened to be talented in that area (and some of them probably were). I now have come to believe that the critical factor is their recognition of the importance in designing effective cues and the willingness to really work at that teaching task.

Finally, the study happily reminded me of an old fascination—teaching different classes with different techniques and watching the results. I know perfectly well that such modest self-study projects lack many of the careful controls required to qualify as research. I also know, however, that they serve to satisfy my curiosity about whether one choice of method yields better results than another. In addition, like some of the formal research investigations in this book, my personal excursions into inquiry tend to turn up unexpected results. Sometimes those surprises can lead to valuable insights. If nothing else, though, puzzling about them serves to keep my fascination with teaching fresh and alive during the familiar routines of a long school day.

 ## Common Ground: Our Shared Perspective

For now, it does not seem unreasonable to suppose that any teaching tactic that engages students as active agents in their own learning is likely to enhance achievement. To that end, it appears that self-talk can have a potent effect, particularly when it uses graphic verbal images appropriate to the age group involved. It also is probable that this technique works best when the tactic becomes an integral part of the entire instructional sequence—from initial demonstration to the forms of feedback used during practice.

> **Any teaching tactic that engages students as active agents in their own learning is likely to enhance achievement.**

Using Environmental Cues to Guide Practice

Sweeting, T., & Rink, J.E. (1999). Effects of direct instruction and environmentally designed instruction on the process and product characteristics of a fundamental skill. *Journal of Teaching in Physical Education, 18,* 216-233.

Terry Sweeting and Judy Rink have long been curious about the possible uses of a teaching trick familiar to nearly all athletic coaches and physical educators. At times, students or athletes are unable to perform a movement skill using the desired "correct form," even after instruction, demonstration, and practice. Sometimes, however, it is possible to change something in the learning environment that then forces, or at least encourages, the learner to produce the desired action. Manipulations of the practice environment can sometimes shape a learner's movements and improve their performance when verbal or visual cues that signal, "Do it this way!" have failed.

Such strategies, for example, have an honored place in the instructional repertoire of anyone who has tried to teach the long jump—whether to beginners as the standing jump (a fundamental movement skill) or to advanced learners as a running jump (a competitive Olympic event). One familiar intervention is to place a target at the desired point of landing, thus encouraging the jumper to execute forward extension of the legs at the end of the flight. Likewise, instructors sometimes introduce a light barrier or hurdle just beyond the takeoff point to force a steeper angle of takeoff. The result is both a more prompt tucking-up of the legs and a higher trajectory for the jump.

Early stages of learning are likely to reveal a number of students who don't seem able to "do it this

way," even after individual feedback and correction. It has therefore been tempting for researchers to explore how manipulations of the environment might be used by physical education teachers to prevent any student from being left behind as a unit of instruction moves ahead. If teachers could have a collection of such strategies and know when and how they might be used to good effect, they could either provide more varied instruction for all students or target particular pupils who appear to be having difficulty in learning a skill.

The problem has been that this particular type of teaching maneuver has existed mostly in the form of *craft knowledge,* the unwritten instructional lore possessed, and sometimes informally shared, by experienced teachers. What has never been explored are the important questions involving why and how environmental manipulations work, with whom they are most likely to show good results, and when in the learning sequence they are best employed. As physical education teachers and present researchers, Sweeting and Rink found it natural (if not easy) to translate their practical curiosity into the systematic inquiry of a research project.

 **The Study**

The purpose of this study was to compare the effects of direct instruction—traditional teaching in the form of verbal cues, demonstration, practice, feedback, and correction—with a form of environmental instruction without traditional verbal instruction, cues, demonstrations, or feedback of any sort. For this study, researchers measured the impact of each method in terms of how far and how well kindergarten and second-grade children could perform the standing long jump.

Participants and Context

From intact classrooms in a suburban elementary school, researchers selected 40 students from two kindergarten classes and 40 students from two second-grade classes as participants in this study. Each group of 40 children was then divided equally into two instructional groups for a total of four groups of 20 children. In that process, the four groups were equated for skill, based on scores from a pretest of jumping skill. Finally, 16 children from a third kindergarten class and 20 children from a third second-grade class were selected to serve as control groups for which no special instructional treatment was provided. These control groups allowed the investigators to monitor any possible effects produced by testing, maturation, or other uncontrolled variables. Thus, a total of 116 children took part in the study.

Design and Method

All children from the two grade levels were given two 6-trial jumping tests: one before instruction (the pretest) and one after 3 days of direct or environmental instruction (the posttest). Both testing and instruction took place in regularly scheduled 25-minute physical education classes. Each of the two testing sessions consisted of six attempts—three on a plain, flat mat and three with a pictured "swamp" to jump over (more on the "swamp" a little later). Researchers recorded the distance of each try and videotaped each attempt. The tapes were later reviewed in slow motion to rate different aspects of each student's jumping form.

At each grade level, the students in both equated instructional groups took 20 practice tries in each of their three classes, for a total of 60 tries. All participants, therefore, had 72 total attempts: 60 in class, 6 in the pretest, and 6 in the posttest. Students in the control groups, however, had only the 12 trials required for their two 6-jump testing sessions.

At least in theory, the only difference between the two groups was the kind of instruction and practice they received—that is, the direct versus the environmental. Carefully designed direct instruction was provided for one group, and a specially de-

signed practice environment without verbal instruction was provided for the other. Otherwise, each of the two instructional groups at each grade level was given exactly the same number of opportunities to practice jumping and had been equated for their initial level of skill.

As mentioned, the direct-instruction group practiced on traditional mats in the gymnasium. The environmental group's jumping lesson, however, consisted of four different practice stations that pupils rotated through during each lesson. The first station consisted of a mat with colored lines placed across the landing area to serve as distance targets. The second station was formed by a light paper barrier set up in the front of the mat so that pupils had to jump over it to reach the landing area. The third station comprised a mat with two such barriers set up about one foot apart so that pupils had to jump over both of them to reach the landing area. Finally, the fourth station was the "swamp," which included a picture of a wet and muddy bog laid out between the starting line and the landing area (the same picture was used in the pre- and posttests).

Results

Some of the results would surprise no experienced physical educator. Both before and after instruction of both kinds, second-graders jumped further than kindergarteners. After instruction of either kind, children at both grade levels could jump further. And although the uninstructed and unpracticed children in the control group did show some improvement across the two testing sessions (probably because the 12 trials helped them get better at taking the tests), their scores for distance and form on the postinstruction test were much lower than those for the pupils who received instruction (of either kind) and an opportunity to practice. So much for what anyone would have expected.

Looking more closely at the results, Sweeting and Rink found something unexpected and much more interesting. The kindergarten children (5-year-olds) and the pupils who scored poorly on the preinstruction tests at both grade levels (those with lower skills that are characteristic of developmental delay) performed best when they took the three test trials involving the pictured swamp—no matter what kind of instruction they had received.

Further, although children in both instructional groups improved their form much more so than pupils in the uninstructed control group, their progress was markedly different. Those receiving direct instruction improved most dramatically in the use of their arms and in their preparation to jump.

Those who only practiced in the special environmental conditions improved most in learning to tuck their legs up during flight.

A Researcher's Perspective

After some thought, the authors found the results less surprising. Each group had learned what each condition taught best. In the environmental practice condition, tucking the legs up was obviously necessary for clearing the hurdles or the swamp, even though no verbal instructions were given. In the direct instruction group, good arm swing during preparation and takeoff was stressed and hence learned, even though there was no way to force the pupils to quickly tuck up their legs in flight.

Given that as a starting place, I expect that most elementary school teachers would predict the following: Because tucking up the legs is the most difficult part of the jumping skill to master, those children at earlier stages of motor development would do best when tested under an environmental condition (the swamp test), which strongly encourages them to pull their legs up. That would be true whether such pupils were younger, such as in kindergarten, or just had developed more slowly—all of which was positively confirmed by study results.

Overall, there was no great difference in how much the two instructional groups learned. Both methods were effective in producing longer jumps and better form. What almost certainly was the case, however, was that for some children, manipulating the environment could help them improve in ways that familiar forms of direct instruction could not. Clearly, when used with the right pupils at the right time, changing the practice environment can be a powerful instructional tool.

> For some children, manipulating the environment could help them improve in ways that familiar forms of direct instruction could not.

A Teacher's Perspective

My attention was immediately drawn to the environmental conditions of pictured swamps, paper hurdles, and landing zone target lines. Each represented a way of encouraging effective performance, and those are examples of what I call golden nuggets. Over time, experienced teachers and coaches collect skill progressions, bits of verbal imagery and metaphors, as well as practice devices (like those in this study), all of which have served to help particular students.

Michele Rusnack, the physical education teacher at Bryker Woods Elementary School in Austin, Texas hangs cow bells from a bar between two cones when children are practicing kicking for accuracy. The task focus during practice is truly extraordinary, as is the delight when one of the students rings the bells. Such devices are the nuggets gleaned from experience, and for the students, many of them are attached to feelings of pleasure and success. Whether recalled in detail or faded into the soft haze of old memories, those are the moments a physical education teacher lives for—when you see the spark light up in a child's eyes as the bits of a progression suddenly morph into the whole performance, when vital change comes in movement after some small adjustment in the cue you gave, or when the missing action in a skill sequence appears exactly on cue because you set up the practice area to demand that it do so.

> Those are the moments a physical education teacher lives for—when you see the spark light up in a child's eyes as the bits of a progression suddenly morph into the whole performance, when vital change comes in movement after some small adjustment in the cue you gave . . .

Because even the best of us can only discover a limited set of nuggets in a lifetime of teaching, sharing that wealth becomes a matter of professional responsibility. If we are going to be equipped to serve all children, learning from each other is not a luxury—it is a necessity. What works to serve the quick learners among our students, those who probably would learn no matter what type of instruction we used, is not an adequate repertoire if our goal is to teach all of our pupils, all of the time. Diverse learner needs can only be met by diverse teacher responses.

Internet discussion groups, in-service sharing sessions, conference presentations, professional visitations, personal contacts, and in this case, research reports, are ways of mining a truly professional and truly necessary collection of teaching strategies. They are not just a bag of tricks. They truly are nuggets of pure teaching gold.

Having given praise for what I found stimulating in the article, I want to sound several cautions. The first has to do with something not discussed in our much abbreviated summary of this report—how the investigators identified the environmental manipulations they were going to employ in the study. They pilot-tested a variety of such inventions. In that process, they discovered some that seemed to have conceptual promise when in fact they actually had an adverse effect on the desired movement. Those adjustments of the environment produced regression rather than improvement in form or outcome—and were promptly discarded.

The same winnowing of clever inspirations has to be performed by teachers. You start by clearly defining the movement you are trying to encourage, then check to see if the intervention truly works to produce that result. If not, it should go into the discard heap, no matter how cute it appears, or how much enthusiasm it elicits from your charges.

Another requirement that may have been obscured within the lengthy story of this investigation is the demand for knowledge about the skill in question. For the researchers, the prerequisite was genuinely having knowledge and experience with the standing long jump. For the rest of us, it could be knowing about any of the skills we must teach. To develop effective environmental manipulations requires that you first have a detailed and accurate understanding of the skill elements to be taught. More than the efficiency of invention is at stake here because a misunderstanding of the elements can lead to misdirection of the learner.

A good example occurs in teaching forceful throwing. Some teachers have incorrectly concluded that stepping forward on the opposite foot is the first and most important key to skilled performance. As a result, they focus almost exclusively on that element, even inventing environmental tricks to elicit that response, such as painted footprints on the floor, all the while wondering why a mature and forceful pattern does not appear in some of the children.

The answer, of course, is that the teacher does not truly understand the essential role of summative rotation in body segments during a forceful throw. Facing forward, front to the target, does nothing to elicit that critical kind of rotation. Simply starting

with the side opposite the throwing hand toward the target will for most children produce a close approximation of the mature pattern on the first attempt. The stepping action of the opposite foot toward the target then becomes a natural consequence of forceful rotation—not the reverse. As that master salesman from *The Music Man*, Professor Howard Hill, asserts in his opening song: "Ya really gotta know the territory!" It is truly so in physical education.

Finally, a little true confession can be good for the soul, even mine. As the teacher member of the team authoring this book, I admit to having to fight off sleep during the first reading of this report in its full, published form. Repeatedly, I had to prop my eyes open, and only the intervention of some chocolate got me through to the end. What was the problem? It was something that never troubled me when considering the other studies. It wasn't the generally negative reaction to research that some teachers report, though it certainly was a lesson in what that might feel like. Some reports actually have me right on the edge with excitement and anticipation, so what is the explanation for my less-than-enthusiastic reaction to this one in particular?

My best guess is that I was overwhelmed by density; that is, this study is quite complex and is reported in full detail. As you already may have guessed, we omitted entire aspects of the report that did not seem essential to the central theme. Although the authors never engaged in a lot of obscure jargon or wrote in a convoluted manner, they did have to go on . . . and on . . . and on. The end result was something that resembled the fine print on an insurance policy. If you are an insurance agent, the long drone of specifics is easy to follow and retain. If you are not, it is hard to pay attention after two paragraphs.

The lesson here is not complicated, and in no way is it a criticism of the competent report prepared by the authors of this study. Some studies of teaching are simply a lot easier to read than others. A word to the wise for those outside the circle of research specialists. Begin with less elaborate studies and shorter reports—they build up your competence and confidence. Those type of reports will yield plenty of nuggets to harvest, but the reading will require a lot less chocolate.

 **Common Ground: Our Shared Perspective**

This study fits well with several others that have examined the same topic with similar results. Together, they should inspire four kinds of action in the field of physical education. First, teachers now have valid reason to try different ways of changing practice environments for their pupils and to observe the impact on different kinds of learners. Second, teacher educators now have sound reason to include specific examples of environmental manipulation as part of preservice courses and inservice workshops. Third, researchers now have convincing reason to push further with investigations of how, why, when, and for whom such strategies are beneficial. And fourth, textbook authors now have good reason to include careful attention to the different suggestions for teaching that can be derived from studies such as this one.

> **Teacher educators now have sound reason to include specific examples of environmental manipulation as part of preservice courses and inservice workshops.**

PART V
The Voices of Students

THE STUDY

RESEARCHER

TEACHER

COMMON GROUND

Kindergarten Children Describe Physical Education

Sanders, S., & Graham, G. (1995). Kindergarten children's initial experiences in physical education: The relentless persistence for play clashes with the zone of acceptable responses. *Journal of Teaching in Physical Education, 14,* 372-383.

Most of the 30 studies presented in this book employ quantitative methods that produce data in the form of numbers. Investigators employing that kind of research strategy have learned to work comfortably with the use of quantities to represent complex human behaviors. This study, in contrast, is a qualitative study that employs words, what people say or write, as the fundamental form of datum for inquiry.

Quantitative and qualitative research often differ (though not invariably) in terms of methods and the kind of data collected. As a consequence, they each produce sharply different kinds of reports, with qualitative studies often seeming more easily accessible and less burdened with technical analysis and specialized language. In addition, most qualitative researchers are comfortable (at least at the outset of a study) with questions that quantitative researchers would immediately regard as inadequately defined. In the world of qualitative research, broad inquiries such as "What's going on here?" are not uncommon starting places. Finally, treating participants' descriptions of their experiences as valid accounts of reality (their reality) is nearly universal among those who do qualitative research.

Many other differences exist between the two approaches to research. Some of those are purely a matter of data collection techniques—interviews and extended field observation, for example, are largely the province of qualitative study. Others, however, are more profoundly conceptual. Among those is the fact that qualitative investigators are more likely to employ inductive forms of analysis versus the deductive reasoning typically used in quantitative studies. For example, the qualitative researcher may ask, "Given these data, what hypothesis can be derived to account for them?" while the quantitative researcher may ask, "Given this hypothesis, what should be observed in the data?"

Such differences notwithstanding, as with all forms of formal inquiry, qualitative research demands careful procedures that produce valid and reliable data. All research reports, irrespective of their format, must face the reader's ultimate question: "Why should I believe you?" Thorough specification of procedures and scrupulous handling of data form the foundation for the investigator's response—whether the data are words or numbers.

If you have opportunity to look more closely at this form of research, you will find a number of initially bothersome differences in vocabulary. Trustworthiness, for example, is often substituted for validity. Despite those distinctions, however, you should have no difficulty in following our summary of this study or the annotations for other qualitative reports included in this book. If you are interested in learning more about qualitative research, we suggest that you consult one of the texts annotated in appendix A.

The Study

The authors refer to the particular form of qualitative research used here as *phenomenological*. In this kind of study, the participants' actual words, as descriptions and explanations, are collected as data. Those data are regarded as meaningful representations of reality as the participants experienced it. In this instance, children were the participants. Along with a careful record of their actions, their words were used to develop a sense of how they viewed one aspect of their reality: attending kindergarten and being in a physical education class.

The investigators employed an explicit theoretical framework for understanding the behavior of children in the physical education context. In this framework, it was assumed that in a play situation, children will persist in maintaining a balance between the opportunities to do things (challenges) and their actual ability to do those things (capabilities for action). If the challenges are too easy, they get bored and will try to alter the activity so that it becomes more difficult. If the challenges are too difficult and beyond their capability, children become frustrated or anxious and will try to alter the activity so that it is within their capacity. So long as there is a balance between those two polarities, challenge and capacity, play will flow along, engaging attention, evoking creative responses, and yielding what children report as fun.

Participants and Context

In a K-5 elementary school, the physical education class for kindergarten children met twice per week for 25 minutes. From the 22 children enrolled, researchers selected 4 students as participants in the study: a less-skilled boy and girl, and a higher-skilled boy and girl. This selection was accomplished with the collaboration of the resident teacher during the first 2 weeks of this 8-week study.

Design and Method

One of the investigators served as the field observer and was present during each class. He took written notes describing what happened in the lesson with specific attention to the behaviors of the 4 partici-

pants (which ultimately produced 350 typewritten pages of field-note data). All classes were videotaped for later review and analysis. In addition to informal conversations with the children, the 4 participants were formally interviewed in pairs in 20-minute sessions on four occasions during the final 4 weeks of the study. The interview format was conversational with interspersed questions. Audiotapes of each interview were later transcribed for addition to the accumulated pool of data.

The process of data analysis required the following steps. First, written descriptions were prepared for the program for each lesson, then for each of the 4 participants as they encountered physical education over the 8 weeks of intensive observation. Next, from those descriptions, themes were developed that displayed the most striking and persisting similarities and differences in the experiences of the 4 students as they were reflected in their words and actions. The mechanical process of developing themes involved clipping out segments of interview transcripts and field notes that related to each theme and pasting them onto separate pages of a 16-by-24-inch sketchpad.

Results

The basic description of the program was straightforward and uncomplicated. Under the direction of the teacher, each of the 16 class meetings followed the same routine. First, one-quarter of the time was devoted to teacher-led stretching exercises performed in unison, with students required to count cadences. Second, one-quarter of the time was used for teacher-prescribed locomotor activities, such as marching, running, walking, skipping. Third, and finally, the remaining class time was employed for teacher-directed manipulative activities, such as throwing, catching, and kicking.

The teacher's behavior was also consistent across the 8-week period. She was precise about how each stretching exercise was to be done and tolerated little variation from the prescribed form of execution. Children who did not conform were scolded and, on several occasions, were not allowed to participate in the remaining activities of the lesson. The teacher explained her emphasis on learning to stretch correctly as a response to the state-imposed Standards of Learning: "In our Standards of Learning we are having to teach the children how to take care of their bodies and this is just the way I have chosen to do it" (p. 374).

In the next segment of the typical lesson, the teacher simply indicated a type of locomotor activity and gave the signal "go." After an interval during which the children moved throughout the available space, she called "stop." She made no attempt at instruction during this period of activity, and she only rarely made attempts to require conformity to the desired kind of locomotion. She explained that the purpose was to "get their blood flowing and muscles warmed up" (p. 375).

In the final (and longer) portion of the class, the teacher specified a manipulative activity, having the children practice a task, such as tossing a beanbag up and then catching it, both individually and with a partner. On occasion, she also employed stations with children rotating through to perform tasks, such as throwing balls at various targets. As with the previous locomotor activity, the teacher allowed a wide variety of responses—some of which wandered rather far from anything resembling the assigned task.

In the report, all of these descriptions and theme statements are documented with brief segments extracted from field notes, video-replay notes, or interview transcripts. For example, the following field-note clip was pasted on the theme page related to the persistence of play. The teacher-designed task for the day was to toss the ball up in the air and catch it, which Brett could do without difficulty.

Brett is now seen kicking his ball in the grass some 30 feet from the rest of the children. He has discovered that by throwing his ball very high the wind on this day will carry it over the short 3-foot fence and into a grassy playground area. (He climbs the low fence to retrieve the ball.) He cannot resist kicking the ball through the grass several times before returning to the group—to throw the ball over the fence and kick it once again. (p. 377)

Additional notes indicated that the teacher did look in Brett's direction, but she made no comment or attempt to bring him back on task. Thus, as you might guess, this excerpt was used to document both a participant's modification of the assigned task to make it more challenging and interesting, and the teacher's acceptance of alternatives to the assigned practice of a manipulative skill.

In another instance, a moderately overweight participant was unable to support herself in the exercise position required by the teacher. Finding herself stuck in place while classmates moved around her, she was observed changing the task.

Holly slowly moves on her hands and knees, [apparently] not having sufficient strength to hold the position required for either the crab or seal walk. There is a smile on her face as she now pretends to be a dog, growling and barking as she moves. (p. 377)

The interpretation provided by the theoretical framework suggested to the investigators that Holly's desire to play led her to adjust the required activity to a modified yet playful task that was within her capacity.

Problems arose, however, when in the persistent effort to maintain the flow of playful activity, these adjustments collided with the teacher's desire for correct execution. For example, this excerpt combines both field and interview notes.

[During stretching], Charlie spent much of his time sitting and watching, legs crossed and hands resting in his lap. This was true even though [the teacher] scolded Charlie for not participating in the stretching tasks. When asked by [the teacher] why he would not participate, he responded, "I don't like to do it." When interviewed, he was only a little more specific stating that: "I don't like to put my hand over my head and do that exercise." (p. 380)

Charlie's opinion was shared by most of the children, and Tabitha observed that the stretching was "boring" and that "we always have to do the same exercises" (p. 380). Brett called the stretching tasks "silly and boring stuff" and in an interview exchange was even more specific about his rationale for nonparticipation.

Researcher: I noticed that you don't do the stretching very often.
Brett: I hate it!
Researcher: You hate it? Why do you hate it?
Brett: I just do. I just hate it! (p. 380)

The frequency of student withdrawal and rebellion observed during stretching was not replicated in the other two time segments. The teacher's less-restrictive standards for locomotor and manipulative activities appeared to allow student modification of tasks to meet their capacities and interests. Investigators labeled these standards as "a wider zone of acceptable responses," and such activities were characterized by better-sustained engagement, obvious expressions of pleasure, and little or no rebellious behavior. That wider zone, however, also had the effect of reducing the actual amount of time devoted to practice attempts, which might have produced improvement in performance of the assigned motor skills.

A Researcher's Perspective

Reading this report gives the distinct impression that stretching tasks as employed in this class had an obvious and significant effect on the participants during their initial experiences in physical education. The data suggest that the activity was a turnoff to the children and that the locomotor and manipulative tasks, as presented in a more playlike atmosphere, provided more enjoyable and age-appropriate experiences. Conditions that pushed children out of their individual zones of competent-but-challenging play had the effect of creating strongly verbalized dislike for the tasks involved.

> **Conditions that pushed children out of their individual zones of competent-but-challenging play had the effect of creating strongly verbalized dislike for the tasks involved.**

As for the theoretical framework, the authors offer convincing evidence that the model of children's play provided useful insights into the events of the class, as well as a way of understanding the participants' verbal accounts of their experiences in physical education. Put another way, the qualitative data collected in the class made coherent sense when viewed through the lens of play theory.

A Teacher's Perspective

Isn't this a real teacher's dilemma? Virtually every day we have to walk that tightrope between focusing on specific learning objectives on the one hand while simultaneously allowing for individual responses, diverse student abilities, and the need to encourage student input into the lesson on the other. There is no doubt in my mind that the struggle to maintain a reasonable degree of balance between task challenges and students' ability accounts for classes that sometimes appear to be directed by little more than the dictum of "keep them busy, happy, and good." The teacher's problem, however, is a difficult one. In pursuing our goal of helping children become physically active for a lifetime, it is not always clear which route will be most successful. Do we concentrate on helping children to have a wonderful time when moving, or do we focus on helping them acquire skills that will help them enjoy activity in the future?

> **In pursuing our goal of helping children become physically active for a lifetime, it is not always clear which route will be most successful. Do we concentrate on helping children to have a wonderful time when moving, or do we focus on helping them acquire skills that will help them enjoy activity in the future?**

Beyond that basic dilemma is an even more perplexing (yet subtle) challenge. The proposition that class activities must maintain an appropriate match of skill and challenge is a useful and powerful idea for teachers, but actually making it happen is a constant problem. The line between a learning focus that turns students off and a freedom for response that keeps them engaged is indistinct and often unpredictable. Nevertheless, if our goal is to help students become physically active for a lifetime; surely happy engagement is a useful (if incomplete) marker on the road to success. Therein lies, however, the ingredients for a truly delicate balancing act.

I think that the frustration the children expressed with the stretching routine was not the result of an irreconcilable clash between the instinct for play and the discipline of orderly learning. The problem was more likely to have been the consequence of inappropriate teaching, the factor that probably produced the lack of focus on learning objectives in the other activities as well. In fairness, however, we should remember that the teacher's attitude toward acceptable responses in the three activities may have arisen from more complex sources than are made apparent in the report.

A key element in the class context was surely the importance of specific movements in stretching, a point much less salient for locomotor or basic skill activities. There are ways to stretch that are contraindicated for reasons of safety, and there are ways to stretch that yield maximum benefit—and both are functions of anatomical and neurological facts. If a teacher does not attend to the criteria for safe and efficient stretching, it can become, particularly with young children, at best, a waste of class time and at worst, a dangerous activity. On the other hand, the same cannot be said for most locomotor movements. A wider band exists of truly safe and wholly acceptable ways to skip, run, jump, hop, and twirl. More explicit goals such as agility, grace, or efficiency can impose some constraints, but the basic rule of relative freedom holds. In the light of those facts, the teacher's decisions may be easier to understand, if not otherwise approve.

The motivation for kindergarten children to persist in practice or play does not come solely from the challenge/competence match used as the theoretical frame for this study. It also comes from the context within which the activity is framed. Among the best kindergarten teachers I know, several made it a regular practice to capture their students in a story that required them to act out the behaviors of characters as a playful involvement in the unwinding plot. This engagement allowed the teacher to evoke a reasonably narrow range of acceptable movement performances, all coupled with other playful motivations, such as creative fantasy. As an accompaniment to the stretching she wants the children to perform, one of those teachers tells a fresh story each day (keep in mind that for kindergarten children almost any simple fantasy line will serve).

The trick, as I see it, is to identify the critical elements that determine the bandwidth of useful responses in practicing any skill. In this, it is important to avoid the mind-set that demands exact replications of a single model and uniformity among children. Variety is important, and spontaneity should be encouraged. When the range is large, create plenty of opportunities for the children to play and experiment. When it is small, provide the support young children need, such as creative teacher inputs, to sustain their motivation for the particular task at hand.

Finally, what children do naturally in balancing challenge and skill in their play activities can itself become a substantial teaching opportunity. Learning how to make adaptations for exercises and active games in thoughtful and creative ways is a reasonable goal for physical education. For example, allow them to play and experiment with the type of ball used, the height or distance targeted, the use of different body positions, and alternative means of propulsion. Encouraging students to experiment can give them a greater sense of personal ownership and control over catching and throwing—and thus make a contribution to their preparation for becoming lifelong learners.

Common Ground: Our Shared Perspective

One can only surmise how children might feel about stretching and warming up, or about physical activities in general, if those same negative experiences were to follow them throughout their school careers. At the very least, if children learn by continually investigating the world through play activities, then it follows that opportunities for learning are lost in situations that do not allow playful experiences.

The authors provide a discussion of what they regard as implications concerning the teacher's choices of method and content. Their position is that the instruction and practice provided for the children was developmentally inappropriate. It is difficult to fault that conclusion with regard to what was observed in the stretching component of each lesson. We wonder, however, whether that same interpretation of the results applies with equal cogency to the "wider zone of acceptable responses" that was documented during locomotor and manipulative activities.

Our own instincts, as teachers, are to be concerned about the fact that adjustments were not made once it became apparent that the practice tasks were too difficult or too easy for some children. It probably would have been best to require them to work on more difficult extensions of the assigned task or, where appropriate, on easier and less complex lead-up tasks—all the while maintaining an emphasis on practicing the intended skill, rather than something else! Doing that seems to be less a problem of adopting an "age-appropriate" pedagogy, than it is a simple matter of sound teaching practice.

The need to create learning environments that hold students firmly on practice tasks is a demand teachers face at every age level. And that remains true even after the teacher has found a way to make tasks appropriate to individual learners. We don't mean to underestimate the tremendous difficulty of meeting those demands for every child, all of the time. This study, with all of its rich detail and sense of authenticity, certainly tells the story of a teacher grappling with a degree of complexity that would make perfect decisions an unreasonable standard.

Nonetheless, if the work of children in school is to learn new skills, then kindergarten is where they must begin to learn about how to learn—although in physical education, much of that new learning can be experienced as playful practice. If the teacher is accountable for creating learning tasks that are sufficiently flexible to meet individual student needs, then it follows that children must be held accountable for persisting in their effort to perform those tasks. Kindergarten, where "the relentless persistence for play clashes with the zone of acceptable responses," is the place it all begins.

> **If the work of children in school is to learn new skills, then kindergarten is where they must begin to learn about how to learn . . .**

Third-Grade Children Describe Physical Education

Ratliffe, T., Imwold, C., & Conkell, C. (1994). Children's views of their third grade physical education class. *The Physical Educator, 51,* 106-111.

As with other studies annotated in this section of the book, the authors here report an investigation that employed the qualitative approach to research. If you have not yet done so, it may be useful for you to review our introductory remarks concerning qualitative research. For that purpose, see Sanders and Graham (1995) in chapter 14.

 ## The Study

From the opening rationale given for the study to the final conclusions at the end of the report, this study is one of the most straightforward and plain-speaking accounts of an investigation in physical education that you are likely to encounter. At the outset, the authors offer just about everything you would need for an introduction. They explain what their question is, why it is important, and how they went about answering it.

It is important to study the actual effects of physical education on children. The best intentions and the most persuasive logic still require verification. Do our physical education classes really accomplish what we intend? Our approach to studying the outcomes of physical education was to investigate its impact on the thoughts, views, and attitudes of children—by talking with children. (p. 106)

Participants and Context

In this study, the 4 children interviewed were selected from a third-grade class at a university laboratory school, and the teacher chosen was an experienced female specialist in elementary school physical education. The selection process was purposeful in that the investigators wanted both boys and girls to be represented, as well as a range of motor skill levels. The participants had daily, 30-minute physical education classes, and the study followed those classes through an entire semester.

Design and Method

After an initial 3-week period during which the investigators simply observed each lesson, the 4 children began meeting once each week for 11 weeks with two members of the research team for a 30- to 45-minute interview. As a group of 4, the children were interviewed together in a private room equipped with an unobtrusive, wall-mounted video camera. All interview sessions were recorded. The children were simply told that the purpose of the interview meetings was to find out what they thought about their physical education class—an explanation that they appeared to accept without difficulty.

During the interview sessions, the children demonstrated typical forms of fidgeting and wandering attention, but they spoke freely with each other, as well as to the interviewers. Review of the video-tapes showed that the conversations were not dominated by any 1 or 2 children, nor did any one child tend to be the first to respond to questions. During two of the interviews, the children were shown a videotape of a recent physical education lesson and asked both general and specific questions about what had been happening. This procedure, called *stimulated recall,* was highly successful in provoking discussions about events that occurred during the class.

The research team reviewed the interview videotape immediately after each meeting with the children. The observations and questions stimulated by that process then served as a basis for developing the interview protocol for the next interview. A copy of a typical protocol is included in the report.

The first stage of data analysis required construction of a record matrix that listed each question and each topic of discussion for each interview. That record allowed not only an inspection of how often particular topics were broached or encountered but how the nature and frequency of topics might have changed across the 11 sessions. In addition, an outside expert in elementary school physical education audited all of the videotapes and prepared an independent list of questions and topics. The match between that listing and the content of the record matrix was quite close, and the small number of discrepancies were fully discussed and resolved.

The second stage of analysis was to identify themes in the children's comments that persisted through all or most of the 11 weeks. In turn, researchers discussed those persisting themes with the teacher and for confirmation in some instances, referred to their notes taken during direct observation of the classes.

Results

The topic of "Why do we have a physical education class?" emerged in all of the interviews. As might be expected, most of the children's responses reflected a concrete and fairly primitive understanding of purpose. For example, the most common view of why physical education was required involved the idea that it was a means to build up the body, develop stronger muscles and bones, and make the students healthy and strong. Learning goals such as developing movement skills or acquiring information about healthy living, physical fitness, and active sports were rarely mentioned.

Discussions with the teacher and observation of many lessons made clear that the teacher's inten-

tions were almost entirely limited to learning goals involving the acquisition and understanding of basic movement skills. Whether spontaneously or in response to direct questioning, what the children said strongly suggests that they either remained unaware of those objectives or were unable to articulate them in discussion with adults.

Expression of likes and dislikes concerning physical education were also scattered throughout the interviews. Most of the negative statements centered on physical discomfort—blisters, getting tired, sweaty hands, cramps and sore muscles, and getting hit by the ball. Other dislikes, though, concentrated on memories of not being successful in class activities, such as not being able to hit the target, inability to get the ball up to the basket, or lacking the strength needed to do an exercise.

Interesting discussions took place about the differences between recess and physical education, a topic that has been explored in previous studies. Both were described as fun and were perceived by the majority of children as serving the same purposes, building up muscles and getting strong and healthy. Although several children offered richly detailed explanations of the difference between the two settings, the adult distinction between a structured class with learning as a primary focus and an environment providing unstructured free choice of activity (without explicit educational intentions), was never articulated. Further, the authors found no evidence that such an abstract distinction was perceived by any of the 4 children.

In several instances, the children assigned interpretations to particular class activities that differed sharply from those expressed by the teacher. For example, at several points in a practice session involving tossing and catching a small ball, the teacher asked the children to see how many catches they could make in 30 seconds (they subsequently chose several children to announce their scores). When asked why the teacher did that, the children suggested "to see if you are honest," "to tell your parents," and "to see who did the most." As you might guess, the teacher's explanation was that she wanted them to experience the benefits of practice, which would then motivate further effort and allow the setting of personal goals.

Finally, the data held one genuine surprise for the three investigators involved in this study. As many class activities involved working with another student, the topic of partner relationships was a persistent subject of comment throughout the interviews. From the children's vantage point, partners were far more central to their class experience than any of the researchers had realized—and the researchers themselves were all veteran physical education teachers. For example, all of the children mentioned that they preferred to choose their own partner, rather than have any procedure that involved the teacher choosing a partner for them. Also, whenever they were asked what they liked or disliked about physical education or what made them feel "good" or "bad" during class, the topic of partners was far more common than references to learning activities or teacher behaviors.

At the heart of their sensitivity to the topic of partners was the desire to work with someone with whom they could get along. More to the point, they wanted to avoid being assigned to a partner who went off-task or misbehaved. Such children were perceived as causes for the teacher to be upset, therefore attracting negative attention and a possible reduction in the opportunity to participate. Children could list strategies for coping with such disruption ("tell the teacher," "ask them to cooperate," and "get a new partner"), but they appeared not to have much faith in the efficacy of such efforts.

A Researcher's Perspective

The investigators reported that their observations of the class indicated that they too would have little faith in the capacity of individual students to be effective in gaining cooperation from partners who were misbehaving. One way of looking at such a difficulty is to start with a different assumption about where the problem lies. Perhaps the frustration students are experiencing is better understood as the teacher's problem and not the students'.

> **Perhaps the frustration students are experiencing is better understood as the teacher's problem and not the students'.**

Student misbehavior, whether in individual, group, or paired partner settings, is best addressed at the level of the whole class—as an instructional problem, a function that properly belongs to the teacher. Further, if students, teacher, and researchers have little faith in the skills children now have for dealing with uncooperative partners, perhaps

some thought should be given to developing a repertoire containing more effective options. Surely such valuable social skills will not automatically be acquired just by being repeatedly confronted by problematic partners in physical education.

A Teacher's Perspective

One of the findings in this study is sure to catch the attention of physical education teachers; mainly so because it is a student concern that is rarely voiced . . . or is it that we are rarely listening for it? Children participating in the study reported being genuinely distressed and frustrated by partners who did not follow directions, went off task, or were otherwise disruptive in class. You may be surprised to read that I actually felt reassured when I read that complaint. I am always working on the difficult task of striking the right balance between managing the class efficiently and creating a freedom that encourages self-direction and responsibility. Where there are students who are frustrated by their partners, there are students who really want to get on with learning and who do not feel I am too strict and oppressive. Dealing with students who are disruptive, of course, is a different matter, as is the problem of how partners are selected.

Over the years I have developed a strong opinion about the consequences of allowing students to choose partners or members of a team. Although students do often report that they like choosing their own partners, it has been my observation that this rarely works without producing some intensely negative fallout. Almost invariably, at least one or two children are left out or are confronted by obvious rejection—no matter how momentary it is or how it is resolved. Because our teaching action sets that rejection up to happen, we are responsible, which is absolutely unacceptable.

No matter how enjoyable and natural children may find the process of choosing their own partners, a process that does harm to any child disqualifies the process as a management tactic. Forcing children to confront rejection, just as with forcing them to engage in a public activity in which they only experience failure, is not justified by the argument that most kids enjoy what is happening. I feel it is necessary to manage both the setting up of partners or other learning and practice groups and the behavior of students toward each other within such social tasks.

Relatively few children are persistently rejected by their peers, but our job is still to find out why and address the situation. If we need to help that child with problematic behavior, help him stay on task or help her invest her effort, then that is our job. If the problem

> No matter how enjoyable and natural children may find the process of choosing their own partners, a process that does harm to any child disqualifies the process as a management tactic.

involves helping children become more appreciative and accepting of differences in others, then that is our job. Whatever the nature of the problem, ignoring it by turning responsibility over to the actions of our pupils is abdication of our role as adults.

Easy for me to say, but is it a lot harder to actually accomplish? Certainly, and the only means to do so takes us right back to the study. So much of the confusion and mixed messages that were reported were the result of leaving students to imagine why particular things were done in class, rather than providing them with explicit reasons. Describing and explaining desirable social behavior, what I call *explicit teaching,* then monitoring students for both their understanding and their actions is tiring work. It can be, however, incredibly rewarding.

We often assume, for example, that the purpose is self-evident. For example, when we want students to understand that they are getting better with practice, we continually pay attention to how they are doing. What this study tells us is that unless otherwise informed, some children may interpret that as an interest in determining who is the best, a distortion that bears all sorts of negative consequences.

The only cure for that problem is to be explicit and to make the motive for your interest in their performance exactly clear. Not only can that effect be accomplished without great difficulty, students' accurate understanding can provide strong and valuable encouragement for those who knew they could never be the best.

Precisely the same rule applies to being a good partner for a class activity. Children need to know exactly what is required in practicing appropriately, in treating a partner with respect, and in supporting (rather than impeding) a partner during different forms of activity. Students also need to be very clear about what constitutes the reverse, the actions of being a poor partner. And elementary children need to be frequently reminded that the way they treat each other matters and how having fun

together results from knowing the right way to behave.

Children have a right to know the intentions behind your teaching actions, and as this study demonstrates, they often do not when left to their own devices. Having a clear idea about what is happening avoids dangerous misunderstandings. It also makes children feel more secure—exactly as it does for adults.

The notion that children cannot understand abstractions such as *purpose* simply does not square with my experience. Questions such as "Do you know why we talk about fitness every day?" or "Why do you think I asked you to count how many times you caught the ball?" and "Why do we stretch before and after class?" can be considered and answered with perfect facility by children in elementary school. It is a matter of us taking the time as teachers to be explicit about why and how. You can see to it that the correct message gets out.

At Davis Elementary in Austin, Texas, Pam Atkins explains social issues such as partner problems to her students in a highly explicit way. She uses a protocol within which she expects partners to debrief each other on a regular basis. She also provides them with prompts to help them understand exactly what issues are to be discussed. In addition, she uses whole class discussions in which students are guided in clarifying the answers to such questions as "What kinds of things can make working with a partner sometimes fun and sometimes difficult?" or "What can you do to help your partner act in ways that will make class fun for both of you?" and "Do you think you can do these three things [selected from the discussion] today with your partner?"

After a period of class activity and some debriefing by individual partners, students report back to the whole class on what their partners did that helped the activity go smoothly. With several changes of partners, this procedure offers ample time and sufficient variation in conditions to provide an effective degree of practice. Pam does not explain poor behavior by citing the shopworn theory of "that's just the way kids are." Instead, she makes positive student interactions the subject of explicit teaching. She wants every student to understand exactly "the way they are to be" in physical education.

Common Ground: Our Shared Perspective

If you examine them closely, we think that the results laid out in this report may lead you to conclusions that are more complex than might be anticipated. On the one hand, the 4 children who participated in this study were missing some of the understandings that are crucial in making sense of the time and effort invested in physical education. Unless their view becomes significantly more sophisticated, that investment will seem less and less reasonable as the years pass in elementary school.

Toward that end, one response is to urge teachers to spend more time with explanations that help children understand the educational purposes served by attending physical education classes. To accomplish the intended goal, however, teachers must give greater attention to finding ways to communicate that are better adjusted to children, rather than other adults.

That assertion, however, raises a question not addressed in this study (though it is recognized in the report). To what extent is it reasonable to expect children in the third grade to understand and value the purposes of any subject matter? It may be difficult to package some abstractions, particularly with regard to our educational intentions, in ways that will be developmentally appropriate for most nine-year-olds.

Two conclusions do seem secure. First, it is highly probable that at least some of the children in elementary school physical education classes don't have a clue about why they are there. Second, if we are serious about our purposes in physical education, we will be well advised to monitor by formal and informal means what children actually are learning—even, perhaps especially, when we are very clear about what we think they have been taught!

> It is highly probable that at least some of the children in elementary school physical education classes don't have a clue about why they are there.

Children Describe
the Mile-Run Fitness Test

Hopple, C., & Graham, G. (1995). What children think, feel, and know about physical fitness testing. *Journal of Teaching in Physical Education, 14,* 408-417.

As with other studies annotated in this section of the book, the authors here employed the qualitative approach to research. If you have not yet done so, you may wish to review our introductory comments about qualitative research (see chapter 14).

Physical fitness tests remain the most commonly used form of assessment in physical education, and the consequences of that fact are far from trivial. As the researchers observe in the opening sentence of this report, "Participating in physical fitness tests is undoubtedly among the most common memories adults hold—for better or worse—of their childhood physical education experiences" (p. 408). It is more than surprising to find that little research has been conducted on how taking such tests influences students' attitudes and knowledge—given such a salient position in how people remember what happened in their physical education classes and given the current emphasis on making fitness tests a means for engaging students in their own health-related fitness goals.

 **The Study**

This study was designed to pursue exactly the point just raised and to do so with regard to the Presidential Physical Fitness Challenge test. The present report, however, is limited to findings for the one-

mile run or walk, which is only one of five items in the battery. Three general questions guided construction of the interview protocols and subsequent analysis of the data (p. 409):

1. "Did children understand why they took the mile-run test? Did they understand what the test item measures? Did they understand the implications of good or poor performance?"

2. "What did the children think, in general, about the mile-run test? What did they like about it? Not like? What would they change about it?"

3. "Were there differences in how students who tended to score well on the test responded to the two questions above, versus the responses of those who scored poorly?"

Participants and Context

Participating children were drawn from two elementary schools (A and B). Reading the descriptions of the two schools may reasonably suggest that they were selected to provide opportunity to examine contrasting physical education environments.

School A, in a rural area, has two full-time physical education specialists, with each having more than 10 years of experience. Physical fitness tests are administered twice each year, fall and spring. Individual results are used as part of a conceptually based health and fitness unit for students in grades 3 through 5. Computerized test results are given to students and used in setting individual fitness goals that in turn are related to fitness-related homework throughout the year.

School B, in an urban area, has three full-time specialists, all with more than 10 years of experience. Here, fitness tests also are given in the fall and spring. Students do not receive the results of their test performances in written form nor are the results employed in any formal health and fitness curriculum, aside from health-related concepts that accompany skill units in the regular physical education program. Students are encouraged to stay active through a voluntary, at-home program. They also took part in a day-long physical fitness competition against students from other schools.

Students selected from the fourth and fifth grades at both schools included 21 who scored above the 50th percentile on the mile-run (and at least two other items in the battery) and 19 who scored below the 50th percentile on the mile-run (and at least two other items). Also included, for a total of 52 students, were 12 students who fell in neither category.

Design and Method

All data were collected by means of interviews conducted during a single school week. The semistructured interview protocol allowed use of the same open-ended questions across all participants, with additional probes where appropriate. Interviews lasted 30 minutes and whenever possible were done with pairs of students selected from the same performance category—that is, 2 students who were both either good or poor performers on the mile-run. All interviews were audiotaped and fully transcribed into a computer for subsequent coding and analysis. Finally, on the first day of data collection, all participants completed a short, 8-minute written quiz, which was designed to test their knowledge of the purposes for each item in the fitness battery. Tests were individually scored, then grouped by school, performance classification, and gender.

The computer program used for analysis of the interview transcripts allowed identification of broad themes that occurred throughout the data. Individual quotes contributing to the development of each theme were pasted on pages of a large, artist's sketchpad so that confirming and disconfirming evidence for each theme could be displayed in graphic form. Once the themes represented in the sketchpad display had been defined and described, an experienced elementary physical education specialist not associated with the study reviewed the results. Questions raised by this external expert with regard to the investigators' interpretations of the data were then discussed and revisions made as necessary.

Results

As analysis of the data proceeded, it quickly became apparent that the results would assume the form of three major themes that ultimately clustered around two of the original research questions. In the report, each theme was presented with quoted materials and test scores to illustrate the recurring nature of the thematic element and to confirm the validity of its definition. The three major themes are as follows.

1. Students' understanding of the mile-run test: "Students did not have a clear understanding of why they take the mile-run physical fitness test" (p. 412).
2. Students' attitudes regarding the mile-run test: "Many students dislike taking the mile-run test, some so much that they become 'test dodgers'" (p. 413).
3. Students' suggestions for change: "Given the chance, many students would change the mile-run test to make it more fun" (p. 414).

With regard to the third research question (concerning possible differences between responses of higher and lower performance students), no evidence from the interview or written test scores suggested that doing well or less well on the fitness test altered responses in any systematic way. Further, some readers might assume that students from School A would show a better understanding of the reason for taking the mile-run test than would students from School B—such, however, was not the case. The authors do not venture a guess as to why, but they do make clear that they believe something far more powerful than the simple quality of curriculum and pedagogy was at work in shaping students' responses.

Finally, in case anyone has wondered, interviews with the teachers showed that all of them had a very clear and accurate understanding of why the mile-run test was given, what the resulting performance scores would mean, and how the five-item battery related to physical fitness and personal health. They also confirmed that they had tried to communicate those concepts to their students. In other words, there was an enormous gap between what the teachers believed they had taught and what the students demonstrated that they actually had learned.

A Researcher's Perspective

Readers who have encountered Piaget's theories on the cognitive development of children may have some advantage in contemplating the question of how the students understood the test. The majority of participants simply did not understand the meaning of the test at all. For them, common responses to probes about the purpose of the test were "to get you exercising most of the time" and simply "to get a time." A few students demonstrated what Piaget would regard as an *early stage*—a concrete, yet incomplete understanding. For instance, an early stage understanding allowed the students in this study to recognize that the mile-run was a test of cardiorespiratory fitness (or endurance), but their understanding did not allow them to accurately elaborate on that connection. As one student put it, "The mile-run is to find out how good your heart is, and if you're bleeding enough when you run" (p. 413). Further evidence showed that a very small number had achieved the level of an abstract understanding:

Researcher: Why do the coaches have you take the mile-run?

Student: It tests your endurance, and your respiratorial system, or whatever.

Researcher: What is your endurance? What does that mean?

Student: Endurance is, I think, is how hard you run it. Like if you don't stop and sit down or start walking, that's not much endurance, but if you keep on running and try your best, then at the end run as fast as you can, all that's your endurance. (p. 412)

Given such uneven responses, I would add that the results concerning student understanding might best be considered through an assessment of whether the conceptual material is developmentally appropriate for children at grades 4 and 5.

For many students, the mile-run was *the* test to be avoided. Although this reaction was common to students who scored poorly, it was far from exclusive to members of that group. Physical pain and discomfort were central in their explanations for dodging the test (by means that will be familiar to any physical education teacher). It is interesting, however, that the "long boring" time consumed by taking the test was also subject to frequent criticism—and with an

unexpected level of passion. Apparently, doing one thing for 15 minutes feels like an eternity when you are a 10-year-old.

For many students, the mile-run was *the* test to be avoided.

The authors close the report with a discussion that raises a number of questions that seem important. For example, they wonder if associating a potentially beneficial activity with a distasteful or painful testing situation might lead students to avoid partaking in vigorous forms of exercise as adults. Beyond that obvious concern, however, they raise some sophisticated questions about fitness testing. They speculate about a possible connection between students who dodge the mile-run and those who exhibit the condition called *learned helplessness*, giving up before even trying an activity. They also wondered about the part played by the students' lack of control over taking the test in shaping their motivation for performing well on the test. In other words, how does "We *have* to do it!" affect them versus "We get to do it." As with so many studies, we answer a few questions but end up with many more.

A Teacher's Perspective

More than anything else, this report made me acutely conscious of a central fact about schools and kids—attendance is not voluntary. Everything in school life is colored by absence of choice. First, there are children who simply would choose not to be there at all. Then there are those who enjoy attending school but not particular activities within the school day, which include lunch, recess, the bus ride, math, reading, show-and-tell, and, of course, physical education. Finally, there are students who usually like an activity but find it unpleasant on that particular day or at that particular hour. Saying "no thank you, not today please" is usually not an option.

I have always wondered what the difference is for the experiences of children whose physical education classes come just before lunch versus just after, or say, at the first period in the morning versus the last period of the school day. I think we are more inclined to treat such questions seriously for adolescents in secondary schools than for children in elementary schools. It is as though their personal preferences and the lack of choice about school and schedules are matters of little or no consequence. The attitude of adults may even reflect the belief that children lack the capacity to care intensely about anything related to school.

So what does involuntary attendance and all that lack of choice have to do with attitudes toward performing the one-mile walk or run as a fitness test in physical education? I am firmly of the opinion that if the qualities of the experience and the associated disposition to like or dislike the activity are what we are concerned about, then we should look first to social and psychological factors, not to human physiology and physical conditioning!

Although we do learn a good deal about the participants' feelings, the report does not tell us how the students were prepared for the running test. In either school, did they have previous training runs on a regular schedule or as often happens, had the test been scheduled for a day between other unrelated activity units that did not involve running? Was the test just inserted into the schedule when rain or other unanticipated events produced time for which no other plans had been made? Had the children been doing some preparatory jogging, only to suddenly be confronted with a stopwatch and the demand for a timed run? It is not hard to imagine how adults would feel under any of those circumstances.

Alternatively, in either school had teachers been leading up to the day by providing appropriate preparatory activities? Had they helped the children regard the test itself as a challenging opportunity to improve on their own previous mark or even as a fascinating chance to match their performance against similar elementary school kids across the nation? The significance and positive values of a difficult or intrusive activity have to be sold to involuntary populations with great skill and persistent care (witness the largely successful campaign for yearly visits to the dentist).

In my own school district, a woman named Kay Morris has started a program called Marathon Kids. In the fall, there is an all-city event at which students and their parents come to run the first half-mile leg of a 4-month long marathon. The children then go back to their own school and log the remaining 25 miles, one at a time, throughout the school year. In spring, another citywide event is held for running the culminating half-mile. The enthusiasm generated by this event is remarkable, with over 10,000 children participating. Through use of careful promotion and marketing at city, school, and class levels, the marathon framework encourages elementary school students to see running as an opportunity rather than as a burden.

Selling any fitness test surely must mean use of a variety of tools to make it seem interesting, important, or at least well situated in what children can regard as a reasonable set of decisions by the teacher. That point makes the absence of any difference—between the students in the study who experienced the integrated health curriculum (and computerized reports on their performance status) and those who did not—all the more curious. Without more detail about the curriculum and mode of delivery, I can only speculate about that outcome. It sure seems clear, though, that something was missing.

In my experience, when the mile-run test is given without efforts to give it some sort of special meaning, the only students who enjoy the experience are those who score at the top of the class. The only exceptions to that rule have occurred when students have been engaged in an integrated health fitness program involving goal setting and a push toward personal improvement, along with multiple opportunities to respond to the challenge. When children are focused on achieving personal bests, nearly everyone can feel good about taking the test.

One such format has consistently worked well in schools where I have taught. A health-based improvement model was supplemented with posttest opportunities to discuss why personal bests were reached and what each person could do before the next time, to improve even more. Then, rather than using the mile-run, we allowed students to run or walk as far as they wanted during a 10-minute period of time. We set a base goal of everyone completing at least four laps, about a half-mile, which is a doable goal for virtually every child. In that context, which included careful recording of results by each student, most kids would push themselves, both toward the goal of a greater distance on successive tests and in preparation activities between tests. The only sources of feedback involved were the sequence of scores on each student's record card and the discussions of who was getting better and why. Comparisons with each other or with normative information were unnecessary to produce the desired outcome.

I would say that based on observation of student responses, the critical elements in that format were the following: (a) maintaining an element of choice, such as how fast to run, being paired with a friend, having music during the test, or choosing the day of the week used for testing; (b) emphasis on personal improvement; (c) running for distance rather than for time so that everyone can finish "at the same time"; (d) continued discussion of the concepts involved and how they influence actual levels of performance; and (e) persistent efforts to keep the running task interesting, such as creating story frameworks (e.g., running the distance to the state capital), inserting cone barriers as hurdles every 30 yards, or dribbling a basketball while running. When students beg to continue running after the 10 minutes are up, you have officially crossed a significant teaching hurdle!

At the end, I found that this study led me to reflect on an old concern that I know many teachers share. In what we try to do for fitness and the encouragement of healthy lifestyles, do we risk winning the battle but losing the war? If we improve times for the mile-run, but leave our students thinking, feeling, and knowing what the participants in this study thought, felt, and knew, then it is a hollow victory indeed. Putting concern for the students' actual experience front and center, with the clear voices of children to back it up, is a perfect example of how research can serve to clarify our thinking and do so in unexpected ways, as in this instance.

> At the end, I found that this study led me to reflect on an old concern that I know many teachers share. In what we try to do for fitness and the encouragement of healthy lifestyles, do we risk winning the battle but losing the war?

Common Ground: Our Shared Perspective

The apparent gap between what the teachers in this study expected their students to learn and the knowledge they actually demonstrated is a reminder of an implacable rule about teaching: *Just because we tried to teach it, does not mean they learned it.* If we really have fitness education as our goal, then we have valid reason to periodically assess, whether formally or informally, what our students really are learning about the content of our lessons.

We also can view the results of this study as a potent reminder of something we all know, but all too readily forget: *Children are not just miniature adults.* They do not have the same attention span, cognitive skills, accumulation of experience, or perception of the world as an adult. Fitness tests, as they now exist as designed by adults, do not seem to mesh well with children's perception of what is important and meaningful. From their perspective, and from perhaps many adults as well, the mile-run and other fitness-test items are viewed as contrived, arbitrary, and unauthentic. We believe that there must be ways to assess components of health-related fitness that are more relevant to and appropriate for children—at any level of their school experience.

> Fitness tests, as they now exist as designed by adults, do not seem to mesh well with children's perception of what is important and meaningful.

Children Describe
What They Learn
in Physical Education

Solmon, M.A., & Carter J.A. (1995). Kindergarten and first-grade students' perceptions of physical education in one teacher's classes. *The Elementary School Journal, 95,* 355-365.

In this study, the investigators started with some assumptions about teaching and learning that have not been widely used in physical education. They decided to adopt the view that learning does not flow spontaneously and directly from the acts of teaching. Instead, they assumed that students play an active role in controlling what they learn and how they go about doing so. It follows, then, that what students elect as responses to instructional events depends on how they understand those events— what the teacher wants, what various instructions mean, and what the purpose is supposed to be.

 ## The Study

The researchers reasoned that if they wanted to improve and extend their understanding of what goes on in elementary school physical education classes, a wise place to begin would be with how exactly students understand what is going on. That led them to a qualitative research design and many hours of listening to students patiently explain things, such as describing physical education to adults, who they clearly regarded as slow to grasp what ought to be perfectly obvious.

That long process of listening, probing, and watching yielded a report that shows qualitative research doing the ideal kind of inquiry—probing the insider's understanding of how things work, knitting together different strands of data into a picture of the whole, and peeling away layers of the familiar to reveal what is unique and even foreign to the outsider. This is not the stuff of questionnaires, skin-fold calipers, or skill tests. This is deep-diving into the world of physical education, as experienced by the people who are doing it.

Participants and Context

The teacher for the study was selected from candidates in several large suburban districts after a preliminary round of observations and interviews. Criteria for selection included specialization in elementary physical education, completion of a graduate degree in the area, a minimum of 10 years experience, a strong reputation for effective teaching among peers and administrators, full-time employment in a relatively small school with a substantial but stable minority population, and teaching in a program based on a wide range of activities and objectives. Ms. Woods (the participating teacher's pseudonym), two of her kindergarten classes, and two of her first-grade classes became the focus for the study.

Design and Method

Researchers collected data for 4 months starting at the beginning of the school year. All classes were observed weekly, either by one or both of the investigators. Field notes were used to record class events, including both teacher and student behavior. Frequently it was possible to speak informally with the teacher after classes for the purpose of adding her explanations or rationales for particular actions to the notes for the day. Although Ms. Woods was not informed of the exact nature of the investigation until the end of data collection, she was aware that her interactions with the students were being observed and recorded. Her comments on the field notes were regularly solicited.

For her pupils, Ms. Woods explained the presence of the researchers as people who needed to watch classes and talk to students so that they would know how to teach other people how to be good physical education teachers. After a few visits, the students appeared to accept their presence as a matter of routine that merited neither notice nor concern.

After the first month of observations, the two investigators began to formulate preliminary ideas based on observed actions and overheard comments about how students understood physical education. They began to talk informally (but systematically) with individual students. With the teacher's assistance, all 104 students were pulled aside at least once over the next 3 months, before or after class (or during water breaks), for interviews that lasted 3 to 5 minutes.

In the course of those conversational interludes, all students were asked the following: (a) what they called the class, (b) what they were learning in the class, (c) whether or not they liked the class, and (d) what they thought the teacher wanted them to learn in the class. Responses to those questions, as well as notes on other spontaneous student comments, were carefully recorded. In addition, classroom teachers agreed in the final month of the study to have all students draw pictures of their physical education class. The investigators then met with each student individually to obtain explanations of the pictures. During that conversation, a research assistant labeled all of the elements in the drawing for which the student provided identification.

After all of the data had been collected and analyzed, Ms. Woods participated in a final interview.

She was given a complete explanation of the study, an opportunity to review a summary of the results, and an invitation to comment on the students' definitions of physical education. Her reactions became a part of the findings and are reported along with the authors' conclusions at the end of the report.

Results

Children typically called the class "PE," "physical education," or "exercise." They consistently said they liked the class because it was fun. They liked the activities, and they liked the teacher. Of the 104 children, 19 of them referred to liking social aspects, such as getting to work with a friend or feeling that they were special in the class. A number also mentioned that they liked knowing that the teacher would help them if they could not do an activity.

In response to the general question about what they were learning, most gave an answer that simply reflected the activity for that particular day. A few, however, indicated awareness of learning that was not limited to content. Some of these were specific to class routines or rules, such as "take turns," or "don't talk when you are in line." A few others, though, ventured into abstractions such as "respect," and "how to exercise."

When asked what they thought the teacher wanted them to learn, students' answers became less content-specific and more global. The dominant theme here was "fitness." Students believed that the teacher wanted them to "exercise so as to be strong . . . to get bigger muscles . . . to grow . . . and to get in shape." Among those that were not content-related were 16 responses (all from girls) that centered on learning the rules of class management and compliance with teacher instructions: "She wants us to learn to do what she wants us to do . . . to pay attention . . . [to have] self-control—not to be bad . . . you don't get to do whatever you want, you only get to do one or two things" (p. 359). None of the boys, however, cited "learning to follow directions" as one of their teacher's intentions. Their replies focused solely on fitness and skill performance.

Student drawings from kindergarten classes tended to show only the teacher, or the teacher and the student. First-grade students were more likely to draw the entire class and include an assortment of equipment. In all, however, the teacher appeared as the dominant figure. Whatever she was portrayed as doing (talking, demonstrating, counting, giving praise), she was drawn as a very tall person, with students shown as no more than knee-high. Of the 104 drawings, 20% did not depict an activity but showed students waiting in line, sitting and listening, or lining up before or after class. Another 20% showed an active student, with others standing in line and waiting their turn. Finally, where numbers of students were shown, they tended to be drawn in groups that were segregated by gender.

The researchers' observations described Ms. Woods in a way that was surprisingly consistent with the children's drawings. A dominant figure in the class, she controlled and directed each step of all activities (she was, however, only of average height). From the start of the semester, she devoted much time and energy to establishing class routines and rules for behavior. Students learned and often practiced appropriate actions, such as getting ready for an activity, taking turns, caring for equipment, and listening carefully.

It was clear that Ms. Woods was sensitive to the problems of gender equity that can infect a physical education class. She was, in fact, remarkably consistent in affording boys and girls equal attention and opportunities to learn. Gender, however, was often used as a managerial tool or as a point of reference during instruction. For example, a frequent class format involved assigning partners so that they consisted of a boy and a girl. Gender also was prominent in the flow of teacher instructions: "Now, when the boys are quiet, I want each girl to . . ." The end result was a class in which efforts to achieve both gender integration and equal opportunity were pervasive and obvious characteristics. It was equally true, however, that children were being informed regularly that gender mattered and that boys and girls brought important differences to their encounters with physical activity.

The teacher's rules and expectations were clear, and she did not deviate from what had been well established from the outset. She did, however, continue to reinforce appropriate behavior, often with public praise, throughout the fall semester. She also generally took time to provide a rationale for all class activities, often relating material from previous classes to new information. A review of key points at the end of class was standard procedure.

Almost all of that would be congruent with current ideals about what constitutes effective teaching. The researchers were entirely open in expressing their admiration for Ms. Woods as an "outstanding elementary physical education specialist and classroom manager." She had been selected with that in mind, and clearly she fulfilled that expectation.

In informal weekly conversations and in the final interview, Ms. Woods expressed well-defined intentions for how she ran the class. The purpose of her early emphasis on rules and routines was to establish a noncompetitive, cooperative, and reassuring atmosphere based on discipline and predictability. Many of the class routines also were a reflection of her sense that maximal use should be made of the available time. The emphasis on fitness activities arose from her perception of the students' priority needs. Finally, her explanation for using gender-based groupings for instruction was pragmatic. It provided a clear and immediate basis for delineating groups or partners. In particular, she believed that putting girls and boys together as partners produced better discipline—girls often served to calm boys down and keep them in line.

The children's definitions of physical education were often logical extensions of what happened in class and what Ms. Woods emphasized as important content. Not once, for example, did any one of the 104 children intimate in any way that he or she viewed physical education as recess or playtime. That was a settled matter.

Although students were equally unequivocal in indicating that they liked physical education class and their teacher, many of their actions, verbalizations, and drawings indicated an understanding that physical education primarily meant following rules, waiting your turn, and standing in line. In this case, however, that understanding appeared not to have the negative connotations it sometimes evokes when students feel oppressed and overly regimented.

Early in the data collection, the researchers began to notice that there were some subtle differences in the way Ms. Woods interacted with girls and boys. Her explanation of using gender groups had acknowledged different behavior expectations for boys and girls, and close observation revealed that she had other ways of acting on that belief. Despite her efforts to create a noncompetitive environment, she sometimes compared boys with girls—and in particular terms. In class, she might say, "Boys, see how quickly the girls have found their personal space," and "Girls, see how well the boys lower their bodies to push hard with their hands." Both messages ostensibly relate to a specific skill, but the former is couched in terms of compliance and the latter in terms of execution.

The persisting theme was reinforcing girls for good behavior and giving boys positive reinforcement for skillful performance. It seems likely that when the children were asked, "What do you think the teacher wants you to learn?" the responses were linked to repeated instructional events. Girls' answers frequently included references to good behavior and following instructions, but boys' answers focused solely on the performance of motor skills.

Ms. Woods' initial reaction to the students' definition of physical education was positive. Content-related definitions, such as fitness, using a variety of equipment, and performing different activities, were consistent with her goals, and social definitions such as having fun with friends were congruent with her values as well. She was not concerned that students often incorporated following the rules and waiting in line in their conceptions of physical education. She argued that those are both essential to learning and valuable skills for daily life.

The evidence that showed how conceptions of physical education in her classes were different for boys and girls was an immediate cause for concern and the source of some discord between Ms. Woods and the research team. The matter was discussed at length, and it became apparent that some of her adverse reaction arose from how that finding distinctly clashed with her personal commitments concerning issues of equity. She saw her actions as designed to ensure that boys did not dominate and that girls had an opportunity to excel. That some of those actions might have served as a hidden curriculum, one that perpetuated stereotyped gender expectations, was a painful and deeply disturbing thought.

A Researcher's Perspective

The perception of physical education as following rules and waiting in line did not arise from mysterious sources. It was founded on an explicit message and was one Ms. Woods clearly intended her students to acquire. Although it might at first seem counterintuitive, it is also clear that students did not find that conception to have negative connotations. Physical education was perceived as fun, something that made them feel good. The teacher's persistence in giving explicit rationales for rules and classroom order seems to have won the students to her views about the importance of rules as a means for achieving order, fairness, and respect for each other.

Her strong belief in a rule-governed class climate was reflected in her actions, perceived by her students, and translated into the way they understood physical education. Likewise, however, her students seemed to have become aware of her expectation that males and females are suited for different kinds of school tasks. It should be no surprise, then, to discover that students also had begun to internalize that differentiation into definitions of physical

education—even though those understandings were in sharp conflict with her intentions.

> **Her strong belief in a rule-governed class climate was reflected in her actions, perceived by her students, and translated into the way they understood physical education.**

A Teacher's Perspective

What I really like about this study is that it provided me with vivid illustrations of two basic rules about teaching physical education that without reminders tend to get lost in the rush of getting the job done every day. First, as teachers, we have valid reasons to care a great deal about how students feel in response to what happens in class, as well as how students understand (or misunderstand) our intentions—and the best way to learn about those things is to ask the children!

Second, because most of my teaching has to be done without the presence of other adults, I have found that it is dangerously easy to be oblivious to subtle patterns in my teaching behavior. Especially when I am working really hard to do the things that ensure a desired outcome, it is all too easy not to notice that other less positive things are happening. Those unintended consequences often are quite apparent to an observer but invisible to us. As this study illustrates, what children report can reflect elements of a hidden and sometimes undesired curriculum, but to tap that feedback requires that we take the time to ask them the right questions.

> **As this study illustrates, what children report can reflect elements of a hidden and sometimes undesired curriculum, but to tap that feedback requires that we take the time to ask them the right questions.**

Before commenting on those valuable reminders, however, I want to draw attention to several cautions about this study. First, evidence derived from children's drawings, even when derived from verbal explanations of the picture, reflects not only their understanding but simply their ability to draw. It is quite possible that (as with adults) children draw what is easy to draw and avoid attempting to portray what is beyond their graphic ability. To some unknowable degree, that internal censor may actually distort what is drawn and so interfere with our efforts to use pictures as a portal to what children think and feel.

Second, the gender differences reported with regard to teacher intentions for learning seem to be well supported by the data. What I find more difficult to accept are some of the inferences drawn by the researchers concerning those observations. Other factors are probably behind the divergent understandings of boys and girls, not just the singular influence of differential treatment by the teacher.

Children probably come to physical education classes fully equipped with societal expectations about gender roles derived from interactions with other teachers, parents, and friends. Girls, for example, already may be far more disposed to accept and internalize messages about the importance of following instructions, and boys may have learned to ignore the same signals. Ms. Woods may have been guilty of not countering undesirable lessons already learned.

Teachers themselves, acting alone or in teams, can use some of the same means to uncover their own insights.

Finally, I always worry when people so easily interpret what students do as a reflection of their gender. Children bring more than their sex chromosomes to physical education classes. For example, boys generally do bring more experience and skill in some forms of physical activity than do girls. What we see in male responses to interview probes (as well as in male behavior during class) may have its roots as much in accumulated knowledge, abilities, and attitudes, as in the simple fact of gender. In this study, the real (or more powerful) variable may have been skill or experience. Gender almost certainly was involved, but everything should not automatically be laid at its doorstep.

To return to the memorable lessons illustrated so well by this study, let's consider the hazards in spending so much time "alone" with children—assuming that our own adult perspectives are shared by our students is foremost among them. Unanticipated results are the rule in something as complex as teaching physical education, and nested within the surprises can be some that are distinctly undesirable.

The strategy of asking students how they understand things is one way to monitor outcomes that may have escaped our notice. For that purpose, interviews and questionnaires are not the only tools. As with the researchers, one of my first instincts is to have students create products that can reflect the meanings they give to what happens in class. At a simpler level, just looking at a videotape of your own teaching performance can sometimes turn up clues to undesired outcomes, if you can discipline yourself not to see only what you expect.

For some purposes, however, there is another strategy to counter undesired outcomes. For areas of your program that you know to be sensitive to such things as hidden messages—and gender equity is certainly likely to be one of those—some problems can be dealt with by a preemptive strike.

A teacher friend of mine (Jim DeLine, an elementary school physical educator in Austin, Texas) has a system for calling on students that ensures gender equity. He has made it a simple and now virtually unconscious habit to alternate, boy-girl-boy-girl. The same strategy is used for assigning tasks, leading groups, and other forms of individualized teacher attention. Yes, the content of those alternating interactions might not be equivalent, as was the case with Ms. Woods, but Jim knows that the distributions of attention and opportunity in his classes follow his personal values concerning equity. A small thing, perhaps, and not a tactic with which every teacher could be comfortable, but it does provide a kind of insurance against doing the unintended.

Common Ground: Our Shared Perspective

The findings that surfaced in this study were produced because two experienced investigators had been questioning students, listening carefully to their responses, and reflecting on what they were hearing. That process, however, does not require either the setting of formal inquiry or special research skills. Teachers themselves, acting alone or in teams, can use some of the same means to uncover their own insights.

High School Seniors Recall Elementary Physical Education

Pissanos, B.W., & Allison, P.C. (1993). Students' constructs of elementary school physical education. *Research Quarterly for Exercise and Sport, 64,* 425-435.

In teaching, there are good days and there are bad days. On the best of them, it is possible to believe that what you are doing will shape and serve your students for a lifetime. On the worst of them, many of us honestly wonder whether any of our efforts will leave the slightest trace, much less be fondly recalled by students as moments of inspired learning.

The joys and agonies of teaching aside, however, the matter of students' memories bears importance far beyond its seeming innocence. If you want to define the bottom line for teaching, one good candidate would have to be, "What do students retain from their physical education experiences 5, 10, or 50 years later?" In confronting that question, the investigators who undertook this study asserted that the answer would have to involve knowledge (facts, skills, beliefs) that had been constructed by each individual student. Much or little, useful or pointless, happy or unhappy, vivid or hazy, and intended or unintended by the teacher, whatever lasted in memory would be the end product of how students understood what went on in class.

If we accept that assumption, then students' memories of elementary physical education can be construed to offer a window through which we can look backward in time. In their recollections, we can trace the outlines of earlier interactions between teacher and student, as well as glimpse the process that links raw experience with the long-term stor-

age of meanings and skills. It was the opportunity to use the window of memory that the investigators hoped to exploit in performing this study.

 ## The Study

This investigation looked backward across an interval of 6 years, with an elementary school physical education teacher (female) and 10 of her former students, now high school seniors and about to graduate. For this study, they reflected on the 7 years of kindergarten through sixth grade that they had spent together. The researchers asked them three general questions: First, what did they remember? Second, what did it all mean to them in retrospect? Third, what factors influenced those meanings and memories?

A powerful theoretical framework was used to design this study and to interpret the data it produced. Called *constructivism,* it represents a particular orientation toward understanding how children learn. Because that viewpoint is particularly complex, we have elected to provide only a brief definition here, relying on our plain-language translation of technical terms and constructs for the remainder of the annotation.

The common perception of what goes on in schools is that students learn by receiving knowledge from teachers. In contrast, the constructivist orientation in education assumes that students are active participants in the creation of what they learn—whether that be knowledge, physical skills, or values. Put simply, what a particular student learns is held to be a composite: what teachers provide in the form of learning experiences gets filtered through and combined with what each individual pupil brings to class.

In physical education, the teacher provides everything from class routines to lectures and practice drills. The students, however, bring their personal characteristics and unique background of experiences, as well as the influences of their social context—for example, their gender, ethnicity, language, and social class. The resulting encounter (sometimes it seems more like a collision) has the potential to leave permanent traces, the cognitive and motor memories we call learning.

In that sense, then, students construct what they learn out of the material provided by their class experiences. They must try to make some sense out of what they see, hear, and do in class, and it is the meanings produced by such sense-making that they take away as learning. From this perspective, what students learn is not defined by some universal meaning that resides only in what the teacher offers. The constructivists hold that in the final analysis, students must create what is learned for themselves. The teacher provides the raw materials and shapes the context for making sense out of them, but the students do the learning. As you can see, while this vantage point on education assigns a critical role to the teacher, it also assumes a very active role for the student.

Participants and Context

The participants in this qualitative study include a veteran teacher of elementary school physical education (17 years) in a small, stable, rural Midwestern community and 10 of her former students. The period during which the students had the teacher was a 7-year time frame that began with the teacher's 5th year of teaching and ended with her 11th year.

The class used for study was selected because the teacher found it to be well remembered, and she recalled it as particularly easy to teach and quite cooperative in pursuing her goals for physical education. Of the 34 students from that class who were now graduating from high school, the researchers selected 10 through use of *maximum variation sampling*. As the name suggests, the idea was to get the greatest possible variety within a single subset of the original group. The factors used in selection were as follows: (a) high to low skill, (b) high to low academic ability, (c) high to low class participation, (d) high (excessive) to low body-weight, (e) high to low creative ability, (f) outgoing to shy, (g) popular to unpopular with peers, (h) verbal to nonverbal, and (i) strong to weak impression in the memory of the teacher. All of the categorizations were derived from the teacher's description of each of the 34 students. Of the 5 males and 5 females selected through the use of those criteria, not one student represented the same combination of characteristics as any of the other 9 students.

Design and Method

The teacher was interviewed by both researchers, providing an audiotaped data record, 2 hours 30 minutes in length. Included were descriptions of her evolving curriculum, teaching methods, and personal teaching goals, as well as recollections concerning particular class groups and students. For the period covered by the study, she also provided unit and lesson plans, teaching evaluations, lesson content source materials, and photographs of students participating in lessons.

The 10 students were interviewed individually over a 4-week period. The open-ended protocol focused on their reflections that concerned the following: (a) themselves, the teacher, and their classmates in elementary school physical education, (b) how physical education was perceived and valued in the school, (c) the content of their classes, (d) the goals and purposes of the teacher, and (e) what they learned in physical education. To stimulate recall, students were shown archival photographs of their class engaged in physical education. The audiotaped interviews lasted from 30 minutes to more than an hour in length. The students were aware that the teacher knew which class had been selected, but they were assured that she would not be informed as to which students had been selected for participation in the study.

The investigators inductively coded and independently categorized the interview data. The resulting analyses were merged and inspected to identify points at which the students had constructed similar or different memories of their physical education experiences. Researchers then matched those memories with student characteristics, data from the teacher's description of the class, and written records concerning curriculum, teaching methods, and school context.

Results

A single predominant theme ran through all of the student recollections. In their minds, the teacher *was* the elementary physical education they had received. The most salient perceptions of their experience were defined by the teacher's particular value orientation, her goals, and her teaching style. Across all of the diverse characteristics represented in the sample group, students used closely similar language to describe the teacher's primary goal—to foster within each of them a strong commitment to do one's personal best.

> We learned how to do our best and to push ourselves to our limits. She taught us to not look back but to look forward and not to say, "I can't," but to say, well, "I can try." She always told us not to give up on nothing. She said just do it and do your best. She said it would come out. That's what we'd do. (p. 429)

Students also were unanimous in remembering that the teacher was consistent and predictable. Whether in or out of class, she listened to what students had to say, made them feel that she genuinely cared about them, and never played favorites. The latter often was recalled with regard to her patience with lower-skilled students.

> You know, the [students] who couldn't throw the softballs and weren't coordinated enough, she really spent a lot of time working with them and demonstrating for them and then doing it herself, and she'd have another kid show them or she would go through the motions, holding onto your arm with you and [be] really, really patient. She always calmed you from being flustered. (p.431)

The teacher was described as having been persistently clear about what she intended and always having a particular intention in class. As one student put it, "She always did what she was supposed to do." The stories students told often connected her clear expectations for pupil performance to her persistent efforts to motivate them.

> Even when you weren't too excited about doing something, you know, or were groaning or something, she would make you want to do it because she'd find a new aspect to make you want to do it. She was really nice but she'd put her foot down and . . . you couldn't walk over her. (p. 431)

Gender was the single factor that was associated with detectably different recollections, all of which related to what was remembered about curriculum content. The broad descriptions provided by male and female students were the same, but they differed greatly in terms of detail. Males recalled much less variety and fewer specifics in the area of sport skill instruction. Females not only identified more sports, but they also described different elements of the sport lessons—and usually in far richer detail than did the males. One female said,

> We played football. Basically, she was more intent on teaching us how to do it than actually doing it. Like, she wanted everyone to learn to follow through when they were throwing and to pull their arm back and to step forward. She wanted to make sure that everyone knew how to do it. (p. 432)

In contrast, a typical exchange with a male participant provided the following:

> Interviewer: What types of things were covered in your program?
> Student: I don't know, probably like, ummm, like I don't know. Oh, basketball. I remember basketball.
> Interviewer: What did you do in basketball?
> Student: Oh, we just threw around the ball, like that. (p. 433)

The researchers offer several explanations for this sharp gender contrast. First, several studies have shown that under conditions of free recall, females are likely to generate much more detail than under conditions of structured recall. The high level of variety and detail among the female students may thus have been a function of the nature of the recall task itself. The interview protocol had maximized their comfort with the process of reminiscence.

A second explanation may lie in the degree to which males tend to establish fairly rigid gender stereotypes about participating in sport. As early as the elementary school years, teaching sport-related skills and coaching are viewed by boys as more gender-appropriate for males. They may have viewed their participation in sport lessons taught by a female as perfunctory. As one participant put it, "She taught us flag football. I got a kick out of that. I didn't think a woman could ever teach it" (p. 433). Thus, the impoverished male recall concerning sport lessons may reflect their stereotyped construction of gender.

With regard to the main result of highly congruent memories in which the teacher's goals and supportive pedagogy were the defining theme, the investigators concluded that this was best explained by the teacher's strong and explicit value orientation—and her persistent efforts to teach in ways that directly reflected that commitment. Clarity and consistency had produced students who could recall many years after the last class exactly what she wanted them to do and learn, and why.

A Researcher's Perspective

From the perspective of a researcher, it seems remarkable that from among such powerful variables as skill level, academic achievement, popularity, and class participation, only gender appeared to influence what the students could recall concerning what happened in elementary school physical education. This surely cannot be taken as an indication that those other characteristics were unimportant in the way students came to understand what happened in class. All of those variables are important determinants of what happens in a student's school experience. What we do not often have opportunity to see, however, is their relative significance when placed in context with the influence of a clear and consistently enacted set of teacher values. This study confirms that what a teacher regards as important educational goals can constitute one of the most powerful factors in how students come to understand their time in the gym.

> **This study confirms that what a teacher regards as important educational goals can constitute one of the most powerful factors in how students come to understand their time in the gym.**

A Teacher's Perspective

What teacher could read this without at least some feelings of envy? Certainly not me! I surely hope that my students will remember a clear message from my classes. To be honest, though, I can only speculate about what they would recall. I know what I intended when I taught them, but with the exception of casual conversations during chance encounters with former students, I really don't know what they remember about their physical education—or about me, for that matter.

> **I know what I intended when I taught them, but with the exception of casual conversations during chance encounters with former students, I really don't know what they remember about their physical education—or about me, for that matter.**

Which leads me to wonder why we don't ask students on a regular basis questions about such recall topics? At the least, we could ask graduating students to provide some simple feedback at the end of their final year. What skills did you learn, what was the teacher's main message, and what do you think was the purpose of physical education? A simple program exit procedure would involve none of the technical difficulties of long-term follow-up. With some carefully phrased questions, not beyond the appropriate level of complexity, we might acquire some valuable information.

Even better, different exit questions could be asked of children at different grade levels. The possibilities are endless: smiling- or frowning-face icons to circle, simple checklists, a reflective writing assignment coordinated with the classroom teacher, or even a cool physical education project, such as designing a brochure describing the just-completed program for parents and new students.

Of course, when I begin to think about what questions to ask, I immediately raise the whole matter of what permanent or long-term legacy do I really want to leave imprinted on my students. It seems to me that confronting that question would be an important exercise for each of us. The memories reported by the participants in this study were impressive, but they surely don't reflect the only possible set of teacher intentions. More important, the authors concluded that the lasting imprint produced by their teacher probably was the result of clearly expressed values and specific learning goals.

I would like to suggest a set of simple steps that could lead you toward a clear sense of the legacy you want to give your students:

1. Identify some specific phrases students would use to describe you as a teacher and what they learned in your program.

2. Identify (and actually write down) some specific actions you take when teaching that are intended to lead students to say those things about you and your program.

3. Figure out a way to check with some current students to see how they describe you and how you teach, perhaps via an anonymous questionnaire given in a class setting away from physical education.

4. Do a similar spot-check with a few randomly selected alumni of your program.

5. Look at that small set of data without focusing all your attention on what the particular responses are. Instead, ask yourself, "Why do my students remember the program and my teaching that way?" If you can, really listen to the messages, even the tone of what the students recall, and try to reflect carefully on what you did that may have shaped them. If you can do so, you should have a powerful tool for creating the legacy you really want.

To close, I wonder if you noted that this study does not tell us much about the content (the skills and knowledge) the students think they actually learned and have retained. Likewise, we find little about whether or not the participants believe they actually ended up with a serious commitment to what the teacher intended them to learn—to always face new challenges by trying hard and doing their best. Those omissions point to a need for further inquiry.

Remembering what the teacher was trying to accomplish is one thing. As desirable as such clear recall may be as an outcome, though, it leaves open the question of what actually was left in the behavioral repertoire and personal habits of the graduates. While self-assessment has its limitations, I wish we could hear how those same participants would respond to additional interview probes about what

they can do now and how they describe the beliefs they hold today.

What is essential is actually doing something to take that next step in assessing an elementary school physical education program's lasting imprint. A legacy that really matters should be detectable further down the line than just the day of graduation. Such data about outcomes, beyond its virtues as feedback to improve program and instruction, would be invaluable as information for our other publics—parents, principals, school board members, and school colleagues.

Common Ground: Our Shared Perspective

This study provides a perfect example of a main conclusion that is almost too obvious to be noticed. The authors of this report noticed it and put it at the front of their closing statement: "Students of a teacher whose value orientation is consistently reinforced through program goals, curricular decisions, and teaching style can learn what the teacher deliberately teaches" (p. 433). That conclusion seems mundane to the point of triviality, until you add the fact that under the right conditions, those lessons can be recalled many years later by every student in the class—and in substantial detail!

> **Students of a teacher whose value orientation is consistently reinforced through program goals, curricular decisions, and teaching style can learn what the teacher deliberately teaches. (p. 433)**

Also of import is the fact that the powerful element here apparently was not content knowledge, pedagogical skill, or program design. At the core of students' memories and what shaped the original class experiences was what a teacher believed mattered most as the purpose of her work. It may be that we have seen a demonstration in this study of why all those elements of knowledge, skill, and design included within a sound teacher-preparation program may be necessary but wholly insufficient in producing an effective practitioner. It is clear and coherent belief that gives life and power to the tools of teaching.

PART VI

Teachers in the Workplace—Training, Experience, and Context

THE STUDY

RESEARCHER

TEACHER

COMMON GROUND

Preservice Classroom Teachers in the Gym

Ashy, M., & Humphries, C.A. (2000). "Don't use balloons on windy days": Elementary education majors' perceptions of teaching physical education. *Action in Teacher Education, 22*(1), 59-71.

In this study, two teacher educators made use of an extensive pool of previously accumulated data, which, in case you wondered, is a perfectly legitimate process and often a very useful form of research. Whenever careful records are maintained over time, whether in a state department of motor vehicles, a hospital emergency room, or a public school, the stored information can be used not only for the purpose of historical research but as a means of answering questions that have direct relevance to the present.

 **The Study**

In addition to their responsibility for classroom instruction, elementary school teachers are often expected to provide physical education. Accordingly, teacher-education programs often include a required course in physical education that teaches methods for all of the student teachers moving toward certification, a training experience usually segregated from courses specifically designed for future physical education specialists.

After teaching such a course for several years, the authors became interested in exploring its educational consequences. They began the process by examining an archive of written materials that was produced by preservice classroom teachers as part of an annual follow-up to a brief field experience in

physical education. The explicit purpose of the examination was to assess the perceptions of classroom trainees in the context of physical education with regard to children, teaching, and themselves.

The Participants and Context

The focus of this study was 424 elementary education majors (402 females and 22 males), who were about to graduate as certified classroom teachers. In most instances, they were destined to assume faculty positions in elementary schools. By their senior year, the participants had completed a brief, one-credit unit that dealt with physical education content and focused on movement skills for elementary children. Before the final semester of student teaching, all were enrolled in a required course that combined attention to theory and field practice for the teaching of physical education. During the field practicum component, the investigators collected the preservice trainees' perceptions of children in the physical education setting, themselves as physical education teachers, and the work of teaching physical education.

Design and Method

The participant group included elementary education majors from 5 consecutive academic years at a single institution. The same protocol for data collection was employed each year. The senior-year field experience that was the immediate precursor of data collection always began 5 weeks into the fall semester and consisted of 10 consecutive class days with first and second grades. Each student planned and taught 30-minute physical education classes on 7 of the 10 days. They performed systematic observations of peers and pupils on the remaining days (copies of the standard recording forms are contained in the original report). Assignments included teaching lessons for small groups of students (5-8), as well as half-class (12-15) and full-class configurations (24-30).

Complete physical education lesson plans were required in preparation for each class. Plans had to include the following: objectives in all three learning domains (cognitive, affective, psychomotor); a warm-up task; an introduction to the lesson; refinement, extension, and application tasks; and a closing activity. In addition, students were required to list performance cues, questions intended to stimulate student thinking, and formation diagrams for all drills and activities.

Immediately following completion of the field unit, students were assigned to small work groups (4 or 5). Groups then spent approximately 90 minutes discussing and preparing written summaries of their responses to the following questions:

- What did you learn about children?
- What did you learn about yourself as a physical education teacher?
- What was the hardest teaching skill to master in the physical education context?
- Which teaching skills helped the children to learn?
- Did you learn anything you wish you had known in advance?
- Were there any surprises?
- What advice do you have for other elementary education majors?

The questions were presented one at a time in serial order, with ample time provided for discussion and negotiation of a group response. In the absence of consensus, each individual student wrote his or her own response.

The two investigators carried out the analysis of data by reading the accumulated response documents independently. They then constructed a preliminary list of thematic categories that seemed to accommodate recurring comments. Rereadings, negotiation, and merging of categories reduced the number of themes so as to retain only those that could be supported by a minimum of 10 participant responses (the original report contains a table presenting the primary themes associated with each question).

Results

Despite the fact that they already had completed school practica in reading and math, many of the participants appeared to be quite unprepared for the realities represented by children outside the classroom setting—particularly their behavior in a setting of open-space activity. Some of the negative comments from the preservice seniors focused on the children's occasional rudeness and disrespect, the wide range of skill levels represented in classes, the lack of social skills required for class participation, and the expressions of poor attitude toward class instruction. It is therefore easy to believe that these student teachers had expected their pupils to be polite, compliant, relatively uniform in abilities, and motivated for the learning activities in physical education.

Evidence also suggested that the student teachers experienced a sudden awareness concerning children with disabilities and special needs. Participants were aware of the necessary adjustments for inclusion policy assignments in the classroom, but they had not thought about how that might be addressed in physical education.

It's not surprising that revelations concerning themselves in the role of physical education teachers centered on management issues. Of the 103 discussion groups, 71 groups produced three or more comments about student behaviors. It is telling that many of the responses were actually teacher-related for the first question, "What did you learn about children?" Responses revealed that children's characteristics were often defined in terms of the management strategies they demanded: "Children need simple and very specific directions."

As mentioned explicitly by 42 groups, the single personal quality cited most frequently as discovered through field experience was patience with children. In some cases, student teachers discovered reserves of patience that they had not known they possessed. More often, though, they realized that to teach physical education they would require a great deal more of it.

The preservice participants did recognize the importance of teaching skills that went beyond those of management. For example, 65 group responses discussed the power that a teacher's verbal cues can have on student learning. Demonstration, feedback, and opportunity to practice were all recognized by some of the groups as helpful teaching techniques. Student teachers realized, however, that to use them well would require knowledge of physical education content—the skills and activities for which they had received only a cursory introduction.

To the admitted surprise of the researchers, responses were predominately at a low conceptual level when preservice trainees were queried concerning physical education as a subject field. Even though lesson plans had included cognitive, psychomotor, and affective objectives, only 2 of the 103 groups made any mention of that fact. For the most part, physical education was discussed in terms of the need for a variety of activities to keep students interested and a recounting of which activities had gone well or poorly in their individual lessons.

The participants' own dispositions toward having to teach physical education were clearly divided. In a substantial number of groups (28), responses indicated that the student teachers liked teaching physical education—or, at least, they discovered that they liked it more than they had expected. Negative responses ranged from the simple "I hate physical education," to the more diplomatic advice for other elementary majors to "be sure to teach in a school where they have a PE teacher!"

 **A Researcher's Perspective**

The results indicate that a brief preservice unit concerning physical education content and teaching methods, accompanied by a limited field experience, can have some value for elementary education majors. That value, however, appears to rest primarily on its service as an introduction. The participants in this study may have improved their understanding of children, their sense of what is required by way of management skills, and their notion of basic requisites for instruction. Nevertheless, the authors of the report reached the conclusion that most of the participants would not be "able to approach the task at a level we consider adequate to sustain growth as a teacher of physical education" (p. 69).

In other words, the investigators characterized the data as portraying trainees who will not know enough about physical education when they graduate to offer any assurance that they will be able to improve their current performance—even if their schools provide resources and continued professional development activities to support their teaching efforts in that area.

> **The investigators characterized the data as portraying trainees who will not know enough about physical education when they graduate to offer any assurance that they will be able to improve their current performance . . .**

The two missing elements the authors identify as critical in this prediction for failure are content knowledge and experience. The authors urge the kind of school support that would allow classroom teachers to grow effectively in their roles as physical educators; however, they also clearly see strong implications for improving what elementary education majors need to know and practice before they embark on their teaching careers.

A Teacher's Perspective

As indicated in the full report for this study, an overwhelming majority of the students preparing to become elementary school teachers are women, who in the past have had severely limited opportunities and encouragement for the development of their own movement competence. This trend has slowly been changing, and I now see more women among majors in elementary education who have been athletes themselves or are currently engaged in such things as running, aerobic dance, or other active lifestyle options.

That is not to say that they possess all of the physical education content background that they should, particularly after completing 12 years of schooling. Nevertheless, many more recruits to elementary classroom teaching have had at least some foundational experiences. Beyond that small advance, however, what all of us must hope for are initiatives that someday improve public school physical education at all levels to produce high school graduates who are physically educated. Teacher preparation should include the same prerequisite expectations for basic movement skills as for the foundational achievement in subjects such as math and reading.

Reflection on this study should encourage physical education specialists to extend their thinking in two directions. First, we need to address the question of how we can best act to support classroom teachers already in the field. No matter what we might envision as ideal, those colleagues must be adequately prepared to provide at least some of the physical education instruction in most schools—and all of the instruction in many more. What we do to support and encourage those teachers is critical and essential in what is delivered to millions of children, both now and in the foreseeable future.

In the other direction, the results of this study once again urge us to do all we can to lobby for the presence of physical education specialists in every school. What is not commonly appreciated is how critical the support of classroom teachers can be in achieving that end. They will be a powerful force in the support of hiring certified specialists when they can (a) express their respect for the subject matter content of physical education and (b) insist that they are properly prepared to do no more than collaborate with specialists in delivering that content.

The task of helping classroom teachers to develop in so many areas—content, pedagogy, management—at once is so overwhelming that even well-conceived efforts such as this one can produce only limited advances in teacher competence. There are particular points at which real progress can be achieved, however, and for the present we must focus on those specifically.

In that regard, I noted with great satisfaction that many of the participants recognized the great benefit of carefully selected verbal cues. Not only is that a key element in the physical education teacher's essential repertoire, it is a demonstration that even preservice classroom teachers can learn directly from watching how students respond to instruction.

At the end of our annotation, I found myself reflecting on how much easier it will be to work with classroom teachers when we finally have de-

> We need to address the question of how we can best act to support classroom teachers already in the field. No matter what we might envision as ideal, those colleagues must be adequately prepared to provide at least some of the physical education instruction in most schools—and all of the instruction in many more.

veloped a solid set of performance indicators. Just such a listing is now under development by members of the National Association for Sport and Physical Education. Coupled with the new national content standards, *Standards for Appropriate Teaching Practices in Physical Education,* specific descriptions of what a physically educated person should know and be able to do will make it possible for preservice and in-service teachers to visualize the goals for their instruction. More particular to the questions raised by this study, such explicit standards will help future classroom teachers understand exactly what physical education provides that is not included in Little League, age-group swimming programs, family outings, or just plain recess activities.

Despite those much-needed clarifications, classroom teachers still have too much to learn during their preservice preparation programs. Personal skills and detailed pedagogical knowledge are required to devise and implement a quality physical education program. They demand investments of training time that are likely to exceed the allotments set aside for preparing classroom teachers in any presently imaginable scheme for teacher education. If all recruits to teaching had previously passed through quality K-12 physical education programs, that fatal limitation might not be true. Such speculation, however, involves circular reasoning. Were such programs the standard in our schools, there would be no need to train classroom teachers in the first place.

 ## Common Ground: Our Shared Perspective

It might be tempting to discredit the main thrust of these findings because of the loose coupling between written group responses to abstract questions about a training experience versus the actual events and consequences of that process. Before doing so, you should consider the fact that the senior author not only taught all sections of the preservice unit involved for all 5 years but served as the clinical site coordinator and primary field supervisor as well. If anyone had intimate knowledge of the participants and their performances in the field, it was she. Further, if anyone had cause to consider the data with an optimistic bias, it was she. In that light, her comments about the findings seem pointedly blunt and devoid of disingenuousness. We are inclined to conclude that she has told us what she honestly believes the data say and that it was not much fun to do so.

> **We are inclined to conclude that she has told us what she honestly believes the data say and that it was not much fun to do so.**

Is Daily Physical Education Worth the Price?

Hastie, P.A., Sanders, S.W., & Rowland, R.S. (1999). Where good intentions meet harsh realities: Teaching large classes in physical education. *Journal of Teaching in Physical Education, 18,* 277-289.

Daily physical education from kindergarten through the 12th grade appears as a recommendation in a number of national initiatives. In response, a variety of legislative mandates have appeared at the state level. These have assumed a bewildering array of formats, some requiring 30 to 50 minutes of daily physical education while others prescribe at least 90 minutes per week—without stipulating a daily lesson. Some of the mandates are couched in the relatively weak language of "recommended policy," but others establish true requirements with which local school districts must comply.

Several factors have served to circumscribe the impact of these political events. Among those is the fact that of the states presently mandating requirements for daily physical education, none provide funding for the necessary increase in the number of teachers. In an elementary school with 400 students and one physical education specialist working an eight-period day, the principal must either inflate class size to 50 students or support an additional specialist, not to mention finding the space and equipment required for scheduling two classes at once.

For elementary schools, it is clear that the initial assumption in many states was that daily physical education could be achieved by more extensive use of classroom teachers. However, as those teachers came under increasing pressure for complex development, planning, and preparation tasks in this era of high stakes testing, their resistance to assuming more responsibility in physical education has grown. The end result for some school districts has been that school principals have turned to the only remaining option for sustaining compliance with the daily mandate—a dramatic increase in class size for physical education.

 ## The Study

In this study, the investigators focused on schools where administrators have opted for the solution of larger class size. They posed two fundamental questions. First, what has been the impact on the physical education delivered to children? Second, what has been the impact on the teachers? The methodology here includes forms of data collection and analysis that are commonly employed in qualitative research—that is, formal and informal interviews. Although the study may best be characterized as having mixed perspectives, you may find it helpful to review our brief comments about qualitative research (see chapter 14).

Participants and Context

Three elementary physical education teachers (all female) were recruited for this study, each from a different K-4 school in the same district. All were experienced specialists with certification and advanced study in the subject field. The state requirement for 30 minutes of daily physical education was met in their schools by combining all students from two or three classrooms to form each physical education class. For the 3 teachers, this policy resulted in the following conditions.

1. Teacher A had a daily workload of 11 classes, ranging in size from 38 to 49. She had been assigned one untrained classroom aide.

2. Teacher B had a daily workload of 9 classes, ranging in size from 44 to 75. She had been assigned one full-time and one part-time classroom aide, both untrained.

3. Teacher C had a daily workload of 10 classes, ranging in size from 43 to 55. She had been assigned one untrained classroom aide.

Although all of the classroom aides had undergraduate degrees, none had formal training for teaching and all were new to both work with children and the subject matter of physical education.

Design and Method

Five of each teacher's lessons were videotaped, including three second-grade and two fourth-grade classes. All of the tapes subsequently were coded to ascertain the amount of class time devoted to four categories: (a) activity time, more than 50 percent of students are engaged in physical activity; (b) instruction time, most students are receiving information about how to perform a skill; (c) management time, most students are not receiving instruction or engaged in activity but have tasks to perform, such as putting equipment away or listening to behavioral reminders; (d) waiting time, most students are not coded in the other three categories but are waiting in line or participating in off-task behaviors.

In addition, researchers observed a random sample of students to ascertain the frequency with which they performed skills, such as practice trials of the movement to be learned, and whether or not they were successful. Finally, researchers closely observed teachers to record how they used their instructional time, with particular emphasis on the categories of refining and extending students' movement skills, or introducing tasks that required simple application, such as scrimmages and games.

Brief, informal conversations with teachers took place when time permitted (most lasted less than 5 minutes). Notes from these were recorded in a field log and served as the basis for constructing questions to be introduced during a 2-hour formal group interview that was video- and audiotaped at the close of the semester. All interview tapes were fully transcribed.

Analysis of verbal material from interview sources involved breaking the transcripts and field notes into conceptual fragments, each containing the expression of a single thought. These were sorted and resorted into categories that were designed to represent persisting themes in the data.

Results

Reliability checks for collection of numeric data from videotapes were satisfactory for each of the several operations. The resulting profiles for time allocation were remarkably similar for the 3 teachers. All came within a few percentage points to the allocation of class time for activity (50%), instruction (20%), management (20%), and waiting (10%), which compares favorably to some current recommendations for effective teaching. Student opportunities to practice specific skills averaged about four tries over each 4-minute interval of observation, with success rates ranging from 70 to 89%. Both opportunity and success rates were higher for students in these classes than those recorded in other research studies.

All 3 teachers organized their lessons around skill themes rather than game units, and they often employed rotation of students through stations representing different concepts within the themes. It is not surprising, then, that students spent the majority of instructional time working on tasks designed to refine and extend skill. The largest expenditure of time for application, in the form of two-on-two learning games, was 24%. Again, this pattern of instruction would compare favorably with recommendations from professional organizations.

The analysis of interview data produced four thematic categories, and we will review each in turn. Considerations of space do not allow, however, inclusion of the extensive quotations with which the authors document the nature of each theme.

1. *Curricular limitations.* The teachers believed that it was impossible to produce lessons that were faithful to their newly designed K-4 curriculum, which is based on skill themes and movement concepts. In addition to the logistic problems presented by student numbers, they regarded space as inadequate for their minimum needs and equipment as insufficient to allow individualized instruction and practice (the district allocated $250 each year for purchase of the equipment necessary for enacting a high-quality daily program).

2. *Safety over instruction.* All of the teachers were deeply concerned about preventing accidents, and they found that double- and triple-sized classes greatly compounded that problem. To ensure safety with bigger classes, teachers had to spend more time organizing plans and had to expend more in-class time on management and transitions, with consequent loss of instructional time. Teachers also found that bigger classes restricted the alternatives for instructional format and required much more attention devoted to monitoring for safety, rather than student skill development.

3. *Administrative constraints.* All of the teachers felt that their effectiveness was compromised by administrative constraints. Among the policy decisions that were viewed as most limiting were the following: (a) no provision for breaks between classes (one teacher was required to be with children for 5 consecutive hours each day), (b) scheduling recess into areas immediately adjacent to physical education classes, (c) scheduling different grade levels into the same physical education class, and (d) absence of administrative support when classroom teachers were responsible for moving children from homerooms to physical education class areas.

4. *Teacher aides.* The teachers continued to experiment with various ways of using their assigned aides, but those efforts were limited by what they regarded as salient handicaps. The aides were untrained, underpaid, often unmotivated, and not available for preclass planning and preparation. Although they regarded the presence of aides as worthwhile, they found the situation more often problematic than supportive. In many instances, aides were delegated to supervision of recreational activities for some fraction of the class so that the teacher could focus on instruction with the remainder. Offers to spend their own out-of-school time in developing the capacities of their aides had been ignored by school administrators.

A Researcher's Perspective

The data reveal some interesting discontinuities. Despite considerable difficulties in the workplace environment created by administrative decisions, the 3 teachers were at least for the present delivering instructional lessons, rather than just activity periods for their students. The data show the bulk of class time devoted to skill practice, with a strong emphasis on developing a sound base of movement capacity. Even when they had to employ teaching practices they regarded as inferior and even when they knew that their classes were by definition developmentally inappropriate for their students, the teachers had persisted—and they delivered as professionals.

What they reported as their daily experience, however, was almost entirely dissonant with that external evaluation. The authors characterize the 3 teachers as feeling isolated from the main stream of life in their respective schools and as perceiving themselves as marginalized into a deep sense of powerlessness. The teachers saw no hope of influencing administrators, who were seemingly being driven by their own demons, and no hope of recruiting support from classroom colleagues or parents (apparently, they had tried without success). Even the one form of compensation offered by administrators, the assignment of teaching aides, had come to be regarded as an exceedingly poor trade for classes of reasonable size.

> The authors characterize the 3 teachers as feeling isolated from the mainstream of life in their respective schools and as perceiving themselves as marginalized into a deep sense of powerlessness.

Perhaps most serious of all, the evidence in the interview data suggested that the teachers felt betrayed by an administrative strategy designed to simultaneously satisfy two needs. By doubling class size in physical education, administrators could meet the state requirement for daily physical education and at the same time provide a needed increase in planning time for classroom teachers. The result was a condition best characterized as "withdrawal" by the teachers. Fighting for change seemed pointless when the creation of their present set of difficult circumstances was used as "the solution" for other problems within the school.

 A Teacher's Perspective

Qualitative research derives much of its power from the clarity with which it describes the experiences of the participants, and this result is made most obvious when those descriptions match what we experience in our own lives. The 3 teachers in this study expressed exactly what the teachers I work with say repeatedly, and they also described teaching conditions identical to some that I have encountered. The enthusiasm of our professional organizations notwithstanding, effective teachers everywhere have serious doubts about the wisdom of a campaign for daily physical education that runs ahead of the political commitments required to fund it adequately.

The strongest and most respected teachers in my district say that they do strongly support the idea of daily physical education, but they would rather have children come to class once every 3 days in single classes versus trying to teach multiple classes that meet simultaneously 5 days a week. Larger but more frequent physical education classes may result in a higher total of "exercise time" but also yield far less progress in learning and a much lower quality of experience for the children.

Dedication to the proposition that the teacher's first job is to teach the subject matter of skillful physical activity—rather than just supervise exercise—has led to repeated clashes between such leading teachers and those who have championed the idea of daily physical education. Veteran physical educators often feel that a lifetime of physical activity can only come from positive learning experiences in which students are successful at developing physical skills. They feel incapable of providing the necessary individualized feedback and adaptations required to produce such positive growth when they also must engage in crowd management. Those who espouse the alternative position (daily physical education through increased class size) see appropriately intense, actual physical activity as the most important (and politically advantageous) educational service to provide to children—with quality interaction, skill learning, and acquisition of related knowledge as desirable but distinctly secondary goals.

So, what should all this say to us? To me, it underscores four factors that appear to be related to the conditions so starkly described in this report. First, we have to get active early in the game, not after the changes that we don't want have already been made. In the schools that I have worked in, I have been taught such a lesson in terms that could not be missed by anyone. *It is far easier to shape and focus policy while it is being made, than to correct it once it is in place.* Some teachers, like Barbara Brantner at Travis Heights Elementary in Austin, Texas, and Frank Tighe from Canyon Creek Elementary in Round Rock, Texas, consistently model what is

required to influence school policy. They volunteer for school committees (particularly those charged with establishing schedules), attend and hold leadership positions in the PTA, speak at school board meetings, and participate actively in their state professional association. In sharp contrast, many teachers wait until the decisions have been made, then, unhappy with the outcome, ask what they should do.

Attending faculty meetings, volunteering for teacher leadership teams, responding in writing and in person to the early signals of coming change, seeking out allies who will support your positions, and just plain speaking out with carefully planned arguments—all of those are part of not waiting for bad things to happen. Is it worth the effort to invest time and energy in being proactive rather than reactive? You bet it is. Your life's work may depend on it!

A second point underscored by this study is the essential role played by the enormous loyalty and professionalism of the teachers—that the 3 participants in this study had all elected to stay on the job has to be something of a surprise. With 50% of teachers now leaving teaching within the first 5 years after entry, what are the chances that those who stay behind believe their mission is to teach rather than just provide activity? It would seem so much more attractive to leave to do personal training, migrate to the classroom, or just seek out positions with more appropriate expectations, particularly when the struggle is against impossible odds in an environment of low respect.

The study leaves me puzzled about a third point—that aside from the teachers involved, nobody seemed to be concerned. For example, one can only speculate about why the parents of the children in this study were not outraged by a policy that put their youngsters in overcrowded and inappropriately staffed physical education classes. Might it be because their point of reference is a varsity football team with 40 to 60 students on the field every day, forgetting that there are 6 to 10 highly trained and motivated coaches to teach and manage them?

And that point leads me to the fourth and final issue documented by this study—that of using unqualified support staff in physical education. Few businesses could survive a policy of not training people who have direct contact with customers. For example, McDonald's puts every employee through a training program, and their employees are paid significantly less than teacher aides are paid. Why don't we require the same priority of training for those who work directly with our children? With the safety and liability concerns that always are present in the gymnasium, it is amazing that this issue remains largely unattended.

Those, of course, are the kind of arguments too often raised after the damage has been done. To be out front and ahead of the curve, we need to make political skills as much a part of professional training in physical education as learning to give clear instructions. We also need to recruit allies who are likely to be effective in their support. We need to avoid the shotgun approach involving hundreds of signatures on a petition; instead, we need to find and nurture the handful of parents and classroom colleagues who will be noisy, persistent, and well informed.

> **We need to make political skills as much a part of professional training in physical education as learning to give clear instructions.**

With regard to the key policy issues, we need to build beyond any of those desirable actions a sufficiently high level of consensus among our own colleagues to give us the political clout required to just say no! Absent that sort of strenuous initiative, the story told by this report could too easily become the course of our own careers.

Common Ground: Our Shared Perspective

The report makes clear that the authors have reached several conclusions. They have come to view their 3 participants as having decided to just "live with the system." The teachers have no faith that any action can now change their lot. They will continue to deliver fundamentally sound lessons under conditions that yield very little by way of personal or professional satisfaction.

> **They will continue to deliver fundamentally sound lessons under conditions that yield very little by way of personal or professional satisfaction.**

In another direction, the authors cannot resist looking beyond the immediate locale of their study to the sources for advocacy of daily physical education in public schools. They (mildly) conclude that if what they have seen is representative of the results created by mandates enacted without adequate provision for financial support, it behooves policy makers to be aware of such realities. We ourselves wonder if that is an adequate expression of what can be learned from this study. What do you think?

The Impact of Inclusion on Physical Education Teachers

LaMaster, K., Gall, K., Kinchin, G., & Siedentop, D. (1998). Inclusion practices of effective elementary specialists. *Adapted Physical Activity Quarterly, 15,* 64-81.

This report provides a perfect example of how an unpretentious study of modest scope can produce findings that truly help us better understand a complex educational problem. This study about inclusion in elementary school physical education supplements questions with the sharp focus of actual examples, and it directs the reader's attention to the salient issues within a tangled debate about policy and practice.

For the purpose of this study, the term *inclusion* refers to a policy in public education that requires students with disabilities to be educated with their nondisabled peers in regular classes. The concept of inclusion reflects a line of reasoning that calls for a more radical approach to class assignments than that suggested by the phrase *least restrictive environment*, which was the traditional nomenclature when dealing with the curricula for students with disabilities. In practice, the primary focus for inclusion has been mild to moderately involved students who bring special needs to the school environment. As a policy initiative that demands substantial changes in school functions, inclusion has roused a vigorous debate among educators concerning the appropriateness of regular class placements for students who would be so classified. In the field of physical education, however, concerns about inclusion have revolved less around social values and politics, and much more around the practical issues

of appropriate pedagogy and the availability of resources to support implementation.

 ## The Study

This investigation was designed to explore the details of what happens to elementary school physical education teachers when the pupil assignment policy of inclusion is applied to their classes. To reduce the confounding influence of other factors, researchers selected participants from schools that were all located within suburban districts with ample resources and uniformly good reputations.

Participants and Context

The 6 elementary school physical education specialists (5 females and 1 male) selected for investigation had participated in previous research studies of teacher effectiveness. As a result, existing evidence suggested to the investigators that the 6 participants could be justifiably categorized as effective teachers, and testimony from principals, parents, and students confirmed such an assessment. In addition, data from direct field observation had documented their positive teaching style, their organizational and management skills, the degree of respect accorded each by peers in their school community, and the degree to which their programs accommodated children of varying skill levels.

Design and Method

Researchers used an extensive questionnaire to obtain demographic and professional information from the participants. Each teacher was then interviewed by the researchers in a semistructured format, which allowed them to use a preestablished list of questions while also inviting teachers to freely share their experiences and insights.

The initial draft of interview questions was reviewed by adapted physical education specialists who provided feedback and suggestions concerning content and phrasing. A revised draft was then piloted with elementary physical education teachers who were familiar with inclusion but were not participants in the study. The final draft of the interview questions was given to teachers in the study group before their interviews with the request that they reflect on their ideas and experiences concerning inclusion. All interviews were then audiotaped and subsequently transcribed by the investigators.

At the first step of the data analysis, the four researchers read the transcripts independently, each coding the documents for themes that seemed both powerful and reoccurring. They then met to share and compare their initial analyses. Through discussion, the full set of thematic categories were winnowed, merged, and reduced to a single set of themes that appeared to be both reliable and well supported by the data. These were identified by four topical headings: multiple teaching responses, student outcomes, teacher frustrations, and differences in inclusion practices. Later in our annotation for this study, we will use the same topics to organize our presentation of the results.

Two final steps concluded the data analysis. First, each researcher was assigned one of the four topical themes. The researchers then read all six of the interview transcripts, this time identifying every teacher statement related to their respectively assigned themes. The resulting collection of supporting and elaborating quotations was then passed to another member of the research team for an additional check on the thoroughness and reliability of the entire process.

In addition to the interviews, all of the participating teachers were observed while teaching classes. Because members of the research team were already familiar with the work contexts, programs, and teaching styles of the participants, these observations quickly served to refresh memories and

ground all of the subsequent deliberations in a strong sense of immediate reality.

Results

As a way of framing the findings, the report offers the following general comments about the impact of inclusion on the work of teaching. First, the ability of teachers to manage their classes is directly related to the complexity presented by their students. That factor is not the only one in the management equation, but it is a powerful one. Certainly, no one can dispute that the complexity faced by the physical education teacher is exacerbated by using inclusion as the guiding policy in making class assignments. In other words, each consequent increase in student diversity represents an increase in complexity. As you will see, that fact had direct implications for the teachers in this study.

How much impact inclusion has depends on a large number of factors, but at the center for most teachers are the following: (a) the total number of students in the class, (b) the number of inclusion students, (c) the particular kinds and severities of handicaps presented by inclusion students, (d) the number of inclusion students with or without Individualized Educational Plans (IEPs) or Behavioral Improvement Plans (BIPs) that address needs and accommodations in physical education, and (e) the number of aides available for in-class support.

As an example of the increases in complexity created by the presence of inclusion students, the 83 class settings for the participating teachers can be described as follows. Grade levels ranged K-6, and all teachers worked with from four to all seven of those levels. Class sizes ranged from 18 to 30 students, and the number of inclusion students assigned to any one class varied from 1 to 11 (the average number present in class was 5). Of the 195 students with disabilities, 33 had IEPs or BIPs that included reference to physical education. (Regulations do not mandate the preparation of explicit physical education plans for each inclusion student if their disability does not require different learning objectives.) Eleven categories of disability were represented among the inclusion students, including sensory impairments, developmental handicaps, severe learning disabilities, behavioral handicaps, and multiple handicaps. In 7 of the 83 classes, aides accompanied one or several of the students. None of the aides had been trained to assist in the physical education setting.

The complexity in those settings is obvious, as is the central demand on teachers to devise appropriate responses. In this study, however, what occupied the foreground of the teachers' awareness was the immediate problem of managing the sometimes problematic students. At one level was the inconvenience created by inclusion students who simply wandered away from class and who had to be immediately located and retrieved. At another level, however, were the more dramatic disruptions created by students with behavioral conditions. Those were difficult to anticipate, and they frequently brought instruction to a complete halt.

Observation and interview data confirmed that the teachers were highly creative in devising responses to such student management problems, but it also was clear that most of those strategies had ancillary costs to both teachers and other students. Such costs tended to be cumulative and to influence individual lessons and entire units.

Setting aside problems related to student behavior, the teachers were uniformly of the opinion that the central response to inclusion had to be the creation of new forms of individualized instruction. From their descriptions, it was clear that from the beginning the teachers had set out to find ways to meet the special needs and capacities of each inclusion student. Those readers familiar with teaching strategies involving individualization will not be surprised, however, to learn that such efforts often create their own set of management dilemmas. As one of the participants observed, "Sometimes you feel like you are trying to teach two lessons at the same time" (p. 72). Those new demands seemed to create a background of tension that was present in the teachers' struggles to accommodate all of their students.

Nevertheless, creation of units based on individualized instruction was the most common response to the presence of inclusion students: "The more inclusion you have, the more individualized it [instruction] would need to be" (p. 72). As might be expected, peer teaching was often employed as a means of individualizing the pace and content of practice. It's interesting, however, that units that were heavy with direct teacher-centered instruction to the whole class also appeared as a common response to the same set of perceived student needs. In such classes, slowing the lesson down, requiring students to respond in unison, and being very specific with instructions were viewed as necessary accommodations to students with special needs. A complex matrix of factors served to push teachers toward one strategy or the other at different times, for different units, in different classes.

Finally, a form of individualization was achieved through modifications of equipment, games, activities, and class structure. Teachers did report that it was sometimes difficult to maintain a sense of authenticity within familiar activities that had been heavily adjusted to meet special needs. Nevertheless, such strategies appeared to be regarded as worth the creative energy invested.

The participants explained that peer teaching could sometimes be used as a way to use pupils without disabilities as tutors and helpers for the inclusion students. The data show that the teachers found this strategy to work well, often recruiting genuine enthusiasm from the peer tutors; however, it seemed to be only effective with inclusion students who presented handicaps that did not involve behavioral problems. Orthopedic, sensory, and developmental limitations were easily accepted, but conditions that produced erratic or disruptive behaviors generally could not be accommodated in settings for peer teaching.

Considering all of the data accumulated under the topic of *multiple teaching responses*, the researchers came to a conclusion that we can paraphrase as follows. These teachers demonstrated creative, energetic, and persisting efforts to adjust to the additional challenges presented in the form of inclusion students. However, their lack of information about the inclusion students' learning capacities, as well as their lack of specific preparation to cope with such a wide range of student needs, made complete and uniformly effective accommodation an elusive goal in their physical education classes.

Under the category of *student outcomes*, researchers divided the teachers' responses into two general categories: social outcomes and physical outcomes. The former appears to have yielded the more positive results of the two, so we will address that one first. By far, the most positive outcome of inclusion to be identified by the participating teachers was socialization—for all students. The teachers appear to have accepted their role in fostering an accepting class climate, and they also appear to have judged themselves as successful in so doing. They repeatedly expressed concern that the positive socialization outcomes might not be generalizing from the physical education environment to the playground, classroom, and cafeteria; however, they all reported their nonhandicapped students as becoming much more accepting of physical and developmental differences among their peers.

As for outcomes in the areas of motor skills and fitness, teachers felt that learning gains and physical improvements among inclusion students were variable and often severely limited. Repeatedly, the primary barriers cited to greater progress in the area of skills and fitness were lack of sufficient time and absence of assistance from aides. Certainly they had doubts about the ratio between cost and benefits, as one teacher put it succinctly, "I don't know how much these students are really learning [in an inclusion setting] that they would not learn if they were with an adapted PE teacher [a specialist in an adapted physical education class]" (p. 72).

The category labeled *teacher frustration and dissatisfaction* was weighted heavily with a small set of frequently repeated stories, comments, and laments. All of the participants expressed frustration with the lack of training during preservice years, which they identified as the main source of their inability to cope with the diverse needs presented by inclusion. The typical requirement of a single undergraduate course was viewed as having been wholly inadequate for the duties they now had to carry out in classes. They simply said that nothing had prepared them for the growing number of students who needed specialized attention.

In turn, feelings of frustration with regard to their preparation were associated with clearly expressed feelings of personal inadequacy—and even guilt. Lacking familiarity with specific needs and disabilities, teachers often doubted that they were getting through to inclusion students. Ultimately, that frustration and doubt led to more generalized questions about the quality of the work they were doing as teachers.

The remaining interview excerpts in this topical category were largely devoted to two specific concerns. The first was a sense that time and energy devoted to understanding and accommodating students with special needs might be working to the disadvantage of other students. Teachers said that other students too often had to wait while the teacher attended to special needs. The second concern (clearly related to the first) was the virtual absence of help from aides—or from adapted physical education specialists who in some cases were actually present at the district level. Opportunities for consultation with specialists and administrators were reported to be infrequent and of only limited value. The participants described workplace lives that were at the margins of a process that made enormous demands without providing even minimal support.

In the final topical category, *differences in inclusion practices*, teacher comments described circumstances that differed markedly across school settings. The result was that at one site the teacher regularly faced classes for which two to four students with severe behavior handicaps had been

assigned, none with IEPs or BIPs for physical education, none accompanied by aides, and always without support staff available for consultation or assistance. In another school, however, the teacher (who also managed instruction in classes that included the most inclusion students) was able to work with intervention teams formed to provide support for teachers dealing with inclusion students who were considered at risk. In some classes she had the assistance of a trained, full-time aide. In addition, a quarter of the inclusion students arrived with fully explicated IEPs for physical education, and the teacher always had access to the services of an adapted physical education consultant.

One of the consequences of the superior (though still modest) level of support in the latter school was evident in the interview data. The participant who worked in that setting showed clear knowledge of terminology, laws, technical categories, and support services related to inclusion policy. It was clear that while the daily struggle continued to be difficult, some support made inclusion policy seem less mysterious and the attempt to cope feel less lonely.

After considering all they had seen and heard, the investigators reached four major conclusions. We have abbreviated them below.

1. All the participating teachers continued to engage the central problem of teaching for inclusion. There was no evidence of "warehousing" or "babysitting," either from what they said about their work or from formal and informal observation of their classes. That persistence, however, seemed directly related to the equally high level of frustration and feelings of inadequacy that were expressed by all.

2. With the ample resources and generally strong reputations of the school districts involved, it is impossible not to give credibility to the argument that the policy of inclusion, whatever its initial intentions, is now being used to reduce or redistribute resources that otherwise would have been available for special education.

3. All of these teachers, even though they were selected for experience and demonstrated effectiveness, were inadequately prepared to face the challenges of inclusion—and they were fully and painfully aware of that fact.

4. The data show frustration, lack of adequate preparation, and a growing sense of guilt about the quality of professional performance among a sample of teachers who are well above the norm by any relevant standard. Can one imagine what these

data might have looked like if the teachers had been selected at random? If this is what is going on in good schools with effective teachers and adequate resources, what is going on in less fortunate schools?

A Researcher's Perspective

As the investigators underscored in the full published report, the 6 participating teachers represented a "purposeful sample." In other words, they were selected for a reason, in this case because they were demonstrably above the norm on criteria for effective teaching. Although the authors go on to suggest that a more representative sample of elementary school specialists might be expected to fare even less well in an inclusion environment, that hypothesis is no more than speculation.

The 6 teachers also represented a sample of "convenience." That is, they all taught in contiguous districts near the college from which all had received their preservice preparation. I do not note any of those facts because the participants were inappropriately presented as representative of a larger population, and the authors certainly made no such claim. The intended point is that qualitative studies of this type always derive their persuasive power from close examination of particular cases, not from appeals to sampling-based generalizability. It is wise for readers to remind themselves of that specific difference from time to time. The data and analysis in studies such as the present example can reflect only the perceptions of the purposefully selected participants.

> **Qualitative studies of this type always derive their persuasive power from close examination of particular cases, not from appeals to sampling-based generalizability.**

If aspects of your own setting and the people within it resemble the 6 participants and their respective schools, then you should feel encouraged to wonder if some of the same consequences might obtain where you work. Responsibility for that leap of logic, however, is a matter for your own judgment, and it cannot be guaranteed by the design and methods used in the study.

What you should look for in a study such as this one is not arrangements for creating a representative sample but the signs of trustworthiness and credibility. Did the investigators appear to have been careful and systematic in collecting data, and were they appropriately cautious in deriving findings and asserting conclusions? In this instance, you have the advantage of our testimony that such was the case. But if you pursue qualitative reports on your own—and they are generally far easier to consume than accounts of quantitative research—you will have to use a watchful eye and some common sense to answer the reader's critical question, "Why should I believe you?"

A Teacher's Perspective

These frustrations certainly hit home for me. Sometimes the complexity of working with diverse groups of students feels overwhelming. The more complex the environment gets in terms of what different children need, the more likely it is that I am going to feel inadequate as a teacher. As this study suggests, the only way out of that trap is to have or find the support required to do the job—training, administrative policy, expert advice, specialized equipment, direct assistance in the class setting, and clear, individual protocols for response to physical or behavioral disability.

Given the nature of the educational world, if that kind of support is going to be assembled, teachers have to begin by knowing the law, pursuant regulations, and local policy directives with regard to children's rights, in addition to their own rights with regard to the delivery of services. Experience has persuaded me that in the absence of a firm foundation of specific knowledge about those rights, those who end up being cheated are you, the children, or both.

What does not change things is the fact that in many cases nobody in the system intended that to be the result. Acting in the best interest of all your students begins with knowing, absolutely and in detail, what they and you have a right to expect under law and regulation. I find that teachers generally do understand that they must be advocates who actively support the right of children to have access to an appropriate physical education. It is less common, however, to find teachers who understand that being an advocate for their own personal rights is part of that larger process. In other words, they have to look out for themselves professionally if they are to look out for their students. In the complexities of inclusion policy, who will be your advocate if you are not your own?

The first step is figuring out what you need, and the second step is getting whatever it is. The latter may consist of nothing more than just being firm and insistent with your principal, or it may require making special appeals to individuals or groups beyond the walls of your school. But I have yet to encounter a system that lacked someone with the power to produce what was truly essential for teaching. Whether the location is in central administration, parent organizations, the office of special education services, the school leadership committee, or local business groups, someone will respond if your appeal is explicit and clear, with the needs genuine and urgent, and the appeals tenacious.

It was interesting to discover that despite the somber tone of this study (and our accompanying comments) I found aspects that evoked real delight. Hearing about how much teachers learn from having children with special needs in their classrooms was without question a significant part of that pleasure. It matches exactly with what I have found in teaching physical education. As with the participants in this study, I have found that developing peer-tutoring systems not only helps the children with special needs but all pupils—and the teacher. Just having to communicate with the tutors about what I wanted everyone to learn helped me become clearer about what I was trying to teach. It often took only one child coming into the class with special needs to stimulate development in everyone there.

A second thing that delighted me was to discover that the participants in the study reported having learned a lesson that I found entirely familiar. Once you begin individualizing instruction for one child, it is inevitable that you will start to think about how you really should be doing that for every child. That thought can easily lead to feelings of frustration or even inadequacy because one teacher just cannot be all things to every child in a class. Some reflection, however, has usually pushed me to reconsider what I could do to create at least some individualized instruction for all students, and the end result has usually been renewed

effort, change, and growth—and fortunately, not depression.

Once you begin individualizing instruction for one child, it is inevitable that you will start to think about how you really should be doing that for every child.

The third and final source of celebration I found in reading this study was that it stimulated me to remember a time of personal and professional development. In helping children in my classes accept children with special needs, I too had grown in understanding the many ways that all children are alike, regardless of individual differences and needs. Amidst all the difficulty in making inclusion work, what a blessing it is to get better and better at seeing the child first, and only then their special needs.

Common Ground: Our Shared Conclusion

The findings of this study urge the conclusion that physical education teachers need more and better preservice training in all areas associated with adapted programs and related pedagogical skills. That they also need far better in-service support may also be true, but that is a much larger and more complex arena. We think that in this instance, however, improvement can and should begin during initial preparation.

We can't avoid noting that from our perspective, one point was made absolutely clear, even though it was not the investigators' intention to do so. Physical education teachers may be at risk if they are not completely familiar with current special education regulations and local procedures in both their state and district. In addition (and more directly applicable to the teachers described in the present study), administrators of special education at the school and district levels are accountable for the scheduling and class assignments that meet the presumptions of applicable regulations.

Physical education teachers may be at risk if they are not completely familiar with current special education regulations and local procedures in both their state and district.

Collaborative efforts between teachers and those administrators should be the first form of action whenever there are problems in meeting the intent of the legal mandate. Beyond that, however, when regulations are not met in an appropriate manner, teachers should employ formal avenues for appeal, mediation, and resolution that are made available through the regulations of every state.

How Five Years of Experience Changed a Teacher

Ward, P., & O'Sullivan, M. (1998). Similarities and differences in pedagogy and content: 5 years later. *Journal of Teaching in Physical Education, 17,* 195-213.

Truly competent programs of teacher education can produce a graduate who is fully prepared to begin becoming a teacher. Once employed, however, it is the following years of induction into the social context of the school and the daily routines of the work that give substance and ultimate shape to a professional career. What we commonly call "experience" is the process of filling in the detail of what formal preparation can only outline. Frequently subtle, sometimes invisible (to the inductee), and always powerful, the first years of experience are an intensive tutorial on the work of teaching and the nature of membership in a school community.

Every veteran teacher has firsthand knowledge of that process, at least in retrospect. Few of them, however, have had the opportunity (much less the leisure) to observe the details and reflect on the consequences—as it is happening to someone else! The study annotated here will allow at least a sample of such an opportunity. Whether your vantage point allows you to look back, or only forward, we hope you will be fascinated by this account of what "experience" can teach a teacher.

 ## The Study

In this study, the investigators took advantage of a fortunate circumstance to provide us with a rare

glimpse into the detail of how time and experience can work to change both teaching and the teacher. As a beginning elementary school teacher (and as the focus of this study), Ian had been a participant in one of the most comprehensive comparisons of beginning and experienced teachers ever undertaken in the field of physical education.

Published as a monograph ("The Effective Elementary Specialist Study") by the *Journal of Teaching in Physical Education* (Siedentop, 1989), the original study had accumulated a substantial pool of data describing each of the 7 participating teachers. Included in the records for Ian were extensive interview transcripts and numerous videotapes that recorded his teaching in a variety of content units. The present research team was able to visit Ian 5 years later in his 6th year of teaching and replicate the same data collection procedures.

Participants and Context

Ian was observed working at the same school, in the same gymnasium, teaching two of the same units (basketball and gymnastics) to students at the same level (fifth grade). Class size remained essentially the same, and the available space and equipment were unchanged. The district in which Ian worked required physical education for elementary school children twice per week for 40-minute lessons.

Design and Method

Data were collected from basketball and gymnastics units that had remained the same in length (10 and 7 days, respectively) over the intervening years. Three units of analysis—class, students, and teacher—provided subcategories for systematically recording observed events in each lesson. For the class level of analysis, five subcategories were used to describe the use of student time: management, warm-up, transition, instruction, and engagement. At the student level, information was collected for categories that included total number of opportunities to respond (practice trials), number correct, and number incorrect. Finally, the teacher's behavior was described in terms of the tasks set for students, instructional methods employed, and number and type of interactions with students. Data for all of these were recorded live during observation visits by the investigators.

Using videotapes taken during the field visitations, a second trained observer, who was otherwise unconnected with the investigation, coded all of the basketball and gymnastics classes a second time. Interobserver agreement was then calculated for those data and the codes recorded during live observation. The mean agreement for class data (the time-based measures of different class activities) was 89%; for student opportunities to respond, 92%; and for teacher interactions (event-based data), 87%. Additionally, scope and sequence charts were prepared from the videotapes for each unit. When reviewed by Ian, he verified that the data had correctly represented the learning tasks in each unit.

As in the original study 5 years previous, the semistructured interviews following each of the two units were based on questions derived from analysis of the videotapes. All interviews were audiotaped, transcribed, and analyzed as follows. First, Ian's assertions in the interviews were triangulated against descriptive data from field notes; second, a manuscript was prepared containing the researchers' interpretation of the interview data; and third, Ian reviewed the manuscript for general accuracy. He suggested no changes for any of the interpretations, but he did offer additional details concerning his choices of lesson content. Those were incorporated into the document and some appear in this report.

Results

With such a large accumulation of detailed information, the data analysis produced a myriad of results. We will present a brief selection from the more interesting points in that large set, then move to the broad themes of change and constancy the researchers identified in Ian's teaching.

For both the basketball and gymnastics units, when class activities were the unit of analysis, time utilization data were not noticeably different in the 2nd year and 6th year. Ian's classes continued to be characterized by little time expended in management and transitions, less than 10% of class time for each, and by a combined fraction of class time devoted to instruction and practice that approached 50%. When compared with other studies of elementary school physical educators, the data indicate that Ian had begun his career as an efficient manager of time and, particularly in terms of engaged time for student learning, continued to be an effective one as well.

In basketball, however, the results for student opportunities to respond revealed that a sharp shift had occurred over the 5-year interval. The mean number of practice trials per class for each student plummeted from 43 to 10, a shift in the per-minute rate from 3 to 1. The difference can be explained in large part by changes in Ian's instructional methods and task assignments.

The predominant instructional method employed by Ian in both years was a variation of the whole-group, teacher-directed strategy. As a beginner, however, he had used stations for that purpose. Five years later he had abandoned the station format because "managerial disorder" in the form of student disruptions had increasingly served to slow down lessons and reduce active learning time. Without multiple tasks occurring simultaneously and with pupils now proceeding only in unison, the number of times each student had an opportunity to have a try fell accordingly. Ian's classes continued to proceed smoothly with few interruptions and low rates of verbal desists, but a price was paid in decreased student practice.

Ian felt strongly that his students were now less capable of self-control than their counterparts during his beginning years, a view he suggested was shared by most of the teachers at the school. Ian attributed the difference to changing home environments, with larger numbers of children coming from homes in which alcohol abuse, drug use, and related forms of violence were commonplace.

The analysis of learning tasks assigned to students revealed further shifts in Ian's basketball teaching. First, in its present form, students spend less time on more tasks and perform fewer practice trials. The unit now covers more content, albeit with less time per task, but Ian devotes substantially less time to introducing and explaining what he wants his students to learn. That increase in "efficiency" might indicate better mastery of pedagogical content knowledge, but changes in the nature of the tasks suggest an alternative explanation.

In his first year, basketball lessons had been directed toward introducing basic tactics, such as the pick-and-roll, that would allow skillful game play. In those lessons, Ian had been observed devoting considerable time to explaining when and why students should use particular tactical skills. Now the goals for lessons were directed toward simple playground activities such as the ubiquitous "horse" and "round the world" games.

His decision to change instructional content from a focus on game play to playground activities was grounded, he explained, in his sense of what his students could achieve. "I don't do games anymore. I've cut back on what I try to teach them. I've tried to teach defense and tactics and there is no way . . . they cannot manage their own behavior. They cannot referee their own games and what they do doesn't resemble basketball" (p. 202). His stated objective is now to give students enough familiarity with basketball to engage in simple games played in social settings. For that purpose, less instruction and practice along with more superficial coverage of content may serve well enough.

The situation was somewhat different for gymnastics. With a sequential curriculum in place, Ian is in a position to help students refine performance across grade levels. He has retained tasks of approximately the same complexity, but he now includes fewer of them, using a guiding philosophy of "less is more" to produce more skillfulness for some students.

As with basketball, however, his overall level of expectations for student achievement has been lowered significantly. For gymnastics in particular, he points to the increasingly transient nature of the surrounding community. With higher turnover in school population, there is less certainty that cohorts entering at each grade level will have the skills required to progress, which in turn would produce more changes in pedagogy and content on a semester-to-semester basis.

The rate of his interactions with individual students in the gymnastics unit has also dropped sharply over time. He explains this decline by suggesting that he now makes better decisions about what is important instructionally: "I need to give you the basics and maybe a key comment or two, but I have figured out that you need time to practice without me hovering over you saying 'No, put your hands here'" (p. 205). He is now able to utilize routines that provide high predictability in lessons. There is little ambiguity, and expectations for student behavior are clear and consistent.

Again, experience appears to have given him a better sense of what constitutes efficient instruction. That efficiency may have a price, however, as routinization clearly has been achieved at the expense of fresh material and any stimulation that might be provided by change. In the interviews, he rationalized the fact that year after year he sticks close to what is familiar in method and content by observing that to do anything else, to try new content, requires too much time for students to learn the requisite new routines. That loss represents a trade he is unwilling to make.

The resulting repetitiveness of his lessons might be seen as tedious for both student and teacher. The researchers calculated that a student who had been present for the gymnastic unit across Ian's 6 years at the school would have repeated the identical learning routines 350 times. In one sense, Ian has found a strategy that works; in another sense, however, what he has found may be less a matter of instructional mastery and more a very deep managerial/instructional rut.

 **A Researcher's Perspective**

After considering the limitations of conclusions based on a single case, the investigators decided nonetheless that the unique opportunity to revisit a teacher justified a further level of analysis. A survey of the within-case generalizations produced by analysis of observation and interview data led them to suggest three recurring themes in Ian's work: pedagogical reductionism, student typicality, and isolation.

Ian reports that over the years he has come to attempt less in terms of goals for his teaching and expect less from his students in terms of their learning. The before-and-after data confirm that those shifts have taken place. One way of interpreting that pattern of "reduction over time" is to see it as a natural gravitation toward what works. We know, for example, that beginners focus on management while experts are able to focus on instruction and learning. We would expect, therefore, that experience would help Ian refine the balance between the two aspects of teaching. But is that what has happened?

Ian reports that over the years he has come to attempt less in terms of goals for his teaching and expect less from his students in terms of their learning.

The overriding theme in Ian's explanation of the changes he has made and his growing sense of frustration had to do with the effectiveness of his instruction. The interview transcripts are full of references to gains and losses in selecting one instructional method over another. He was continually frustrated in that search because no method could produce the level of student skills he desired. He saw this deficiency in part as the result of changing student abilities that undercut his expectations for their achievement and also in part as the consequence of a system that prohibited him from using powerful methods such as personalized instruction—that is, the system in terms of length of class time, total time assigned to physical education, and the number of students in class. In the light of those issues, he may simply have reduced his pedagogical options to a one-size-fits-all approach.

Other studies of teacher development in physical education affirm that part of growth is the ability to make increasingly accurate estimates of what constitutes the "typical" student in a class. Ian says that experience has indeed improved his ability to make that assessment, but he also complained that what was "normal" now changed from year to year. He saw students in his 6th year, for example, as less competent than those in the previous year: "Students enter school less ready, less capable of learning" (p. 209). What worked in his 1st year didn't work in his 6th because his students, he believed, were different.

Moreover, this perceived change in students affected Ian in terms of his enthusiasm for teaching. In his words, "The joy is missing . . . I think teaching can be extremely fulfilling, but if the joy is sucked out of it, you're just on the assembly line" (p. 209). We must take Ian's report of how he feels at face value. However, what are we to believe about his assessment of changes in student abilities and their readiness (or willingness) to learn? Nothing in the data can confirm or deny those assertions. All we can do is wonder about alternative explanations for what the data show.

The authors of this report suggest that Ian's pedagogy can be made more understandable by framing it in terms of such constructs as reflection, mentorship, and professional development. Over the years, Ian has spent a great deal of time reflecting on questions about his teaching. In that process, however, he always was both speaker and listener. In mentoring, or collegial forms of professional development, the perspective of another teacher enhances the process of reflection. Comparing one's own practices, experiences, and ideas with those of other teachers allows growth that is simply not possible when working alone. In that light, consider Ian's response to the question, Whom do you talk to about physical education?

Ian: "Nobody."

Interviewer: "All year long, there's no one?"

Ian: "No one. Our district never has us meet as a PE contingent." (p. 210)

Ian has been effectively isolated from the common opportunities that teachers use to judge their own work. While he claims that in his 6th year he gets along with everyone, he noted that during his initial years at the school he was shunned by fellow classroom teachers: "It took a while to be accepted into the school. It's just the tradition here to try to ice you out for 3 or 4 years" (p. 210).

The shunning, however, may not have been entirely one-sided. He also reported that in the early years he often ate his lunch in his office because he didn't like the atmosphere in the teachers' lounge. Also, as school and district level professional development workshops focus on classroom teaching or coaching interscholastic sports (which do not interest him), he does not attend, using the time instead to catch up on unfinished work or rest.

From the outside, it is easy to suggest changes that would reduce his isolation and consequent feelings of entrapment. From the inside, however, Ian is not optimistic about achieving any improvements. Now, he even senses that he may not survive without some change in his workplace. "I don't want to get out of teaching. Could I see being driven out of teaching? Yes!" (p. 211)

The study shows that Ian's world now is both similar and different from his 1st year of teaching. It has stayed the same in terms of his use of time, his instructional and managerial routines, and his isolation as a professional. It is most different in terms of his sense of what students can learn and what is appropriate content for gymnastics and basketball.

A Teacher's Perspective

Reading about this study raises so many issues! I am going to pick just a few and concentrate all of my attention on them—though I would not be surprised if other teachers found different concerns to be more urgent. For this discussion, however, I'd like to talk about the following: the importance of student data for interpreting the results from this study, the matter of how we understand the problem of transient student populations in schools, and the topic so poignantly raised here, that of teacher isolation.

Regarding the importance of student data, I was struck once again by the fact that the investigators and all who read their report have been left to struggle with problems of interpretation that can't be resolved without additional information. The study documents changes in Ian's teaching behaviors that he attributes to changes in his students and his consequent search for effective ways of adjusting to those changes. Fair enough, and the description of what he did seems well supported by both the data and a thoughtful analysis. Nevertheless, for me to make sense out of that situation requires another kind of information.

First, we are given nothing about whether the population of the school over the 5-year period actually has changed to become either more transient or more heavily weighted toward students from lower socioeconomic backgrounds, both of which Ian asserts to be true. Second, he likewise tells us that what students learned in the early years was markedly different from what they learn now. Third and finally, the investigators suggest that in making his classes run more smoothly he has created monotony for students.

All three of those points are subject to a degree of empirical verification. In other words, those points need observable, verifiable data to support the validity of the claims made by Ian—and the interpretations made by the authors. To really make sense of what has happened in this fascinating story, we need some additional evidence with which to frame the judgments made!

This is not a matter of catching anyone in a lie or in a miscalculation. It is simply a matter of creating some background that helps us to understand the data. For example, if the student population at Ian's school has not changed nearly as much as Ian suggests, we don't then discard his testimony—instead, we attempt to understand it very differently. Similarly, we can rea-sonably guess that what feels monotonous to an observing researcher might not seem so at all to students who are new to the school, attend physical education only twice a week, and then move on to another school after a few months. We must be careful about assuming more than the facts will bear.

The addition of just a few data points would have made the qualitative data much more powerful for me. Obviously, I think a little information about student demographics at Ian's school would have helped to frame some of the results. Beyond that, the study could have included data on some of the performance indicators for basketball that now are available from professional organizations. With such information, I could have derived much more from Ian's assertions about what his students did and did not learn in the 2nd and 6th year.

At the least, the voices of a few students concerning their experiences in his program would have helped me make better judgments about what to conclude from the study. More specifically, additional data from students would go a long way toward developing a relevant (and richer) context for understanding Ian's story.

Turning now to the question of how Ian appeared to understand the impact of transient students, I wish the researchers had done more to underscore the selective nature of his response. Over 5 years, most of his adjustments dealt with reducing the number and complexity of his goals for student learning. To frame that response properly, you have to realize that an alternative might have been changing his goals to include more attention to confronting the needs of a new population—for example, helping them develop more self-control, if indeed it was lacking.

There is a dangerous tendency to put blame for the problems and dilemmas of teaching onto the backs of students. The alternative view is to blame nobody and just to describe such often very real learning barriers as indications of what has to be taught by us and mastered by our students within the context of our curriculum.

Please don't take that comment as one belittling the impact of high rates of student turnover in physical education classes. I have taught in schools with student transient rates as high as 40%. Little more than half of the pupils who started the year in my classes were still present at the end. It sometimes seemed as though I spent half of my time updating class lists. Turnover is a serious issue that presents a myriad of problems.

As many teachers learn from hard experience, student transience is not just a matter of spending a little extra time to teach class procedures or finding easy ways to alter roll books. The time and effort required to establish management routines for new students in the middle of an ongoing academic year is far out of proportion to the initial investment in September.

Worse, as soon as that in-process effort starts to have some effect, the new class citizens are gone and other unfamiliar faces have appeared. Amidst all of that, we know almost nothing about the impact of transience on the students who do remain. Whether Ian's account of changes in his school arose from his perception or from actual empirical facts (or some of both), he has put his finger on a genuine issue and one that deserves more attention from researchers in physical education.

Finally, the theme that emerged concerning Ian's sense of isolation weighs heavy on my heart. He indicated that he ate lunch by himself at first because he didn't like the atmosphere of the teachers' lounge, although he also indicates that with the passage of time he now gets along well with those same colleagues. More particularly, he notes that he has come to share their view that students have changed in the direction of being less capable of learning.

> **The theme that emerged concerning Ian's sense of isolation weighs heavy on my heart.**

Unfortunately, that all reminds me of my own experiences with enthusiastic new teachers being dismayed by the negative talk about students that occurs in some schools. In the teachers' lounges of such schools, kids are described primarily in terms of their inability today for doing or learning X or Y, always the things that used to be the standard expectation for students.

From the data presented, it is at least possible that Ian tried to avoid being sucked into that negative world; therefore, he found himself painfully isolated. Ultimately, though, he gave in to become one of the gang who now share low expectations for what students can achieve. I know that even some old-guard teachers assigned as mentors in an induction program can spread the same educational poison. In any case, my point is that alternative interpretations of Ian's story are far from impossible. We just don't know enough about Ian's first 5 years, given the limitations of the data available in the report.

It seems fair, however, for me to use the study as an occasion to offer some advice to teachers who are new, either to the profession or just to a particular school. To avoid being isolated, you only need 1 or 2 colleagues, not 25. Identify people who you admire, whose outlook seems mostly positive, and find ways to spend some time with them before or after school, at lunch, or during planning periods.

Contacts with colleagues who work in subject areas other than physical education (or school services other than teaching) are particularly worth cultivating because of their potential for revealing new perspectives on the school, more diverse kinds of information, and a better understanding of how the system works. What begins with a few can gradually be extended to others without the risk of being co-opted into the vortex of complainers, naysayers, and student disparagers. Whatever your interpretation of Ian's story—it does not have to be your story.

Common Ground: Our Shared Perspective

Certainly, Ian's world in his 6th year is not what he would have predicted in his 1st year, nor is it a world in which he is happy. The investigators were persuaded that he knows what has to happen to improve the situation. The difficulty for Ian, as for most teachers, is that systemic changes require both the inclination to act and the power over the resources required to accomplish an action. It is tempting to assume that he knows what has to be done to improve his situation but lacks the necessary support to make the needed changes. Given what we can learn from this study, however, it also is inappropriate to make those general assumptions.

This study could describe the similarities and differences in Ian's lessons, but it cannot help us understand the political and social structures that surround his gymnasium. For now, at least, he must confront that problem alone. In that final fact, his professional isolation, may rest the most powerful explanation for what has happened to him and to his teaching—5 years later.

> **This study could describe the similarities and differences in Ian's lessons, but it cannot help us understand the political and social structures that surround his gymnasium.**

How Veterans and Rookies Planned a Class

Griffey, D.C., & Housner, L.D. (1991). Differences between experienced and inexperienced teachers' planning decisions, interactions, student engagement, and instructional climate. *Research Quarterly for Exercise and Sport, 62,* 196-204.

Many ways exist to design studies about teachers and the work of teaching physical education. At the outset, one of the most important decisions facing investigators is whether to frame their question in broad and general terms or to narrow the inquiry to a single, specific focus. There are advantages and limitations to either choice, and the final decision is often as much a matter of personal judgment as it is a function of hard and fast scientific rules.

 **The Study**

In this study, the researchers elected to take a wide view, setting up their procedures so as to record observations of different kinds, all related to the basic question suggested in the title above: What are some of the important differences between veteran practitioners (those with many years experience) and rookies (those just graduating from their programs of professional preparation) when asked to plan and teach actual lessons? In addition, some of the experienced teachers used in the study have strong reputations as effective physical educators. The contrast between how they approach and execute a lesson versus how the study's inexperienced beginners perform the same task therefore offers an opportunity to clarify exactly the valuable lessons

teachers have learned on the job that preservice programs did not (or could not) provide.

As teacher educators themselves, Griffey and Housner were looking for findings that might be instructive for developing stronger training programs—for skills, knowledge, or even habits of mind that might give their graduates a stronger push toward mastery of important professional skills. They knew full well, of course, that not all the lessons related to effective practice can be absorbed by a trainee or even by a new teacher navigating the difficult early years of teaching. Some things can be appreciated or understood only after substantial experience has provided the foundation of an appropriate perspective on the work of teaching children. In addition, younger teachers can approach some issues only after they have mastered the basics that cause distracting anxiety, which usually include the difficulties of class management. Indeed, there even may be things that certain veteran teachers are able to do with great success that should not even be attempted by a beginner.

Those reservations notwithstanding, many things veteran teachers do could have a place in preservice study, even if they served no purpose other than to alert novices to the vital opportunities for professional growth that lie ahead. Moreover, all of this is not just relevant to the work of preparing new physical educators. What effective teachers do are clues that can help us understand the nature of effective practice, particularly when those acts can be associated with desirable outcomes. Any teacher, irrespective of level of experience, will for that reason have an interest in what distinguished the performances of the veterans and rookies in this study.

Participants and Context

Identified by peers and principals as effective practitioners, 8 urban elementary physical education teachers were matched with 8 preservice students who had been prepared as elementary physical educators but had not started their first year of teaching. All data for the study were collected in the venue of a university summer sports camp.

Design and Method

The participants in both groups were asked to plan and teach two lessons, one on dribbling in soccer and the other on dribbling in basketball. The study therefore involved a total of 32 lessons, each class consisting of 4 students ages 7 to 9.

For audiotaping purposes, teachers were asked that while planning their lessons they "talk aloud" all of their thinking processes, including concerns, intentions, and final decisions. All were provided with any information they requested concerning students, teaching context, and equipment, and all of the lessons were videotaped for subsequent analysis of both teacher and student behaviors. The planning audiotapes and lesson videotapes were then used to extract a wide range of information, including such things as teacher instructions, student-teacher interactions, student engagement in learning tasks, and class atmosphere. For the present purpose, however, we will just focus on how the teachers in the two groups went about planning their lessons.

Results

When planning, teachers in both groups asked for the most obvious points of information: "How many students? How old? What previous experience? How much time? What materials and equipment?" Experienced teachers, however, asked for much more information about the lesson environment itself. For example, nearly all of the veterans asked to actually see the lesson site in advance, a request that did not occur to most of the novices. Further, the experienced teachers asked a much larger num-

ber of questions than did the rookies. For instance, they wanted to know a great deal about the ability and previous experiences of their students—again, a point that received little attention from the inexperienced instructors.

As for the specifics of the instructional plans, the topics treated by both groups appeared at first glance to be quite similar. Both included general plans for use of time, class structure, formations, and learning drills. The differences, however, rested in several specific areas that reside just beneath the broad outlines. First, the veteran practitioners made explicit plans for what to do if the students had unanticipated characteristics or responded to the original lesson in unexpected ways. In short, they anticipated the need for adaptations when things did not go as planned. Second, they specified exactly what points would be emphasized in each activity, including even the precise words to use to describe key points. Third, they were much more concerned with smooth and economical management, which included considerations such as transitions between tasks, placement of demonstrations within the lesson, frequency and type of feedback, and how to start and stop activities. None of these three categories of planning attracted more than minor attention from the beginners.

If you wonder whether those differences in planning were associated with any clear differences in the 32 lessons actually taught, the answer is yes—absolutely—and in many different ways. It's not surprising that virtually all of the results from analysis of the videotapes favor the lessons executed by the experienced teachers. What you might find less readily anticipated, however, is the fact that many of the things observed could have been predicted on the basis of those "think aloud" plans. Teachers who make contingency plans, for example, tend to handle the need for lesson adjustments much more smoothly than do teachers who are caught entirely off guard. The report contains many examples of this kind of fit between plans and various aspects of the actual lessons. Discussing individual instances is beyond the scope of this annotation, but all are reported in the original study in a clear and nontechnical style, completely accessible to practitioners and lay readers alike.

 **A Researcher's Perspective**

The differences between the plans of experienced and inexperienced teachers left me with a rather strong overall impression. The veterans did not simply plan a sequence of activities that would fill the available time; instead, they created managerial schemes for efficiently using those activities to change what particular children knew and could do. To do that, they thought it important to plan in much greater detail than did the novice teachers. They chose to give more thought to the adjustments that might be needed, the possible problems that might arise, the efficient use of time, and an exact definition of what they expected students to learn.

Some of these differences certainly must have arisen from the fact that the beginning teachers lack accumulated experience on the job, which leaves them with much less to think about when faced with planning a lesson. When making plans, you surely can't consider what you never have encountered. Is that, however, the whole explanation for what Griffey and Housner observed? Were there some aspects of novice planning that were ignored or insufficiently considered, not because the inexperienced teachers had never done full-time teaching in real schools but because those aspects were not presented in their preservice preparation programs (or were not given sufficient emphasis and opportunity for practice)?

For example, planning for how to move students from one activity to another is a small point and one mostly ignored by the rookies, but it appeared to be associated with the much greater waste of instructional time in lessons taught by the inexperienced teachers. It is my judgment that attention to transitions when planning a lesson does not require extensive experience. At this point, you might find it interesting to go back and consider the other differences between the plans of the two research groups. Which ones do you think really require the accumulation of years in the gym, and which ones might profit from serious attention before careers begin?

> **Planning for how to move students from one activity to another is a small point and one mostly ignored by the rookies, but it appeared to be associated with the much greater waste of instructional time in lessons taught by the inexperienced teachers.**

A Teacher's Perspective

This study brings to mind the idea that teachers go through various stages in their careers. At first, they worry mostly about being liked by the kids, and their definition of a successful lesson is one in which they don't end up looking foolish. They then gradually begin to focus more on creating lessons that work, in the sense of simply not falling apart. Only later do they reach the stage where they are more concerned about whether or not the students are learning what the lesson was intended to teach. In this study, some of the beginning teachers may even have been most concerned about whether their lesson plans looked professional to the researchers.

I do have some takes on the behaviors of those rookie teachers that are a little different from the interpretations of the authors. Looking at the greater number of questions asked by the experienced teachers, I suspect you may be seeing that one of the benefits of experience is confidence—in this case, the kind of confidence in your own ability that allows you to feel comfortable asking questions. Having learned the value of background information, the veterans were not uncomfortable in asking for it. Teachers who are at that level are not concerned with "looking bad" or seeming to show their ignorance. From the perspective of the other direction, the beginning teachers may have stopped asking questions because they simply didn't want to seem less than prepared to do the teaching.

> **Having learned the value of background information, the veterans were not uncomfortable in asking for it. . . . the beginning teachers may have stopped asking questions because they simply didn't want to seem less than prepared to do the teaching.**

That way of looking at the study leads me to think that we need to focus more on helping inexperienced teachers believe that asking questions and getting information is an okay thing to do, an important way to learn and something that is really valuable when you are designing lessons. That adjustment would begin, of course, by treating all of their questions respectfully.

Another way to look at the difference in the number of questions asked by the two groups of teachers is to think about it in the same way that Graham, Holt-Hale, and Parker (1998) have analyzed skill acquisition in their book *Children Moving: A Reflective Approach to Teaching Physical Education*. In the beginning of skill acquisition, learners proceed through what the authors call the stage of *precontrol*— that is, if the learner succeeds at anything, it is by accident. Then they begin to *control* some parts of the movement and can therefore be more successful, but only if they can really concentrate completely on what they are doing. Once they can do the movement while noticing other things, such as what other players might be doing, and are really able to use the skill in actual performance, they are at the level the authors term *utilization*. Finally, the students learn to do what a skilled athlete can do—pay attention to everything going on around them, let their movements run on autopilot, and execute the skill without any conscious control.

My guess is that young teachers go through stages that are a lot like the way Graham, Holt-Hale, and Parker describe learning a physical skill. At first, they have to concentrate fully on one or two aspects of teaching—giving information, organizing the class, providing feedback—but the moment they have to pay attention to anything else, such as some kind of student misbehavior, their lesson falls apart! Then they can't even remember the learning cues they were going to focus on.

The end result is that the novices in this study may have been wise in not asking for more information than they possibly could use. A lot of the questions the experienced teachers asked may have dealt with teaching decisions the beginners were not even going to attempt—and perhaps at some level, they already knew that.

I had read this study some time ago, and one of the things that is not reported in our summary is the fact that in the actual lessons, the beginning teachers allowed a lot more comments and input from their pupils. My first reaction was to think that doing so reflected the simple fact that novice teachers do not have as good a sense about when to draw the proverbial line and get on with the lesson. You can learn to push on like that only when you have a lot of confidence in yourself.

On the other hand, we also know that pupils always feel a lot more involved in a learning activity if they have had some input into decisions about what that activity is and how it is run. My own experience tells me that when you can manage to create that sort of student involvement, it can have a positive influence on both practice and learning. In that regard, it might have been helpful if the study had included some record of how the pupils rated the lessons. Perhaps we might learn something or at least be reminded of something by considering what the beginners did—that the veterans did not do.

Finally, although I do value the organizational skills of expert teachers, I sometimes wonder if we haven't lost track of other values in learning to run really smooth classes. Quite simply, I miss the opportunity for relaxed fun with children. Class management is important, but it is not the only thing that matters. Perhaps there are times when an unstructured format might teach us a different lesson about what is effective in the gym.

Common Ground: Our Shared Perspective

Results from this study match almost perfectly with results from other investigations that explore the nature of effective teaching, many of which use very different methodologies. The use of teachers with sharply contrasting levels of experience also helps to clarify and sharpen what we have come to understand about effective teaching. The inclusion of lesson planning as a variable in the design allows one conclusion that we have found particularly useful. There are many people, some physical educators among them, who harbor doubts about the importance of planning as an influence on what teachers really do and particularly on its relationship to what are known to be effective forms of instruction. If you are among them, perhaps you will want to think again.

> **There are many people, some physical educators among them, who harbor doubts about the importance of planning as an influence on what teachers really do . . . If you are among them, perhaps you will want to think again.**

Many factors influence the end result of planning: how much time teachers have to plan, if they plan every day, whether or not they typically commit their plans to paper, and which of many formats they employ. The questions asked in this study, however, have allowed us to learn something unequivocal about the 8 veterans involved. First, they knew how to plan; second, they planned in sophis-

ticated and complex ways; and third, they created plans associated with lessons that were in many ways superior to those produced by inexperienced teachers. We conclude that teacher educators and practitioners, at all grade levels, with all degrees of experience will find it helpful to match their own habits of lesson planning with those of the 16 participants in this study.

PART VII
Assessment As Part of Teaching

THE STUDY

RESEARCHER

TEACHER

COMMON GROUND

Using Skill Assessment to Build Effective Lessons

Kelly, L.E., Dagger, J., & Walkley, J. (1989). The effects of an assessment-based physical education program on motor skill development in preschool children. *Education and the Treatment of Children, 12*, 152-164.

This modest investigation offers perfect illustration for a number of the points we have emphasized in our reading guides. First, some studies are valuable simply because they deal with people or topics that have received little attention. Here, for example, the study deals with a program of physical education for preschool children, a topic and an age group that have received little attention by researchers. Second, even a small study that has obvious limitations can nonetheless be conducted with great care and precision. In this instance, not only did both teachers and external evaluators receive special training, but their work was also carefully monitored to ensure that they performed their assignments reliably. Third, sometimes a truly important result has little to do with the intended purpose of the study, as is the case for what you are about to read.

 **The Study**

This research was designed as a quasi experiment to test how well children would learn when taught with a particular method—and the findings indicate that they learned very well indeed. In fact, they learned significantly more than similar students in a control group who did not receive instruction. For some readers, an equally interesting fact, however,

might be that they did so in a 12-week unit, using classes that met only twice each week. It was a program of truly modest intensity.

Participants and Context

In this study, 47 preschool children (27 female and 20 male), ages 3 to 5 years, came from two preschool programs. One offered two 50-minute periods of physical education each week, and the other one offered daily, supervised recess periods with no physical education.

Design and Method

For 12 weeks, the children taking physical education received instruction in six basic movement skills: underhand ball roll, two-hand catch, instep kick, overhand throw, horizontal jump, and sidearm strike. The teachers were trained and certified in use of a basic skills curriculum model that emphasized direct instruction in specific motor skills and frequent checks on student progress. In turn, that progress information was used continually to design and revise lesson plans that would best meet the needs of individual children and the class as a whole. Meanwhile, children at the other school continued with 12 weeks of supervised free play during recess.

Results

The performance of all 47 children on the six motor skills was tested both before and after the 12-week program. Trained investigators used videotapes to rate the performances through use of carefully devised standards. In one respect, the findings confirmed what every teacher knows. Although they were basically the same at the start, the group with physical education classes had after 12 weeks improved substantially in all six skills and the recess group had not changed at all. Even with a fairly simple research design such as this, we can be certain that some combination of instruction and practice (and, perhaps, familiarity with having adults watching and evaluating performance attempts) had produced learning. But, surely, you could have predicted that outcome. If so, of what value is the study?

A Researcher's Perspective

If you adjust the perspective just a bit, I think you might find the results both useful and intriguing. First, were you truly certain that children in preschool would profit so dramatically from formal and rather highly structured physical education classes? If you were to look at the accumulated research studies that have been done on that topic, you might not have been so sure because there are very few and I know of none that could be considered definitive. Provided that the students in this study are reasonably representative of preschool children everywhere, this study should give you confidence that many of them can learn a wide range of basic motor skills without serious difficulty.

Second, what part do you think was played by the effort to continually adjust daily lesson plans on the basis of feedback from evaluations of student progress? Was keeping close track of learning just a frill and another burden on the teachers' limited time and energy? Did using assessment information to revise lesson plans as the unit went along have enough payoff to make the extra effort worthwhile?

Again, this simple experiment cannot provide an unambiguous answer to those questions, but several conclusions are certain. Clearly, using progress information makes logical sense. It did not harm or limit learning, and it is here associated with gains in mastery of complex motor skills that would otherwise be considered impressive for any group of

learners. To me, that sounds like a reasonable basis for preschool physical education teachers to invest some time in reading the original study and perhaps trying some of those ideas in their own classes (the original study, by the way, has a great deal more detail about the program and the task of assessing student progress).

Finally, did you notice how small the investment of time was relative to the results? That topic was not the focus of the investigation, but a smart reader pays attention to all of the findings—whether intended or not! Do the math: 50 minutes, twice a week for 12 weeks provides 20 hours of instruction and practice. As any experienced teacher knows, the total learning time was probably substantially less, even in a well-organized class. At the end, 47 children had made progress toward mastery of six important skills that can serve them for the rest of their active lives: catching, kicking, striking, throwing, and rolling objects, as well as jumping. Those are the kinds of results that parents and school administrators like—important in nature, substantial in degree, dependable across pupil variations, and economical in cost.

> **At the end, 47 children had made progress toward mastery of six important skills that can serve them for the rest of their active lives . . .**

A Teacher's Perspective

My immediate response to this study is "Yes! Yes! Yes!" Although physical education teachers believe that teaching does make a difference in how students perform motor skills, a great many people do not share that view. Among the people I talk with, including some classroom teachers, it is much more common to believe that children are either born with the ability to move skillfully or they are not. The possibility that physical education classes and instruction can be a potent factor in that equation is simply not considered. It is a curious fact (at least to me) that the same people will honor the ability of athletic coaches to develop motor skills in the same children. How often we hear, "Oh yes, Andrew had a great coach in Little League who really taught him sound fundamentals."

At the most basic level, what this study does is show the teacher that it is possible to actually demonstrate, rather than just claim, that good teaching makes a noticeable difference in what the students can do. Usually, you teach your heart out and truly believe that you are making a difference, but it is difficult to show that difference as a hard fact. If we really tell the truth, sometimes even we find it impossible to be sure about what has happened to the performance of each student. There are simply too many pupils, too much going on, with everything moving too fast, and the next class already waiting at the door. Clearly, putting the improvements in the simple and clear terms of black and white is the way to go, but there's the rub.

Faced with heavy schedules, large classes, and reduced contact time, physical educators have tended to see formal assessment of learning as a luxury they can't afford. Anybody who actually has tried to teach in the typical school context surely can understand that response. That understanding, however, does not change the fact that it is utterly demoralizing when you work hard to produce results that most people don't believe are really there.

> Faced with heavy schedules, large classes, and reduced contact time, physical educators have tended to see formal assessment of learning as a luxury they can't afford.

So, the first thing this study did was to bring me right back to a problem I have struggled to solve over my whole career as a teacher. How do I get information about the learning of students in my class? In the study, the investigators had the instructor and trained evaluators, as well as a teacher aide and a supervisor (neither of whom were mentioned in our brief research summary), to collect assessment data during each class. The teacher then had time to reflect on and discuss that information after each session as part of planning for the next class. I'd love to have that kind of support, but it certainly has never been the situation for any school in which I worked!

In struggling to get out of that catch-22 trap, I have devised one simple way of gathering information about students' progress—without having to use other adults and without devoting too much attention to the recording process. On a sheet of paper, I print out repeated columns of the names of students in a class: five or six such columns, in landscape orientation, on each side of the sheet. At the top of each column, I pencil in a note indicating a key aspect of the skill we are working on that day, such as "side to target" or "opposite foot."

Then, during class I watch for students who are performing that aspect correctly and just draw a line through their names. For students who are really having persistent difficulty, I circle their names. The whole process takes little time, preserves most of my attention for other teaching tasks (feedback, management, encouragement), keeps me focused on the main goals for the lesson, supports my often fallible memory, and creates a hard record of progress for individuals and the whole class.

An added benefit of this technique is that once the names of children who have mastered the skill have been crossed off, the remaining names fairly leap off the page! Such highlighting of students who are having a persisting problem with learning helps me to focus my attention exactly where it is most needed.

A second result of reading this study was to attract my attention to the protocol for lesson plans, training materials, and assessment tools used by the investigators. Some of that information is printed in the full report, but what I want to do is compare the researchers' full protocol for the study with what I am already doing in my own classes. If they were that effective, I want to find out why, which means sending a note to the lead researcher who gave his address in a footnote and invited interested readers to contact him. How convenient—and respectful of readers!

My third response to the study is to point to something that was not emphasized in our summary. This is one of those things that are so obvious that we tend to take them for granted and thus underestimate their importance. When the teacher knows ahead of time exactly what performance factors will be evaluated, they have a powerful tool for focusing what they do when teaching.

It is amazing what focus can do for learning! You can use specific cues as part of instruction; you can check on specific elements of movement during practice; and you can give feedback that is specific to one particular outcome, rather than a lot of other outcomes. When there is a close match between the primary focus for a lesson and what the teacher talks to students about during practice, the feedback is called *congruent*. There can be little doubt that the power of congruence had a part in producing the results found in this study.

I don't at all intend such a comment to be taken as a criticism of the study. It seems to me that the investigators set up exactly the right situation, the one I just described and the one we all should work to achieve. Knowing exactly what you want students to learn, specifying exactly what that learning looks like as a performance, then teaching it for that desired outcome is powerful (yet basic) stuff.

Which skills to focus on and in what order to teach them is, of course, a different problem that also requires a lot of thought and probably some help from motor development research. So, one thing at a time. The lesson in this study is one that all of us need to hear over and over until it really sticks. Find the elements that seem crucial to the performance aspects of each motor skill, then focus on a small set of them in each lesson (two or three, at most). Then, as this study reminds us, devise a simple way to monitor the learning that results.

 **Common Ground: Our Shared Perspective**

This small study can be useful in at least three different ways. First, it encourages us to believe that young children can profit from time devoted to formal physical education; second, it offers provocative clues about how tracking and regularly assessing student progress might contribute to particularly effective teaching; and third, it might even be helpful as evidence in the political process needed to persuade people that such classes are a reasonable investment of educational resources. Certainly the conditions for instruction in this study were much closer to ideal than is typical for public schools, and, of course, there is a great deal more that we must learn about preschool physical education. Nevertheless, we believe it would be hard to find a better place to begin.

> **This small study . . . might even be helpful as evidence in the political process needed to persuade people that such classes are a reasonable investment of educational resources.**

Is Peer Assessment Both Practical and Accurate?

Hill, G.M., & Miller, T.A. (1997). A comparison of peer and teacher assessment of students' physical fitness performance. *The Physical Educator, 54,* 40-46.

Textbooks and teacher educators often assert that multiple benefits accrue from the practice of making students responsible for various aspects of their physical education class. From simple assignments, such as distributing and collecting equipment, to more complex tasks, such as those presumed by reciprocal (peer) teaching, it is suggested that when properly prepared, students can assume important roles in the conduct of their own program. The purported advantages are higher levels of student engagement, a greater sense of student ownership over the learning process, opportunity to practice personal responsibility, and (not incidentally) more efficient use of class time.

For the most part, as attractive (and logical) as those suggested benefits may sound, such outcomes remain unconfirmed by any body of research evidence. In this study, however, the authors give close examination to one form of student responsibility—the task of scoring test performances (for themselves or peers). That particular practice lacks the usual positive consensus of opinion about student participation and has been subject to some debate among physical educators, facts that may lend more than ordinary interest to your consideration of this study.

The Study

On cursory inspection, this study appears to do little more than offer a straightforward answer to a relatively simple question: Can students in fifth-grade physical education classes score and record the fitness test performance of classmates with the same accuracy as a trained adult? In fact, the report does describe both the investigation and the answer to that question, but in the process it accomplishes considerably more.

The deeper issues probed here go well beyond the matter of using peers to obtain assessments of fitness test performance. They pertain, directly or indirectly, to the entire matter of assessment in physical education—whether the measures involve learning movement skills or changes in physical status such as physical fitness. It is a simple fact that most physical educators do not make much use (if any) of student achievement assessments that go beyond the informal and impressionistic. Among the multitude of explanations for this is the fact that large class sizes limit instructional time, and heavy teaching loads make the logistics of formal testing an unsustainable burden.

It has been commonplace for various outsiders to offer advice intended to encourage teachers to use creative strategies that circumvent those logistic barriers. One of the most common recommendations is using students as scorers and recorders for the test performances of peers. The idea is to economize both class time and teacher effort, as well as gain whatever advantages there may be in fostering student responsibility for serious assessment tasks. Practitioners have responded less than enthusiastically, however, citing concerns about the accuracy of such peer-generated information and the new logistic/management problems created by peer testing. And so the argument goes round and round, without much change in the gym.

The authors of this report do not pretend to have resolved the complex issues surrounding the uses of student assessment in physical education. What they did attempt was to tackle head-on the question of whether conditions could be designed that would allow students to accurately score each other's fitness test performances. Both their method of investigation and the results obtained may hold some interesting surprises for you.

Participants and Context

While working in small groups that rotated through testing stations, 54 students in two fifth-grade physical education classes scored and recorded each other's performances on four strength and flexibility items selected from the Fitnessgram fitness test battery.

Design and Method

In each class, students were assigned randomly to work groups, within which they cycled through the roles of test taker, scorer, and recorder at each station. All selection and testing was accomplished in a single 1-hour class meeting.

A number of important conditions formed the context for the peer-testing effort. First, it occurred at the end of the semester and had been preceded by an earlier teacher application of the same tests. Second, the teacher used students to model correct form for each test and specified exact procedures for scoring and recording results. Third, signs with diagrams and keyword reminders were posted at each of the test stations. The fourth and final element in the testing environment, however, was an unusual provision for assessing the accuracy of the scores produced. Four previously trained adults were present (one at each station) to score and

record all of the student test performances. Students had been told, however, that the adults were rating members of the work groups on how well they cooperated with each other. The students wore name tags, ostensibly for the purpose of distinguishing among group members but actually to allow assignment of individual fitness test scores. In the end, the test session was completed without incident, all score sheets were completed in correct fashion, and students gave no indication of having detected the "deception" employed in the research procedure.

Results

Appropriate analysis of the scores produced by students and those by the adults revealed close agreement. For two of the tests (trunk lift, sit-and-reach) the scores were either identical or only fractionally different. For the two others (push-ups, curl-ups) the separation was small and of neither statistical nor practical significance—for example, the average number of curl-ups counted by adults was 31 while the students counted 35. The latter test items require a degree of subjectivity in determining whether a given performance meets the test criteria for correct form; thus, they might be expected to produce a slightly greater variation in scoring.

For all practical purposes, peer scoring produced scores that were just as accurate and usable as those produced by trained adults, and this included either giving formative feedback on student progress or calculating a summative measure of student achievement. Further, the testing had absorbed only a single hour of class time and the investment of only modest teacher effort in planning and preparation.

 **A Researcher's Perspective**

Many questions can be raised concerning this study and what we might learn from it. As part of their report, some of the most important questions were raised by the investigators themselves, a fact that always should increase your confidence in the credibility of what is claimed. They point out, for example, that it may have been the presence of unfamiliar adults (even under the conditions of deception) that constrained the students to be so careful and accurate in scoring their peers. They also acknowledge that the same assessment procedures might not work well with tests requiring more complex scoring and that younger students might not be able to perform with the same reliability.

I feel sure that you could devise ways to confront some of those problems. For example, random teacher checks on accuracy of scoring during the testing might be one way of replacing the influence of adult observers. It is clear, too, that preparation of students and standardization of scoring procedures would be critical elements in any attempt to use peer assessment. There is one limitation within this study, however, that may not be so easily resolved.

In addition to what you may learn about the possibilities for peer assessment, we believe this study gives you an opportunity to consider several important ethical questions. What do you think about deliberately deceiving the participants as a planned part of any research study? What harm might be caused by such action? Does it make any difference that the participants here were children and probably not volunteers? Do the potential benefits of the research and the arguments supporting the lack of other alternatives for methodology make it okay to lie to children? Should the journal have published this particular study?

> **What do you think about deliberately deceiving the participants as a planned part of any research study?**

Those are difficult questions that touch on issues of real substance. Part of your consideration might include speculation about procedures that could have been used to avoid or reduce the problems associated with deception. Investigators must do exactly that in many kinds of studies. For instance, inert starch pills are given as placebos in some medical studies. Although the participants are made aware that some patients will be receiving them rather than the test medication, they also know that neither they nor the investigators will know which pills went to which patients until the completion of the study (such designs are appropriately called *double blind*). A kind of deception still remains in such studies, but it is largely mitigated by careful and honest explanations.

Might the researchers in the present study have introduced the adult observers and simply said they were there to "help if needed"? A degree of deception would still exist, but no outright falsehood. If

adults had been present during lessons in the past, perhaps a better option would have been simply to say nothing about them at all.

A Teacher's Perspective

While they may not be so obviously troubling as the issue concerning deception in research, the problems that attend the reliability of student-reported assessment data are also of real concern to teachers. Assessment loses most of its value if we get incorrect information. In fact, there are actually two issues here: first, the children's ability to make the judgments, measurements, and so on, and second, their willingness to report their findings correctly. Either or both can be inadequate to the task of providing accurate information.

In the first case, wherein mistakes are unwittingly made, future decisions based on the data will be faulty. In situations where this is likely to be a problem, it is better not to spend the time on assessment than to conduct it in ways that yield unreliable information. Counting push-ups and body curls may be well within the capacity of students when, at the same age, counting resting and exercising heart rates is well beyond their ability to produce reliable information. I suspect that many fitness units that depend on the students' counting of rapid pulse rates are encouraging those students to present and use data that they know full well are no more than wild guesses!

Clarity about procedures and the rubrics involved in judgment are the absolutely essential foundation for accurate measurement, which means spending time on explanation, demonstration, and practice. The impressive accuracy shown in the findings from this study were a product of the care taken in preparing the students to do the assessment tasks correctly. If you are interested in trying to use a complex form of self- or peer-assessment in your own classes, I urge you to take the time to see how that can be done by reviewing the original report.

When the capacity to make accurate judgments or measurements is adequately developed but conditions are present in the class that lead children to be deceptive (such as fear of being unsuccessful) a different set of problems emerges—and with those problems there is more to lose than just the accuracy of information. I see it as irresponsible to create an environment in which students may be encouraged to fabricate information (lie) without helping them to deal with the practical and ethical issues related to doing so.

A key element in creating the social forces to which students are exposed when they do peer- and self-assessment tasks is the intended use of the information. When the assessment is being done to provide feedback on progress and instruction for subsequent practice (formative assessment), there is little motivation to provide inaccurate results. In fact, there may even be some intrinsic motivation to be careful and honest in reporting findings.

Conducting self-assessments and partner assessments present the lowest level of ethical risk when they have the least summative consequence—grades, fitness awards, final rankings. If students are made real partners in the learning process and if teachers are prudent about the formative and summative uses of assessment data, the motivation for dishonest reports will be absent for most children.

> If students are made real partners in the learning process and if teachers are prudent about the formative and summative uses of assessment data, the motivation for dishonest reports will be absent for most children.

All of these problems offer a wonderful opportunity for some important teaching. Just describing how assessments can help in planning future actions and what goes into a meaningful measure can be helpful in preparing students for responsibility. Just because the child is not presently able to accurately perform an assessment task does not mean that they should not be exposed to the reasons we have for checking on motor and cognitive achievement. A question even very young children can understand is simply, "How do you know you are getting better?"

I want to close this comment with an encouraging note taken directly from my own classes. The results of this study reflect exactly what I have found in my dealings with student self-assessment. When given clear information about what the standards are, children can be right on the money in their judgments. In one recent class, students rated their performance in the physical and social skills covered at the end of a 6-week period. For example, specific statements such as "I can dribble the basketball while moving around and keeping my head up without losing control," were rated with B for *beginning* ("can do once in a while"), L for *learning* ("can do so long as I am concentrating"), M for *mastered* ("I can do it without even thinking about it"), and P for *problems* ("I am having problems with doing this"). Each time I compared their letter ratings with my own records of their performance during class, I would find almost complete agreement.

One of the most interesting things that turned up in this self-assessment process was the fact that the students who marked P (problems) for the statement "I listen carefully during instructions," were the students who had obvious difficulty in maintaining attention. They knew perfectly well that they had problems—even in such a highly personal and sometimes subtle area of behavior.

Did any students provide what I saw as questionable ratings? The honest answer is yes. A small number would mark M (mastered) for every statement. The 2 or 3 who did so (out of 300) had without exception multiple behavior problems that involved acting out, clowning around, and asking for constant attention. It may be that the need for approval and support for their fragile self-esteem simply overwhelmed their ability to accept their own learning needs.

In contrast, students who took the risk of marking P for their lack of progress on particular motor or social skills opened a wonderful opportunity for me to ask them what they felt caused the difficulty and how I could be helpful. The ensuing conversation led us to a real team effort toward improvement and for me, a much better understanding of what life was like from their perspective. Responding in a reflective fashion was so much more powerful than my simply rating their behavior or skill level as a problem—and *then* trying to help them. Important benefits, such as allowing the child to be in control of identifying problems, can lie beyond such technical matters as accuracy and reliability.

Common Ground: Our Shared Perspective

Your reaction to this study, like ours, will be a matter of personal judgment. We can tell you this much, however, with complete confidence. When it comes to deception, there is at least one standard of behavior among researchers upon which all agree. If people are misinformed about the nature of their participation in a study, the investigator is obligated to later give them a full explanation of how and why that was done (a process called *debriefing*). In that regard, we must tell you that although they may have done so, the authors of this report make no mention of whether their deception was ever explained to the students involved. Reports cannot by their nature include a great many of the small details that go into completing a study. This is one item of information, however, that never should be omitted.

What would be your judgment about this use of deception in research, and how would you decide? We do not want to take a "higher standards than thou" approach to this matter, but it offers an opportunity to discuss one of those difficult issues that both investigators and readers have to think about. It is important for all of us to understand and remember that the answers do not come easily—and especially not without poststudy thought and reflection.

> We do not want to take a "higher standards than thou" approach to this matter . . .

PART VIII

The SPARK Studies: A Program for Teachers and Children

THE STUDY

RESEARCHER

TEACHER

COMMON GROUND

The Impact of SPARK on Children's Fitness and Activity

Sallis, J.F., McKenzie, T.L., Alcaraz, J.E., Kolody, B., Faucette, N., & Hovell, M.F. (1997). The effects of a 2-year physical education program (SPARK) on physical activity and fitness in elementary school students. *American Journal of Public Health, 87*, 1328-1334.

Insiders to the world of physical education will know that in the United States, there have been continuing threats of cuts (and in some states, significant depletions) to the cadre of elementary school physical educators. One result has been an increase in both the number of itinerant teachers who see students only once or twice each week, and the frequency with which three or four classes are combined into a large group for mass instruction. The result is that many elementary school students receive most of their physical education under less than optimal conditions. The same erosion of positions for subject specialists means that in many school districts it is the classroom teachers who must provide the bulk of instruction, if the children are to receive any physical education at all.

Until support develops for hiring more specialists, if there is to be significant improvement in the quality of physical education delivered in public elementary schools, it will have to involve classroom teachers who have had little or no previous preparation to teach that subject. In other words, what will be needed is not only a program with content and methods that reliably produce the desired results with children but intensive in-service teacher training that prepares and sustains classroom teachers in doing the job.

 **The Study**

This study is not only large and complicated; it is one in a closely connected sequence of such investigations that all had as their general purpose the improvement of the quality of physical education delivered to elementary school children. In this quasi experiment, the treatment variable was a specially designed, health-related physical education program for fifth- and sixth-grade students.

Among the many research questions involved were four that lie at the heart of the matter. First, does the program produce the desired outcomes? Second, with training and on-site support, can classroom teachers implement the program? Third, when taught by classroom teachers, does the program produce the desired outcomes? Fourth, when on-site support is eliminated, do classroom teachers persevere in using the program? The entire effort encompassed nearly a decade of work, and the report that served as the source for this annotation described a 2-year study performed near the middle of that period.

Participants and Context

Seven schools participated in the study: two in which all classes were conducted by certified physical education specialists who were trained to implement the program Sport, Play, and Active Recreation for Kids (SPARK); two in which all classes were taught by classroom teachers who were trained to teach the SPARK curriculum; and three in which all classes were taught by untrained classroom teachers who continued with whatever was their usual contribution to physical education. All seven schools were provided with the same level of material support for physical education classes (balls, cones, etc.). Program results were measured for two entering cohorts of students (955 fourth- and fifth-grade pupils) whose beginning and end-of-year scores were obtained over the 2 years of the study. Classes in the four SPARK schools met for an average of 3 days each week for a duration of at least 30 minutes.

Design and Method

Creators of SPARK designed the program as a health-related curriculum that emphasized increasing the amount of moderate-to-vigorous physical activity, both during the physical education classes and out of school. The program involved units that were enjoyable to children, included the teaching of motor skills, and promoted high levels of physical activity. To help the children generalize SPARK program content to regular physical activities outside of school, teachers included a substantial self-management component in the curriculum. Taught in weekly, 30-minute classroom modules, this part of SPARK included goal setting, self-assessment, self-reinforcement, self-instruction, and problem solving. Out-of-school activity was monitored through use of accelerometers—small sensors that when worn by children could detect and record the frequency, duration, and intensity of their physical activity.

All teachers using SPARK were given instruction in program content, instructional skills, and class management, and they were also provided with supervision and on-site support. Researchers observed teachers and their students throughout the study to ensure that the SPARK curriculum was implemented as intended. Measures of muscular strength and endurance, cardiovascular endurance, and level of out-of-school physical activity produced data that were used to assess the impact of physical education as provided under the conditions in each school.

Results

The three conditions for physical education produced substantial differences in what happened in classes, as well as in the test scores for children. It will not surprise you that the children in the non-SPARK programs taught by untrained classroom teachers had test scores that were at the bottom on just about every measure used in the study. If you are not an elementary school veteran, however, you will be surprised to learn that a contributing factor in those lower performances was the fact that children in those schools simply had a lot fewer physical education classes. No matter what standards were urged or how much equipment and space were made available, classroom teachers just did not manage to get their pupils into the gym as often. Without the encouragement and support of a strong in-service development program, it seems that there were too many other important things to do.

Even when there actually were classes in the non-SPARK schools, the children engaged in significantly less physical activity. Put another way, the students taught by the SPARK-trained specialists had twice as much moderate-to-vigorous exercise during class as children taught by classroom teachers who lacked preparation and support, with pupils in the classes of the SPARK-trained classroom teachers falling between the two. That pattern was in fact often repeated in the results for class observations and test scores: specialist-led classes at the top, trained teacher-led classes somewhat behind, and untrained teacher-led classes lagging far to the rear.

Of particular interest is the fact that in a number of fitness and activity areas, girls made significant gains from baseline to the final measurement. Girls in the specialist-led classes obtained the largest fitness-gain scores in cardiorespiratory endurance as well as muscular strength and endurance. Although some of that happy result reflects the fact that boys have much higher levels of fitness at baseline (and thus have less margin for improvement), it always is important to find a circumstance in which girls can begin to close the gender gap.

 **A Researcher's Perspective**

When a sound physical education program is tracked over a lengthy period of time (researchers call such studies *longitudinal*), can it show positive results in elementary school children's physical status? The results here say yes, and they do so emphatically. That finding may vary somewhat with different fitness and health measures or it may be shaped by how well the program is planned and implemented, but the answer is the same in the end—yes! Can classroom teachers implement such a curriculum with reasonable fidelity if they are given training and continuing support? Certainly they can; the results make that absolutely clear. But at the end of the year, will their students show the same superior test scores as the pupils of real physical education specialists? Unhappily, the answer there is a firm no, and by a substantial margin. They will outscore their peers who spent the year with untrained classroom teachers, but they will also have missed out on benefits they might have gained with physical educators.

There was a subsequent study in the SPARK series, one that examined what happened when the 2 years of on-site support was gradually phased out. We won't attempt to report its findings, if only for the reason that they are more complicated than you might expect. Two facts from that study, however, were simple and clear, with both good news and bad news. The SPARK-prepared classroom teachers persevered and continued to deliver a physical education experience that was superior to that offered by their untrained peers. For example, they maintained physical activity levels at about 88% of what had been observed while the original SPARK study was in progress. In that same follow-up period, however, they tended to move away from dedicating time to really trying to teach motor skills and instead drifted toward the familiar pattern of just playing the games as a recreational activity.

In the end, our minds were pushed in the direction of a less than happy conclusion. Both in the study reviewed here and in others in the SPARK research program, the data make clear that if classroom teachers are to be responsible for the physical education of children in this nation, they must be provided with well-designed preparation and continuing on-site encouragement, supervision, and support. Even under those conditions, the resulting impact on children is likely to be inferior in at

> **If classroom teachers are to be responsible for the physical education of children in this nation, they must be provided with well-designed preparation and continuing on-site encouragement, supervision, and support.**

least some respects to what we might have obtained through the use of trained specialists. If that is true, then we can only conclude that in the long run it would be more cost-effective to have employed physical education specialists in the first place.

 ## A Teacher's Perspective

Does this study mean anything to us as physical education teachers? Well, it certainly gives us some cause to celebrate. Even if it only validates a subjective impression among us that is nearly universal, it should improve our self-esteem by simply substantiating the fact that as specialists we do deliver a better educational product than classroom teachers. In addition to that implicit message, I gained several other impressions that were less obvious but perhaps more important.

The specialists trained to deliver the SPARK curriculum produced classes with substantially more student activity time than what you will find in previous studies of classes taught by physical education specialists. This means that many of us might well take a close look at the instructional methods used in the SPARK program as a means for ensuring that our own classes match the activity levels observed in this study (copies of the SPARK curriculum are available from the San Diego State University Web site at **www.foundation.sdsu.edu/projects/spark/index.html**).

In addition, there are sobering implications in the gender-specific results. Scores for the girls on the sit-ups approached those of the boys after 2 years in the SPARK program. No parallel shift was seen for girls in the 3 control schools where untrained classroom teachers delivered the physical education program. Although boys' scores may have been suppressed by a ceiling effect, the significant gains by girls opens the possibility that in the control programs their potential for performance and improvement had somehow been restricted. A thought that should give us serious pause is the implication that physical education classes taught by classroom teachers might actually suppress girls' natural expansion of physical strength and ability, as well as their motivation.

A thought that should give us serious pause is the implication that physical education classes taught by classroom teachers might actually suppress girls' natural expansion of physical strength and ability, as well as their motivation.

Another aspect of this study that attracted my attention was the fact that for their instructional roles in SPARK, classroom teachers received 32 hours of in-service training (7 half-day sessions over the school year). That commitment of time and resources exceeds any time awarded to in-service training for any subject matter in districts with which I am familiar. And yet, in terms of gains for health and fitness, the classroom teachers' pupils continued to trail those of the specialists by a substantial margin.

Data from rigorous studies such as this should be brought to the attention of school board members at the time of budget construction. These types of studies have implications for the support of teacher development that go far beyond our immediate concern for the slice of resources reserved for physical education. Significant improvements in teacher performance require investments of time that are far greater than those usually allowed. What may account for the often disappointing results produced by efforts at school reform is the sharp contrast between what usually passes as in-service teacher development and the 2 weeks of fully paid training provided annually for my friends who work in local industries.

Finally, to end on a happy note, every reader should notice the interesting tools and ideas for measurement that are contained in the report. A carefully validated, self-report physical activity checklist was developed as part of the SPARK program (Sallis et al., 1993). Think of the potential uses for such a tool, both to encourage out-of-school activity and to detect changes in the level of children's engagement. Also, I can't resist thinking about how much fun it would be to purchase several of those accelerometers used by the investigators to track out-of-school physical activity and to clip them onto my own students during regular physical educa-

tion classes. The feedback would be valuable for me and would offer the basis for some wonderful teaching moments about a variety of topics. Having videotaped classes and then attempted to gauge individual student activity levels while watching a monitor with stopwatch and clipboard in hand—I could very easily be romanced by the efficiency of such a new toy!

 Common Ground: Our Shared Perspective

It would be neither prudent nor completely fair to the investigators for you to draw hard and fast conclusions here without having perused all of the studies in this excellent research series. We have read those studies, however, and it is our job in this text to share what we think we have learned from research. Taken on balance, the SPARK effort must be regarded as an important success, for it shows what can be done in a variety of areas related to the health of elementary school children.

The SPARK effort must be regarded as an important success, for it shows what can be done in a variety of areas related to the health of elementary school children.

We make that judgment not only for the investigators' ambitious research agenda but also for the SPARK program and its sophisticated implementation. That all of their strategies did not work as hoped is, to us, far less important than what the research team found conclusively—that given sufficient investments of time and money, such interventions in the lives of elementary school teachers and children can be successfully designed, implemented, and evaluated. Although the evidence shows that the SPARK curriculum did not produce desired results in every area of measurement, the fact that we have hard evidence that it worked admirably for some outcomes is more than sufficient for us. There are very few elementary school physical education programs about which we can say that much.

The Impact of SPARK on Catching, Throwing, and Kicking

McKenzie, T.L., Alcaraz, J.E., Sallis, J.F., & Faucette, F.N. (1998). Effects of a physical education program on children's manipulative skills. *Journal of Teaching in Physical Education, 17*, 327-341.

The study reported here is a companion to the one presented in chapter 26. Accordingly, you may find it helpful to review the introductory sections of that annotation.

 **The Study**

While the current study focuses on outcomes for manipulative skill development, the earlier investigation (Sallis et al., 1997) examined the impact of Sports, Play, and Active Recreation for Kids (SPARK), an elementary school curriculum and professional development program that focuses on components of physical fitness. With other investigations, these two were products from a federally funded line of inquiry initiated at San Diego State University.

Participants and Context

Seven schools participated in the study, each being assigned at random to one of the three treatment conditions. The first group was composed of two schools in which all classes were conducted by state-certified K-12 physical education specialists (PES) who were also trained to implement the SPARK

program. The second group consisted of two schools in which all classes were taught by classroom teachers (TT, for teacher-taught) who were trained to teach the SPARK curriculum. The third group comprised three schools in which all classes were taught by untrained classroom teachers (CO, for control group) who continued with whatever was their usual contribution to physical education. All seven schools, and the 56 fourth- and fifth-grade physical education classes within them, were provided with the same level of material support for physical education. Classes in the PES and TT schools were scheduled for three 30-minute classes each week (the state requirement was 200 minutes every 10 school days). Frequency and duration of CO classes continued to be effectively under the control of classroom teachers, which resulted in an average of 18 minutes of physical education per week.

Design and Method

Creators of SPARK designed the program as a health-related curriculum that emphasized increasing the amount of moderate-to-vigorous physical activity. The program involved units that were enjoyable to children, and it included the teaching of motor skills while promoting high levels of student engagement. All teachers using SPARK were given supervision and on-site support in addition to initial instruction that included program content, instructional skills, and class management, along with detailed lesson plans for each unit. Teachers and their students were observed throughout the study to ensure that the SPARK curriculum was implemented as intended.

The 28 classroom teachers in the TT group were trained during the first 2 years of this 3-year intervention. They received 32 hours of teacher development during the 1st year and 9 additional hours in the 2nd year. On-site follow-up support included grade-level planning meetings, modeling for lesson segments, and verbal and written feedback after observation of their lessons.

One-third of the students in each fourth-grade class and (one year later) in each fifth-grade class were randomly selected for participation in skills testing. The pretests were given in the fall 6 weeks after the school year began, with posttests given approximately 6 months later in the spring. Three manipulative skill tests—throwing, catching, and kicking—were given in random order in the seven schools. All tests were administered by a team of eight trained, paid, adult assessors, none of whom were members of the primary research team. Complete sets of data were collected from 709 children (358 boys and 351 girls).

At all of the school sites, the children's physical education teachers were unaware of test specifics. They were not informed of test results, and they did not have drills prescribed in their programs that closely resembled the testing conditions. Multiple and diverse drills and games for throwing, catching, and kicking did occur, however, as natural parts of instruction and practice in many of the SPARK units—notably, Frisbee®, basketball, softball, soccer, and other field games.

Results

A complex data analysis for the three tests produced a lengthy list of results. Four of the findings will be of particular interest to readers concerned with elementary physical education, and two of these were not unexpected. Both baseline performance and learning gains were greater by substantial margins for boys than for girls. This difference applied to the three skill tests individually, as well as to total scores for all measures. Likewise, scores of fifth-grade students were generally higher than those of students at the fourth-grade level, although the differences favoring older students were not as large as those favoring males.

A third finding, however, came as a pleasant surprise. After only 6 months of program implementation, the three study conditions had produced differential effects for two of the three skills. Students in the classes of SPARK-trained classroom teachers (TT) showed significantly more improvement in throwing and catching than did students in the 3 schools using untrained teachers (CO). Gains in the PES schools followed the same pattern of superiority for catching and throwing, but the scores fell just short of the cutoff for statistical significance. The surprise here was that previous studies of physical education at the elementary level have generally failed to provide evidence of significant learning gains over such a limited period of study (6 months).

Finally, among the results that we regarded as particularly informative, the fourth finding was one that was initially less obvious. It takes some reflection to understand its significance, but our plain-language translation of the statistics should make it accessible. Although both gender and grade influenced the initial level of performance on the three skills and how much students profited from instruction and practice, SPARK had a positive effect on student learning irrespective of grade or gender, whether under PES or TT conditions. Put simply, SPARK worked for everyone.

The authors speculate that the strong skill gains may have resulted from the combination of a predesigned curriculum with the application of a professional development program that included follow-up support in the gymnasium. Observation data collected during the study did reveal that students in the PES and TT schools spent more time actively engaged in vigorous activity and skill practice than students in CO schools. At the same time, CO students spent significantly more minutes each week in free play than either PES or TT children. Finally, the specialists and trained classroom teachers provided more active instruction during lessons in the form of verbal prompts and performance feedback than did control teachers.

A Researcher's Perspective

The three manipulative skills were measured by simple tests under closely controlled conditions (the protocols are briefly described in the report) rather than by elaborate rating systems of form, or assessments of skill execution made during game play. Those sharply restricted test formats may have served, however, to sharpen and clarify the results for student learning. These were outcome-based tests. Either you could perform the skill or you could not. Either you could catch the ball (or kick the distance, or hit the target) or you could not. Form, the actual topography of the performance, was not considered. There is no doubt that assessing correct performance might have added useful information, or that assessing use of the skills in actual game play might have provided a more authentic evaluation. However, creating and applying valid and reliable tests for either of those factors would have enormously complicated the problem of achieving uniform measurements across 7 schools, 57 classes, and 709 children. Perhaps using uncomplicated measures of skill that yielded unambiguous data ("either you can do it or you cannot") was what allowed the learning superiority of the experimental conditions to show itself.

It also is true that I could have thought of many other motor skills that could have provided a meaningful assessment of program outcomes. Nevertheless, throwing, catching, and kicking are fundamental and generalizable manipulative skills that are prerequisites to successful participation in many school and community programs for sport and recreation. Acquisition of these skills has to be an important objective for any elementary school physical education program.

> **Throwing, catching, and kicking are fundamental and generalizable manipulative skills that are prerequisites to successful participation in many school and community programs for sport and recreation.**

Finally, the large and persisting score differentials that show girls trailing far behind boys in mastery of these basic skills must be cause for concern. It is clear that simply instituting a sound program taught by trained teachers is not in itself a sufficient means to address that problem. Even with the absolute gains provided by the SPARK program, the fifth-grade girls were further behind relative to boys at the end of the year than they had been a year earlier in the fourth grade.

If girls are to have equal access to a wide range of physically active play activities, something else is required—and it may be that the requirement can only be met at the elementary school level of physi-

cal education. Such special attention to the skill development of girls may be no more complicated than a modest amount of additional time for instruction and practice, but that supplement will be essential if we are to achieve a reasonable measure of gender equity.

 # A Teacher's Perspective

Here is another study confirming that high-quality instruction does make a difference. Although we may know this in our hearts as teachers, it is rare to have data to back up our assertions about that fact. Better still, the design provides specific evidence to affirm that instruction really is superior to practice in the form of free play. Wherever the long debate still rages over whether or not recess can substitute for physical education, this study ought to be cited, explained, and affirmed. In fact, when we are playing our formal role as professional educators, we should mention this study in conversations with parents, administrators, classroom teachers, and community leaders as a part of a standing protocol for such interactions—whether private or public.

> **Wherever the long debate still rages over whether or not recess can substitute for physical education, this study ought to be cited, explained, and affirmed.**

The study can also serve as a model for what we can do on a smaller scale as teachers. We can identify three basic skills that we believe could serve as indicators of whether students in our program have been learning what we intended, then do exactly as the authors did by working out simple, efficient, and reliable measures. With careful planning and with some parents trained to help with the administration of tests, we could validate our program, identify students needing additional help, and gain useful publicity. Of course, that can't be done for every skill, but a few each year might provide a tool that would serve multiple purposes.

From another perspective, two aspects of this study are distressing for me. The first, of course, is that the girls' performance indicated that they not only had poorer skills than boys at the outset but that they fell further behind over the course of the study. Ouch! Such an observation is both discouraging and confounding, even with the usual caveat that this study does not indicate that all girls are less skilled than boys, which is an erroneous assumption that the data directly contradict. To reflect on the question of why, however, brings us back to the study and the second source of my distress.

One explanation for the lagging female scores may rest in the hidden aspects of SPARK or any other curriculum. Researchers reported no observations of the number of skill trials by gender during classes. Other research will tell you that in physical education classes, boys often get many more practice trials than girls. Whether this is explained by male assertiveness, teacher and student expectations, or stereotyped role behaviors is an interesting academic question. But the result is the same—on average, boys learn more and girls fall progressively further behind.

Affirming girls' right to learn and their need to learn how to attend to their own learning sometimes seems inadequate and a bit stale to me. That is, it will seem inadequate until I stop being aware of all the messages I get every day from society that say as a woman, I am not as capable as a man, should not be as assertive, and should not expect to assume the same professional place. Although we may have come a long way, those messages are still out there and all around us, not least in elementary physical education classes. We have to be vigilant in detecting the hidden parts of curriculum that are not mentioned in the official course outline but that have powerful consequences for our students. Once detected, we are accountable for teaching in ways that eliminate or blunt whatever works to harm our students.

Best teaching practices require equity of opportunity for all students, which includes opportunities to try. Whether than means a ball for every child or small-sided games that are structured to ensure an equal distribution of touches for every player, the environment has to be manipulated to produce the needed result. Such provisions are a part of the SPARK curriculum. Beyond that, however, it is clear that a further intervention dealing directly with gender role expectations should be devised, tested, and added.

My distress can be set aside, however, in the light of a far stronger response. This study reflects important work. Reading reports about the impact of SPARK on student fitness and skills yields strong testimony for quality physical education. Further, positive ratings given by teachers participating in the study lend an additional kind of support.

That is not to say that SPARK is pie-in-the-sky. The teachers thought the activities and learning goals were valuable for children, and they also thought the pedagogical skills demanded were well

within their capacity to learn and implement. All of which leads me to want a copy of the SPARK curriculum for my own use. If you feel likewise, visit the SPARK Web site at **www.foundation.sdsu.edu/projects/spark/index.html**, or write to SPARK at 6363 Alverado Ct., Suite 250, San Diego, CA 92120.

Common Ground: Our Shared Perspective

The results from this study suggest that quality physical education programs delivered by trained physical education specialists or trained classroom teachers can improve children's manipulative skills. There is a vital caveat here, and the authors make it very clear.

It is important to emphasize, however, that the gains produced by the classroom teachers came as a result of implementing a carefully designed and tested PE curriculum and that this curriculum was accompanied by substantial training, monitoring, and follow-up support. (p. 338)

If we are serious about achieving learning outcomes in return for the time and resources assigned to physical education and if we also wish to continue employing elementary school classroom teachers as physical educators, there will be a significant cost. It is unclear whether that additional price is best met by institutions of higher education during preservice training or by school districts through induction and staff-development programs (or by resource inputs from both institutions). It is clear, however, that the resources will have to be made available.

There is persuasive evidence to demonstrate that SPARK offered a significant improvement over what passes for physical education in many elementary schools. SPARK, though, did not come cheap in either human or fiscal terms. As always, the question here is, What are we willing to pay for?

There is persuasive evidence to demonstrate that SPARK offered a significant improvement over what passes for physical education in many elementary schools.

How Well Do Children Like Various Physical Education Activities?

McKenzie, T.L., Alcaraz, J.E., & Sallis, J.F. (1994). Assessing children's liking for activity units in an elementary school physical education curriculum. *Journal of Teaching in Physical Education, 13,* 206-215.

This study was conducted during the first year of Project SPARK (Sports, Play, and Active Recreation for Kids), a 5-year program funded by the National Institutes of Health to evaluate a comprehensive approach to promoting physical activity among elementary school students (other studies from this project are annotated in chapters 26 and 27).

 **The Study**

Although SPARK was a multifaceted program, the present study was limited to students' assessment of their enjoyment of activity units within the experimental school curriculum. The decision to pursue the matter of how well students like various activities as part of a curriculum development process represents something of a landmark in our research literature. It is difficult to find evidence indicating that student perceptions have been systematically studied and used in the design of school physical education programs. For the most part, curricula at the elementary level have been shaped primarily by theories about child development, local traditions, and physical context, as

well as by the personal interests and beliefs of teachers.

In contrast, this early version of the SPARK curriculum was field-tested to obtain feedback in the form of student opinions that could be used in making modifications and refinements that would improve the program. Students' liking of what they encountered in class was presumed to be critical if the program was to influence continued participation in physical activity. Accordingly, the data provided by this study were used in the final revisions of the SPARK curriculum and the research program that followed.

Participants and Context

The pilot curriculum was implemented for 1 year in the fourth- and fifth-grade, coeducational classes of two suburban elementary schools. A credentialed physical education specialist who was hired, trained, and supervised by the investigators taught physical education in each school. Both specialists had master's degrees and more than 4 years of experience teaching at the grade levels included in the study. Equivalent space and equipment were available at both schools.

Design and Method

The SPARK curriculum was designed specifically to promote high levels of student engagement in physical activity and skill practice. It included a detailed yearly plan that was divided into two types of activity units: those emphasizing health-related fitness and those emphasizing skill-related fitness. The former included activities such as aerobic dance, jump rope, fitness circuits, and running programs while the latter units focused on developing motor skills, particularly as they related to body-limb-object coordination and sport skills such as basketball, Frisbee, soccer, softball.

The yearly plan called for classes to be taught 3 days per week throughout the entire school year with each lesson divided into two distinct parts. The first half was devoted to a warm-up with a transition to health-related fitness activities; the second half consisted of motor-skill activities that transitioned into a period of cooldown and closure. Skill units differed from traditional sport activities in that they were modified to stimulate more student activity, such as playing small-sided games. The full curriculum contained nine specific activity units of each kind (health-fitness activities and motor-skill activities).

Following cooldown and closure activities, each student was given a pencil and rating form. The form contained two questions: "How did you like the fitness activities today?" and "How did you like the sport activities today?" Printed below each question were four happy/sad faces and the accompanying words *excellent, good, fair,* and *poor.* The teacher reviewed the day's activities relating to the two questions, then the students anonymously circled the face indicating their response. The forms were collected and later scored via numerical values (*excellent* = 4, *good* = 3, *fair* = 2, *poor* = 1).

Data were only collected for complete classes that implemented the full lesson for that day. Throughout the year, students were frequently reminded that their opinions about their physical education activities were very important because they would be used in development of a curriculum to be used in many other schools throughout the nation.

Results

Over an 8-month period, students in the eight fourth- and fifth-grade classes reported 16,032 scores for 648 different physical education lessons, averaging 24.7 responses per lesson. The ensuing data analyses used several different permutations

of the scores. For our present purpose, however, it will be sufficient to assume that they are simple averages (means) for raw scores.

Mean scores combined for all classes and students showed that students liked all 18 units (all means were above 3) but liked some significantly more or less than others. For example, softball and the motor-skill activities involving parachutes received the highest ratings (above 3.5) while teacher-led exercises and the walk-jog-run unit were at the bottom (both means below 3.25, still rated *good* but much less enthusiastically so). Generally, units that emphasized engagement in cardiovascular activities at relatively high intensity received the lowest ratings.

Close inspection of the data revealed no significant differences for day of the week, schools, grades, or teachers. Those factors simply did not exert a strong influence over how students responded to activities in the SPARK curriculum. Readers with some experience in teaching children will be interested to learn that time itself, in terms of the number of repetitions for a unit, did not appear to influence scores. The initial level of liking a unit did not change appreciably as students had more experience with the learning activities that composed the unit.

Students generally liked the activities included in the nine motor-skill units better than those in the nine health-related fitness units. The margin of superiority was not large (the means were 3.40 and 3.30, respectively), but it was persistent and certainly not due to chance. The only health-fitness activities to assume positions in the top nine ranks were aerobic dance, obstacle courses, and fitness circuits. The only skill-related activities to drop into the bottom nine ranks were Frisbee, soccer, and field games.

 # A Researcher's Perspective

You can be sure that the SPARK investigators were gratified (perhaps even relieved) when they found that the average student felt all activities in the curriculum deserved ratings between *good* and *excellent.* As one of the goals of the program was to engender positive feelings toward physical activity in the participants, that finding was a critical one. If daily attempts to provide positive teacher-student interactions, high rates of success, ample equipment, and carefully controlled small-group competition had not won student approval, it is difficult to imagine what would have.

Two bits of physical education folk wisdom were brought into question by the findings. Contrary to what I might have expected, students did not show any signs of becoming bored by repetition of units. For example, there were 84 lessons across the eight classes involving Frisbee activities. Likewise, some readers will be surprised by the fact that improved student skills and much encouragement from the teacher did not lead to indications of greater enjoyment of an activity, at least not over the time span encompassed by units in this study. In short, it appears that students simply liked what they liked!

> **Contrary to what I might have expected, students did not show any signs of becoming bored by repetition of units.**

In contrast, the clear preference for skill-related over health-related activities was not entirely unexpected. Other studies have shown that children prefer less strenuous activities. They also like using a variety of equipment, which again may give the advantage to skill-based units. Children at these grade levels also come to class far more familiar with activities such as basketball, softball, and gymnastics, than with endurance activities such as running, calisthenics, or jump rope. All of that interpretation notwithstanding, only one-tenth of a point separated the means for the two types of activity (a 3% difference). The primary interpretation remains that the children liked all of the activity units.

 **A Teacher's Perspective**

Finally, someone has asked the question of how well particular activities are received by our clients! I think that represents a great advance, and the investigators did it in a simple, straightforward format that even I could use. Just a sheet with two quick questions. I may not have all of the time and resources they had for tallying results, but I do have the option of limiting the burden of tabulation to the number of students in just one or two classes.

If the point is to get some sense of how students are feeling about a class or specific activity, the options are endless. I have seen one local teacher (Judy

Howard at Brown Elementary in Austin, Texas) use a "totem pole," actually an upright broomstick that is banded with different colors. As kids leave the gym, they touch the pole at the level (color) that reflects how well they participated in the class or on other days how much fun they had. It may give the teacher no more than a quick impression and one not protected by anonymity, but even that much seems important to me—especially if the children's consensus conflicts with the teacher's own impression or if students touch unexpectedly high or low levels of the color-coded response.

Just by considering students' feelings, the researchers of this study make a special contribution to physical education research literature. Nonetheless, I still wish they had told me a bit more about the data and gathered a bit more of it than they did. For instance, I think it would be important to know whether a mean response of 3.4 represented mostly 3s and 4s, or actually consisted of a large set of 4s and small sets of 1s and 2s. In other words, I am interested in whether an activity was well liked by nearly all children or was detested by some and a source of real joy to others. Those two very different patterns would lead me in quite different directions. Most particularly, I'd like to know a lot more about the experiences of those recording the 1s and 2s. Insight into their feelings might be the most valuable outcome of any such evaluation.

> **I think it would be important to know whether a mean response of 3.4 represented mostly 3s and 4s, or actually consisted of a large set of 4s and small sets of 1s and 2s. In other words, I am interested in whether an activity was well liked by nearly all children or was detested by some and a source of real joy to others. Those two very different patterns would lead me in quite different directions.**

I mention that point about noticing and responding to children whose experiences are not like those of the majority for a particular reason. Like most teachers, when I am in a hurry or just not thinking carefully, it is all too easy to interpret the occasional negative reaction by two or three students as an indication that they are the ones with the problem. Sometimes that may be an accurate assessment—but not always. As the responsible adult, I owe every student at the least an honest moment of reflection on the question, Is there something in the activity, my teaching, or the class context that is producing a bad experience for some students?

That concern, of course, is the sort that can't be addressed by data from a 4-point scale, which leads me to make a general observation about studies of this kind. What puts a very real limit on what can be learned is the absence of an open-ended opportunity for students to comment on what was liked, what was not liked, and why.

For example, the authors mention as a finding from other studies that it might be the strenuous nature of the fitness activities that lowered students' numerical ratings. Nevertheless, no student data is given here that would lead to that conclusion. Since small-sided games are both fairly strenuous and well regarded by the participants, my own suspicion is that the real issue for the students was the continuous (or repetitive) nature of some fitness activities.

Given the opportunity, kids will run hard in short bursts, then rest. In my experience, asking them to run slower but continuously is attractive to only a small number, perhaps the future distance runners. Most of the others quickly show signs of simple boredom—not fatigue! I really believe this observation fits the present data just as well as speculation about the level of physical demand. It is further supported by the fact that aerobic dance, with its music and rapidly changing movements, was rated fairly high, despite that it was fully as strenuous as many of the other fitness activities.

All of this is speculation, of course, until someone (perhaps you?) asks students to record one or two words that anchor the numbers they report for likes and dislikes. It would take just a few key words jotted on a card or even feedback left behind on a tape recorder with an open microphone. I bet it would not take long to clarify whether some fitness activities are rated lower because of their strenuousness or because of their unrelieved repetitiveness. That kind of information would enrich and extend the important beginning already made in this study.

> **Novelty and variety appeared to play important roles in determining student reactions.**

 # Common Ground: Our Shared Perspective

The most general conclusion to be drawn from the findings of this study is that elementary school students can evaluate components of their physical education curriculum. Although the reactions were generally positive, the data allowed sufficient discrimination among units to offer considerable guidance in curriculum construction and revision.

To cite but one example of how consumer reports such as this might help in program design, the authors note that novelty and variety appeared to play important roles in determining student reactions. For example, aerobic dance, fitness circuits, and obstacle courses involved a variety of activity components and at the grade levels used in the study were unlikely to have been experienced outside physical education. The researchers therefore reasoned that those characteristics—high variety and novelty—probably account for why those were the only three health-related fitness activities (of nine) to be ranked in the top half of the scores. In that connection, we note with interest that the "astronaut drills," the least-liked unit in the entire curriculum, also involved novel fitness challenges, but those exercises were among the most physically demanding of the health-related activities.

The lesson for curriculum designers is clear. A variety of new activities can serve as a powerful attractor for a unit.

Finally, we can draw no conclusions concerning skill level and liking because the anonymity of rating forms precluded identification of individual students. Likewise, we have no information about the influence of gender or factors such as ethnicity or cultural tradition. It would simply demand a great deal more information to move from what children actually liked to the question of *why* they liked the activities they encountered in SPARK.

We intend that observation to be less as a criticism of the study and more as an encouragement for teachers who might wish to take the preferences of their students into account when planning curricula. By doing so, teachers might enhance the acceptability and ultimate effectiveness of their programs. We think this study provides a useful starting place.

PART IX

Reviewing Studies
of the Effects
of Physical Education

THE STUDY

RESEARCHER

TEACHER

COMMON
GROUND

The Legacy
of Elementary School
Physical Education

Shephard, R.J., & Trudeau, F. (2000). The legacy of physical education: Influences on adult lifestyle. *Pediatric Exercise Science, 12,* 34-50.

The publication to be discussed here is not a research report. It is a review of research pertaining to a particular topic—the impact of participation in physical education programs, during childhood or adolescence, on subsequent adult patterns of activity and indicators of health. In short, this is about research on the short- and long-term outcomes of physical education.

Writing an annotation for a research review involves one problem of which the reader should be aware. What follows here consists of our explanations of the explanations given by the review authors of the original research reports in which investigators explained what they did and what they found. Given all those steps, it may quickly become difficult to identify exactly whose voice is being heard at any given point in the annotation.

Aside from trying to be very careful about sticking close to what the review authors actually said, we found no perfect resolution to that potential problem. In the following sections, however, we have put text that consists primarily of our personal commentary and judgment in brackets. Explanations and descriptions, as well as quotations and paraphrases based directly on the review, are not in brackets.

This annotation follows the general pattern of the review by attending first to the importance of fol-low-up studies and the difficulties involved, then by moving on to related efforts such as research on short-term program effects and tracking studies. Finally, we summarize findings from a small set of regular experimental studies.

 ## The Review

Shephard and Trudeau provide a brief overview of findings from 100 publications that comprise research reports and previous research reviews. Their review includes a detailed discussion of what the authors regard as the most significant research contributions in this area of inquiry—the long-term follow-ups of the Trois-Rivières growth and development study (a series of investigations, several of which we have annotated in chapter 30).

Most physical educators have assumed with little questioning that childhood physical education programs have a positive influence on the subsequent physical activity patterns of the adult. After all, that long-term outcome is one of the basic arguments for including the subject of physical education in the elementary school curriculum. But what does the evidence actually show about that fundamental assumption? Does high-quality, daily elementary school physical education return its considerable cost in the form of tangible benefits manifested 20 years later when today's child has become tomorrow's adult?

As this review shows, a single and wholly unambiguous answer to that question simply does not exist. Of course, there is a wide range of very different questions that can be raised about the outcomes of physical education. If investigators wish to assess the impact of a program on children at the end of a school year, it would lead them to a particular set of research questions. On the other hand, evaluating a program in terms of measurements made 20 years after students have left elementary school would require some very different questions. Likewise, it is one thing to examine the influence of program participation on cardiovascular risk factors, but it is quite another to assess how much health-related information former students remember, how often they exercise, how positive they feel about their bodies, or how confident they are when performing basic movement skills.

As you might expect, investigators have posed a variety of those questions, tried different measurement techniques, sampled a number of populations, and timed their research to follow program participation by intervals ranging from a few days to 20 years. Given such a scattered and largely unsystematic effort, it is not surprising to find that there are almost no points on which there is both wide agreement and extensive evidence.

The explanation for such poverty is not difficult to find. Until recently, evaluating the outcomes of elementary school physical education has not been an attractive field for inquiry, in large measure because it is difficult and expensive. Among many problems, there are daunting technical and logistic complexities in doing longitudinal research (studies that track individuals across substantial periods of time). For example, in an increasingly mobile population, it often is difficult to locate participants after an interval of only a few years—let alone the decades that separate elementary school attendance from adulthood.

[Locke and Lambdin: That single difficulty guarantees that it will be difficult (and perhaps impossible) to do small and inexpensive studies that can settle questions about the long-term influence of school physical education programs. Nevertheless, we have yet to hear anyone argue that longitudinal follow-up studies are anything other than absolutely essential to the survival and future development of elementary school physical education.

The studies reviewed here were early efforts in a tremendously challenging area of inquiry. That they were undertaken at all is a tribute to the investigators involved. Our decision to include this review (and the related research annotated in the following chapter) was intended a celebration—not a critique.]

The passage of time and the forces of social change now give questions about the impact of elementary school physical education a degree of urgency they once lacked. Consider, for example, the following facts. The level of physical activity for the average child has decreased progressively over the past half-century as a result of various technological and demographic changes. Those include television and computer games as well as the growing concentration of population in large cities with limited opportunities for physically active play. Concurrently, we have seen significant increases in the prevalence of childhood obesity and other cardiovascular risk factors. In addition, over the same time span a steady erosion of physical education programs has surfaced in North American schools. [Locke and Lambdin: It does not require much thought to conclude that those facts might somehow be related.]

Program Evaluations: Short-Term Benefits

The authors of the review began with questions related to short-term dividends from physical education programs, in the form of improved performance on various tests of physical fitness given during or immediately after a period of program participation. Here the answers are reasonably clear. The studies briefly noted here indicate that when physical education includes a component of vigorous physical activity at the appropriate levels of intensity and duration, it will yield modest but generally reliable fitness benefits for children (chapters 26 and 30 provide further illustration of this generalization). Many of those gains, however, are transitory, being lost after only a few weeks of inactivity.

Such short-term outcomes, however, are not the results that really matter for the present purpose. Transitory changes in physical performance are equally available to anyone, at any stage of life, with or without prior exposure to physical education programs. What does matter are persisting style-of-life outcomes that can be linked (however loosely) with antecedent school programs for children and youth.

Program Follow-Up Studies: Long-Term Benefits

Of greatest consequence would be confirmation of a legacy that persisted over the long term and that gave measurable advantages to graduates of quality elementary school physical education programs. Those benefits should include well-established skills, knowledge, and dispositions—the tools and habits that support and encourage a physically active lifestyle. [Locke and Lambdin: What would secure the place of physical education in the elementary curriculum is reliable evidence indicating that instruction and practice during childhood is a strong predictor for quality of adult life.]

If the primary concern is with the influence of elementary school physical education programs on adult behaviors, many of the longer-term follow-up studies reviewed here have value that is indirect at best. For example, findings that deal with the impact of middle school and high school programs are of only limited interest, as are evaluations of elementary school programs that follow graduates only into their middle-school years. Such investigations do not touch the central question of how elementary school physical education influences health and physical activity patterns 5, 10, or 20 years later.

The Tracking Studies: Following Individual Patterns

Another form of inquiry that offers at least peripheral relevance appears in what are called *tracking studies*. These investigations follow individuals over time to ascertain the extent to which characteristics measured at one age can be used to predict the status of those factors at a later age. Variables that have been tracked over periods ranging from 1 to 20 years include attitudes about fitness and exercise, measures of physical activity (such as type, frequency, and intensity), physical fitness, motor fitness, and clinical variables (such as obesity, cholesterol, aerobic capacity, and blood lipids). Such studies are not experiments that require provision of actual school programs; most rely on self-report for data concerning current and retrospective experiences. They are therefore not prohibitively expensive or logistically complex. Accordingly, this area of the research literature has modest depth and offers some basis for confidence in the findings.

The logic that argues for the relevance of tracking studies is quite simple. Suppose it was found that the children who were the most physically active at age 10 (fourth-graders) were also the most active at ages 15, 20, or 25. That would open a door of possibility: A strong physical education program that encouraged fourth-grade children to engage in vigorous physical activity every day (at home as well as in school) might, at least in theory, exert an influence on the later behavior of those children as adults. In other words, tracking would have successfully demonstrated that such a behavioral influence could persist over time. Tracking studies could not provide direct evidence that the program caused the adult behavior, but they clearly could make that appear to be a logical possibility.

Findings from a dozen tracking studies in seven nations (Netherlands, Belgium, Denmark, Finland, Canada, Sweden, and the United States) were noted in the present review, and despite many procedural differences, their findings appear to have a surprising degree of consistency. If you ask about the persistence of some particular variable over time, the answer will be, "It depends on the variable and the time span." If you ask, however, whether the door appears to be open for elementary school physical education to influence variables such as adult health, fitness, or lifestyle, the answer will be yes—although the opening is not large. On this latter point, the authors of the review provide a succinct summary.

A substantial number of authors have examined the extent of tracking of physical activity, usually from adolescence into adult life. At best, interage correlations have been weak to moderate [most lie in the range between .15 and .30]. It is unclear how far such data can be extrapolated to infer the impact of physical education programs on adult lifestyle. (p. 39)

It is important to note, however, that all of the correlations have been positive, despite being relatively small (with the exception of retrospective data that reflect having been "forced to exercise" during childhood and adolescence), which leads to the next question: If the door for long-term influence is ajar, what happens when investigators make a deliberate attempt to open the door further? That question, of course, is another way of asking for results from actual interventions in the form of experimental programs.

Experiments: Follow-Up for Planned Interventions

Seven of the studies reviewed here do qualify as true experiments. In those, relatively large numbers of participants who had attended a deliberately designed physical or health education program were compared with others who had not been exposed to that curriculum intervention. Initial differences were controlled by random assignment of schools, classes, or individual children to treatment or control conditions. The participating populations ranged from students in the third grade to the ninth grade, and researchers conducted follow-up assessments after intervals ranging from 2 to 11 years. The measurements used included factors such as level of physical activity, type of physical activity, health knowledge, body fat, and aerobic capacity.

Granted, the number of studies using experimental procedures is small, and the results depend heavily on particular features present in the design of each experiment. Nonetheless, it is quite fair to ask, "What do they tell us?" The authors conclude that when taken together, these studies largely confirm what was suggested by tracking research. The long-term impact of school-based educational programs on physical activity and health can be detected, but it is limited in magnitude and not consistent in its appearance. Put another way, most longitudinal studies employing experimental formats have revealed relatively modest and often inconsistent influences on the later lives of participating students.

For example, when girls in an experimental sixth-grade physical education program completed high school, they showed modestly higher levels of physical activity than control-group peers did—but that benefit did not extend to boys who attended classes in the same program. In another study, an experimental program included regular physical education classes, supplemented with health education units. The activity levels of participants were checked 3 years later, and the boys (but not the girls) were found to engage in significantly more "moderate" physical activity than members of the control group. The same was not true, however, for "vigorous" activity where boys from experimental and control classes reported similar levels of engagement.

Such ambiguities were a common feature of the experimental studies considered in this review. For every instance of apparent success, there were instances of "no significant difference," or as indicated previously, findings that were mixed in unpredict-

able ways. If we were limited to the results from the experimental programs reviewed in the present effort, we could accurately say that not all produced adults whose activity behaviors, knowledge, and physical status were detectably different from those who experienced typical elementary school programs or no physical education at all.

The authors of the review expressed considerable caution about results from these initial attempts at long-term follow-up based on experimental design. At the heart of their concern was the fact that many experimental programs suggested that their designers might have been confused about the constructs of sport, physical activity, physical education, and physical fitness. With the exception of one study (Trois-Rivières), the result is that the researchers have persistently overlooked the fact that programs focusing on lifetime physical activities should logically have the greatest potential for carryover to adult life—certainly more so than programs consisting primarily of competitive sports.

[Locke and Lambdin: Although they do not say so in direct terms, we believe the authors have elected to withhold their final judgment about elementary school physical education until there have been long-term follow-up studies of the impact of programs that were explicitly designed to have a lasting influence on behavior. That certainly is our own position. If elementary school physical education is to have a genuine opportunity to demonstrate long-term influence on adult living, it must be conducted with attention to the importance of lifelong participation in physical activity. Program content must be designed to move children toward attitudes and behaviors that characterize what is typical in healthy adult lifestyles—walking, jogging, bicycling, aerobic dance, weight training, tennis, hiking, and swimming—rather than (exclusively) toward complex team sports, such as basketball, football, and baseball. Helping students become comfortable and enthusiastic movers is an essential objective for any elementary school program, but so too is introduction to the full range of vigorous physical activities.]

The Trois-Rivières Studies

The final section of the review was devoted to a summary of results from several studies that involved attempts to follow participants from both the experimental and control groups in the original Trois-Rivières investigation in Canada. The review authors assert that as a single undertaking, these 20-year follow-up efforts represent "the only study that has yet attempted to examine the impact of enhanced physical education [at the primary school level] on adult behavior" (p. 40). Because we have annotated three of those investigations in the following chapter, we include here only an assessment of the results drawn directly from the review: "In confirmation of inferences from tracking and shorter-term intervention studies conducted elsewhere, the long-term impact of the [Trois-Rivières] study upon physical activity and health [of adults] was relatively limited" (p. 43).

A Researcher's Perspective

I think it is important to keep some perspective when considering research reviews such as this one. Readers must remember that examining how particular experiences play out over the years leads into very deep water. Our lives are terribly complicated, and the origins of any belief or behavior are likely to be multiple, tangled, and obscure. It should be no surprise that it is difficult to find direct and unambiguous ties between a particular elementary school curriculum and anything that appears in our lives 20 years later! In short, this is a situation where modest differences may very well indicate important consequences.

> **It should be no surprise that it is difficult to find direct and unambiguous ties between a particular elementary school curriculum and anything that appears in our lives 20 years later!**

Further, every reader can cite particular teachers, courses, books, activities, and events that taught well-remembered and greatly valued lessons. Why should physical education not be so honored in memory and action? It is, of course, for at least some of its clients. Twenty years later, 40% of the participants in the Trois-Rivières experimental program rated it as "very satisfactory," versus only 12% in the control cohort. Across the always uncertain bridge of memory, that outcome must be regarded as substantial.

If it is unreasonable to expect too much from program evaluations based on longitudinal research, it is equally so to expect nothing whatever! Such a

dilemma leads directly to a question we think all of us must consider: Are findings of weak influence the result of inadequate programs—or of inadequate research?

 ## A Teacher's Perspective

For me, a review of studies on this topic leads directly to a single, powerful question: What would I want as follow-up measures of my success as a physical education teacher? That is a very tough question to answer, but it deserves a lot of thought because the answer should guide both my teaching and my selection of class activities. I can't help but wonder if any of the researchers in these studies formed advisory boards of veteran teachers to guide them in selection of variables for investigation of long-term program effects?

My own sense is that we do need follow-up of both short- and long-term program results. It does matter that we produce some changes in our students right now, as well as encouraging adult or adolescent behaviors. For instance, for some of my students, being competent and confident enough to start playing on a school team during junior high might make the difference between being involved in basketball—or in a street gang. Likewise, there is evidence to show that in their early years, teenage girls involved in school sport programs have significantly lower rates of pregnancy. The point here is that factors such as gang membership and pregnancy have long-term consequences, but they may themselves be influenced by short-term effects from high-quality physical education programs.

I do also care about what my program does for my students in the long term. It seems reasonable for me to believe, however, that if I can't see positive changes in my pupils—right now—they are not going to be there 20 years down the road. In other words, these are the kinds of questions about short-term results for which I would like to have answers.

- Affective/Social
  1. How many of my students really love physical activity and find themselves feeling cheated on the days they don't have a chance to be active?
  2. How many of my students feel confident about their physical abilities and their capacity to learn new skills?

- Cognitive
  1. How many of my students can list the health benefits of physical activity?
  2. How many of my students know safety measures for exercising—proper training, heat precautions, protective gear, and so on?
- Physical
  1. What are the cholesterol levels, bone density, glucose levels, and resting heart rates of my students? Are they in healthy zones?
  2. How many of my students have mature basic motor skills by the time they leave the fifth grade?

When I can have answers to questions such as these that deal with short-term benefits, then I will be ready to think about how to measure their continuation into adult life. In addition to my inclination to place more value than the authors of this review did on short-term program assessments, I also am less inclined to be discouraged by the inconsistency of some of the findings for long-term program influence. If, as happens to be the case for the Trois-Rivières study, significantly more males in the experimental group were nonsmokers as adults when compared with males in the control group, then I find it to be a matter of interest and concern that this was not also true for females. I do not see, however, how that inconsistency diminishes the truly remarkable and enormously consequential finding for males!

Finally, I want to make clear to our readers that I do not think physical education teachers should sit on their hands and wait for the slow engines of research to produce information about program impact—either long- or short-term. If you look in our national and state journals and at the efforts currently going on in our professional organizations, it will be clear that teachers are directly involved in questions that are an intrinsic part of this research review. What are the performance indicators that can be used to signal outcomes in the areas of our educational objectives? What are the benchmark assessments that are essential in understanding the results of our programs? Questions of that order

It seems reasonable for me to believe, however, that if I can't see positive changes in my pupils—right now—they are not going to be there 20 years down the road.

require answers from teachers—and, subsequently, translation by research experts into procedures for reliable measurement and evaluation.

Opportunities always exist to be a player in this important game. You need only select one or two results that would indicate whether you were successful or not, then go after them. If there are opportunities coming up to gather long-term data, such as a class reunion or an alumni mailing, then why not go for it? If there are not, then examination of indicators for the here and now will be just as important in understanding your work and your program.

Common Ground: Our Shared Perspective

To do justice to the authors, they present arguments that could be used to indict both programs and research. Their concerns about research, though, do not include what we regard as one of the most problematic components—the variables, or criteria, selected as measures of program influence. Neither blood cholesterol nor self-reported hours of vigorous physical activity per week (both used in the Trois-Rivières studies) seem at all close to a teacher's daily experience with student learning in physical education. Granted, this review focuses primarily on health-related aspects of adult lifestyle, but even within that arena, the measures of program outcome still seem rather remote.

As physical education teachers, all of us see students acquire new skills, grow stronger, achieve better control over their impulses, become more adventuresome, take time to help a classmate practice, remember to bring their gym shoes, or work diligently to improve a fitness test score. And, to that, we say, "They are learning, getting better at things, growing, and that is what the program is supposed to do—push them along in things that will matter in their lives." But where are those learnings in the follow-up protocols of longitudinal research designs? Do researchers include criteria that are sensitive to what successful physical education accomplishes at ground level?

Do researchers include criteria that are sensitive to what successful physical education accomplishes at ground level?

Allow us to provide an analogy. If the history courses of a modern high school were to be judged by the voting behaviors of their graduates after they became adult citizens or by their 30-year-old former students' recall of the dates of the Peloponnesian Wars, there probably would be little evidence to support the place of that subject in the curriculum. Moreover, history teachers would cry foul and appeal for more appropriate outcome measures. The same holds true for physical education and its practitioners.

If we have some of the same concerns about measuring the legacy of elementary school physical education, then it is incumbent upon us, exactly as it would be on history teachers, to suggest more appropriate places for researchers to detect the long-term consequences of our programs. If follow-up for your program is not to be limited to percent of body fat and minutes of vigorous physical activity per week, what would you add to that measurement agenda?

PART X

The Trois-Rivières Studies: Long-Term Effects of Physical Education

THE STUDY

RESEARCHER

TEACHER

COMMON GROUND

Twenty-Year Follow-Ups of Participants in a Model Program

Trudeau, F., Laurencelle, L., Tremblay, J., Rajic, M., & Shephard, R.J. (1998). A long-term follow-up of participants in the Trois-Rivières semi-longitudinal study of growth and development. *Pediatric Exercise Science, 10,* 366-377.

Trudeau, F., Laurencelle, L., Tremblay, J., Rajic, M., & Shephard, R.J. (1999). Daily primary school physical education: Effects on physical activity during adult life. *Medicine & Science in Sports & Exercise, 31,* 111-117.

Trudeau, F., Espindola, R., Laurencelle, L., Dulac, F., Rajic, M., & Shephard, R.J. (2000). Follow-up of participants in the Trois-Rivières growth and development study: Examining their health-related fitness and risk factors as adults. *American Journal of Human Biology, 12,* 207-213.

The noted three reports all deal with follow-up analyses of the long-term influences exerted by a single physical education program. This is not, however, an instance of "milking" one study to produce multiple publications (a form of scientific misconduct). Despite their common origin, each report reflects a separate and legitimate undertaking. The reports are addressed to different audiences; the follow-up protocols involved examination of different variables; and the studies utilized independent subsamples from the original participant population, as well as data from other comparison groups. Because the source study employed a single elementary school physical education program, however, we have combined the findings from the three follow-up reports into a single annotation.

You may find it helpful to review chapter 29 as background for the present annotation. In the re-

search review discussed there, the authors identify the Trois-Rivières growth and development study (the original source for the three investigations considered here) as the only attempt to examine the impact of an enhanced elementary physical education program on subsequent adult health status and activity behaviors. So far as we are aware, that unique distinction remains true.

 ## The Trois-Rivières Study

The Trois-Rivières experiment took place over 6 years between 1970 and 1977. The follow-up studies began in 1995 and extended through 1998 (21 years after the end of the original study). At the outset, a total of 546 elementary school students were assigned to either experimental or control conditions. The experimental group (EG) received 1 hour per day of specialist-taught physical education from first grade through sixth grade, whereas students in the control group (CG) received the standard provincial physical education program of that era—a single, 40-minute period each week of exercise and games supervised by their homeroom teacher. The experimental intervention was terminated when the children left elementary school at ages 11 to 12, but they subsequently were recalled for various follow-up measurements when they had reached ages 30 to 33.

The experimental program consisted of an age-graded curriculum in which activities were matched to developmental levels and in which instruction was aimed at maximizing the active engagement of each student during each class period. Over the 6-year period of the original study, vigorous activity averaged between 20 and 30 minutes for each class meeting, with telemetered heart rates in the range of 157 to 175 beats per minute.

Efforts were made to develop student interest in and positive attitudes toward a wide range of physical activities, including pursuits with strong potential for carryover into adult life. Class units included track and field, team sports, gymnastics, swimming, dance, and outdoor activities, such as canoeing and cross-country skiing.

The short-term effects of participation in the daily program were dramatic. Those included an overall level of physical activity outside school hours (notably on weekends) that was substantially greater than that displayed by students enrolled in the control condition. In addition, physiological outcomes (measured each year) for EG students included scores that were significantly superior to CG students in tests of aerobic power, muscular strength and endurance, and a variety of motor skills. Finally, despite a 14% loss of time for classroom learning in academic subjects (the result of assigning an hour each day to physical education), there was no negative impact on the scholastic achievement of students in the experimental program. In fact, their academic performance remained equal to, or in some subjects slightly superior to, that of control students who spent significantly more time at their desks.

The First Trois-Rivières Follow-Up

Procedures to locate participants in the original study were initiated in 1995. In the first follow-up study (Trudeau, Laurencelle, Tremblay, Rajic, & Shephard, 1998), a health survey questionnaire was mailed to 178 experimental and 141 control students. Returns were received from 150 of the former (84%) and 103 of the latter (73%).

Principal results from analysis of the questionnaire data indicated the following trends. First, more EG women exercised (or labored) at a high intensity three or more times per week than did CG women. Second, EG men and women more commonly perceived their health to be *very good* or *excellent*. Third, EG women reported significantly fewer incidents of lower back problems. Fourth, EG men and women reported greater psychological dependence on exercise—that is, they felt that something was not right when they did not exercise. Finally, although all participants in the original study retained a generally favorable impression of the physical education programs they received in elementary school, the proportion of former students in the experimental group who now report being very satisfied (40%) was much larger than that for the control cohort (12%).

The Second Trois-Rivières Follow-Up

In a second study (Trudeau, Laurencelle, Tremblay, Rajic, & Shephard, 1999), certain technical problems in the analysis of longitudinal data were resolved by substituting a much larger control sample, which consisted of participants who had concurrently taken physical education at other schools in Quebec in the traditional once-per-week format. Thus, questionnaire data from 147 members of the original experimental group were compared with responses to the same questions from 720 respondents who were matched for age, gender, and socioeconomic status.

Again, the analysis revealed that EG women reported significantly higher rates of vigorous physical activity on 3 or more days per week than was the case for CG women. Further, it was observed that women in the experimental group were more likely to select activities with a potential for high intensity—for example, aerobic classes, power walking, jogging, mountain biking, and swimming. In addition, smoking was significantly less common among the male participants in the experimental group. At 31%, the CG males were far more likely to report a regular smoking habit than men from the 1970-1977 program of daily physical education (11%).

The Third Trois-Rivières Follow-Up

Finally, a further sample of participants in the Trois-Rivières study was recruited to provide 32 males and 36 females from the experimental group, and 30 men and 35 women from the control cohort (Trudeau et al., 2000). In this later study, the participants were tested for indexes of physical fitness—physical work capacity, handgrip strength, abdominal muscle endurance, sit-and-reach flexibility, and balance performance. In addition, blood lipid profiles and waist-to-hip ratios were recorded as measures of cardiovascular health.

Again, the findings were sharply defined and unambiguous. Only results from the test of balance (the Flamingo Stand Test) showed a significant advantage for men and women in the experimental group over their control group peers. In light of their 20-year earlier superiority on many of the physical indexes, it is reasonable to conclude that most of the physiological and anthropometric advantages achieved by the Trois-Rivières participants did not persist in the absence of continued stimulation across the span of time into middle adulthood. The best that can be concluded is that the balance test involved a component of motor skill that (in theory, at least) may have been more permanently established through practice during the 6 years of daily elementary school physical education.

A Researcher's Perspective

Reading the findings from the three studies is considerably complicated by their use of different subject samples. For example, men in the 1998 study who had participated in the experimental physical education program reported less smoking than men in the comparison control group. The magnitude of that difference did not reach statistical significance, though it was noted as a trend. With a different and much larger control group as the basis for comparison, however, the gap between smoking rates for the two groups of males from the 1999 study widened substantially, more than meeting the test for statistical significance. That shift in results is not particularly surprising, but it does require careful interpretation.

In the spirit of full disclosure, I must note a further complication. Several of the studies contain minor but nonetheless confusing errors and omissions. None of these appear to reflect fatal flaws of research procedure—in fact, most could be characterized as oversights or the products of careless editing—but they made an already complex task of reading and interpretation all the more difficult.

Setting aside those complaints, I suspect that whether you regard the findings from these studies as cause for celebration or discouragement depends on your expectations. My own positive assessment of the Trois-Rivières follow-up studies is based on three considerations that allowed me to be impressed by the effort and pleased with the admittedly modest outcomes.

First, the actual number of longitudinal studies of elementary school physical education that follow students into the adult years is limited. The research literature provides almost no context to help us understand and evaluate the findings from the Trois-Rivières experiment. The authors of the three follow-up investigations, if not flying blind, were piloting their efforts with few visible landmarks for navigation. Whatever else, we must be thankful that they took the necessary risks and expended the substantial resources required to give us at least an initial glimpse into the long-term workings of elementary school physical education.

Second, longitudinal studies are rife with technical problems, many of which must be resolved by less than perfect compromises. For example, use of a control sample in the 1999 study that was external to the original experiment was made necessary by the risk of cross-contamination between experimental and control students. Many students continued to live in the same communities and inevitably could be expected to talk with each other about their very different experiences in elementary school physical education. Such communication could influence subsequent responses in follow-up assessments, attenuating or enhancing differences in unpredictable ways that had nothing to do with the students' actual school experiences.

Third and last, given the complexity of our lives and the often imprecise nature of our measuring tools, it seems to me little short of a miracle that the impact of a particular school program could be detected at all—especially in data gathered 20 years later. Many instances occurred in which those data revealed no particular advantage for having spent an hour in each school day in physical education classes. The analyses also demonstrated, however, a number of "miraculous" connections, most of them the sort that an optimist might expect. The three studies annotated here give us some basis for believing that something profoundly secular was at work. That quite unmiraculous source may have been a sound program of daily physical education.

> **It seems to me little short of a miracle that the impact of a particular school program could be detected at all—especially in data gathered 20 years later.**

A Teacher's Perspective

It will be no surprise that my reactions here are quite close to the ones expressed at the end of the previous chapter. Having already expressed some specific concerns, however, I feel as though it is appropriate to move on to some more general reflections.

These three studies made me wonder about how my students will be different 20 years from now having been in my program. I find this surprisingly difficult to do because what I want for my students is just what I want for everyone—joy in each new day, good health, positive relationships with other people, strength and endurance to do exciting things, confidence in the ability to learn, and the physical capabilities needed to feel excited about opportunities to move. Those are the things I try to share in every class, every day, but where and with whom do I really connect? What part of those teaching efforts will my students still have 20 years from now? Questions on that scale seem almost too large for my imagination.

Where I can connect more easily with the ambitious agenda of those Canadian researchers is at the level of thinking about what my students will need to take with them into middle school and high school. I truly can contemplate what they need to know and be able to do, right now, if those next programs are going to be powerful experiences that continue the push I have given them toward living vigorous lives.

> **Where I can connect more easily with the ambitious agenda of those Canadian researchers is at the level of thinking about what my students will need to take with them into middle school and high school.**

Knowing how important quality physical education can be is one piece of equipment they are going to need. Students who feel that they have a right to a quality program, who know the hallmarks of effective physical education, and who are not willing to put up with less—they are the ones who are really equipped to move on.

As part of achieving that goal, some of the teachers in Round Rock, Texas (Terry Condrasky at Great Oaks Elementary and Charly Brown with Sandi DiBari at Caldwell Heights Elementary) do a project with the fifth-grade students who are ready for middle school. The purpose always is to educate both the students and the community. For example, they research a health issue, think about how physical education can affect it, then plan and give a presentation of what they have learned to the local school board. That is an example of physical education designed to leave an indelible fingerprint on the later lives of students. They are being equipped to move on and speak out.

As for the specific findings from this study, sure, I was pleased to learn that my efforts might contribute significantly to the ability of my students to sustain their balance as adults (when I will be just a dim memory). As I watch my 80-year-old mother struggle with balance problems, I can see the enormous importance that aspect of physical education has later for the quality of life. The capacity she has built up by being active throughout her entire life has been crucial in maintaining her independence and safety. We need, however, to demonstrate long-term outcomes that go much beyond superior retention of balance capacity, and the only way to find those outcomes is to look. Long-term follow-up studies of program outcomes are ways of looking, and when what is seen can be shared with parents, educators, and political decision makers, we will have powerful tools for championing what children need and deserve—quality physical education throughout their school careers.

Common Ground: Our Shared Perspective

There is one conclusion for which we may feel absolute confidence. Universities, professional organizations, and political entities (such as federal, state/provincial, and local governments) should plan, support, conduct, and disseminate longitudinal studies of the long-term effects produced by exemplary physical education programs. Only such studies can produce the sort of guidance required to shape wise educational policy. Our reading of the Trois-Rivières studies leads us to believe that physical educators have nothing to fear and everything to gain from more and better inquiry into the impact of quality physical education for elementary school children.

Our reading of the Trois-Rivières studies leads us to believe that physical educators have nothing to fear and everything to gain from more and better inquiry into the impact of quality physical education for elementary school children.

CONCLUSION

Finding Different Ways to Make Research Serve Teaching

At this juncture, we have done our part. We have tried to present 30 studies in a reasonably accessible form, and we have tried to serve as a catalyst for your thinking by commenting on the studies and by providing the reactions of a veteran practitioner. Our hope now is that you have become sufficiently intrigued to find yourself thinking about the next possible steps in the form of plans that will move you from reading to action. If you decide to use any of the valuables found in this book in your own teaching, you will become one of an elite group of teachers who have taken the long step to cross the gap between research and practice.

More than a century ago, the first American psychologist, William James, described such a gap between research and practice more succinctly than anything we ever could compose. He was lecturing to a class of future teachers when he observed that "teaching is an art, and sciences never generate arts directly out of themselves. An intermediate, inventive mind must make the application, by using its originality" (James, 1983, p. 15). If you want to make something happen in your gym that will apply a valuable idea gleaned from research, that "intermediate, inventive mind" must be yours.

Applying Research

We can't tell you what will work in your school because we don't know your school. It may be a well-worn teachers' aphorism, but the following rule is true nonetheless. Every classroom and school is unique, and only the people who are there can determine what is needed and what is appropriate. It follows, then, that if research-based ideas are to be used to change and improve anything in your classroom, it is you who will have to determine what and how.

The process of making that determination is commonly called *research application,* but such a phrase is dangerously misleading. Its implication is that you simply take "how to do it" off the pages of a book or journal, then insert the process into your daily practice. On rare occasions, that may happen, but far more often the process of fitting an idea or research finding to local conditions involves adapting rather than just applying. New teaching strategies inspired by research have to be stretched, shaped, and tailored to meet the unique characteristics of your students, program, school environment, resources, teaching style, and educational objectives—which is exactly why James said that in inventing what to do with research, the educator's mind would have to "use its originality."

How Teachers Select Studies for Application

After many years of watching students and teachers rummage through stacks of research studies, we have acquired various observations about the application process that you may find useful. First, they are almost unfailingly able to select particular studies to serve as the basis for designing their own application to test in class. Those selections seem to fall into one of three broad categories:

1. Studies with applications that reflect teachers' concerns about problems that are evident in their workplace, whether pedagogical, programmatic, political, or social

2. Studies with applications that reflect teachers' desire to move students toward particular educational outcomes, whether physical, cognitive, or affective

3. Studies with applications that reflect teachers' encounter with a topic they had not previously

given attention, but about which they discover some special interest, curiosity, or personal concern.

If you reflect for a moment on your responses to the studies we have annotated in this book, we are sure you will identify particular examples that reflect how your own responses fell into one or more of those categories. If those are some of the common reasons for deciding to try a research-based idea in the gym, what exactly is your next step? How do you go from an attractive-looking possibility to an actual application in action? There are too many answers to such a question to even begin a discussion in this limited space, but there is, however, a general pattern to a teacher's efforts to make use of research-based ideas—a pattern that might offer some guidance should you decide to take the next step yourself.

A Model for Common Paths to Application

At least in physical education, most efforts at research application seem to follow one of three well-defined paths. We have tried to describe them, and in doing so, we have labeled them simply as Paths A, B, and C (we are running low on creativity at this point). In addition, we have provided a figure (see p. 174) that diagrams the essential elements defining each route. You may want to consult that illustration as you consider the notion of alternative paths for application.

We caution you that like all such diagrammatic representations, this one is a vast oversimplification. In the real world, the paths are not so nicely separated and linear but richly interconnected and full of branches. It is common for teachers to proceed along one and suddenly discover that they really need to be on an adjacent path. What makes the most practical sense is to start out by considering which path best fits the opportunity offered by a study. Avoid getting locked into a bad choice or failing to consider alternatives that are not even included in our figure. Diagrams are just abstractions about a world that is far too complicated to capture with little boxes and arrows.

Path A

Path A is the fast track to application. Research studies invariably turn up ideas for action that are simple, low cost, low risk, and intuitively attractive. Remember not to make application into a big production—just make a simple plan for what you want to do and try it out on Monday morning. In this text, chapters 4 ("Modifying Equipment to Fit the Students"), 5 ("Reducing Disruptive Student

Behaviors"), 12 ("Can Learners Guide Their Own Practice With Self-Talk?"), and 13 ("Using Environmental Cues to Guide Practice") may fall into such a category for certain teachers.

The protocol for checking out a possible application follows the advice given in many of the Teacher's Perspective sections of the preceding chapters. Keep it simple; start with just one class; use simple tools to economize time; prepare your pupils for any change in routine; watch for things that might improve a second try; and finally, don't expect to be perfect the first time around. Our own experience suggests that for most applications of this type, a recursive loop (not shown in the figure) often leads back to planning and thus to further trials.

The most common mistake in following this route is to fail to plan for some explicit method of deciding whether or how the application worked. In other words, how will you be able to tell if the application was successful or not? You do not need elaborate provisions for evaluation at the start, but you do need at least a simple strategy for noticing the consequences of change. With some evidence or impression of what the application actually produced, the decision about keeping, revising, or discarding becomes simple.

Path B

This path leads first to collecting information, rather than some immediate effort at application. In the case of certain studies, their potential for application really cannot be assessed until you know exactly what is already going on in your classes. A perfect example in this book is provided by chapter 2, "Who Gets the Teacher's Attention?" We have found that when prodded a bit, most teachers (ourselves included) will admit that they are not altogether sure about their distribution of attention in classes. The topic seems important and worthy of a teacher's inquiry. The first step, then, has to be an assessment of what already is happening with regard to who gets your attention.

As Lambdin pointed out in her practitioner's commentary, the process of gathering data to establish a baseline for how you distribute attention to students need not be elaborate or costly, so long as you limit your effort to easily observed behaviors. In fact, the real problem is often forcing yourself to look at the findings of such preliminary self-assessment with honesty and a dispassionate eye. The outcomes of that first step are displayed within our figure as (in your judgment) either satisfactory or deficient in some regard. The latter, of course, may lead to the design of an intervention suggested by the study in question—in which case the full report of that investigation often can provide some useful leads.

Paths to the Application of Research in Physical Education

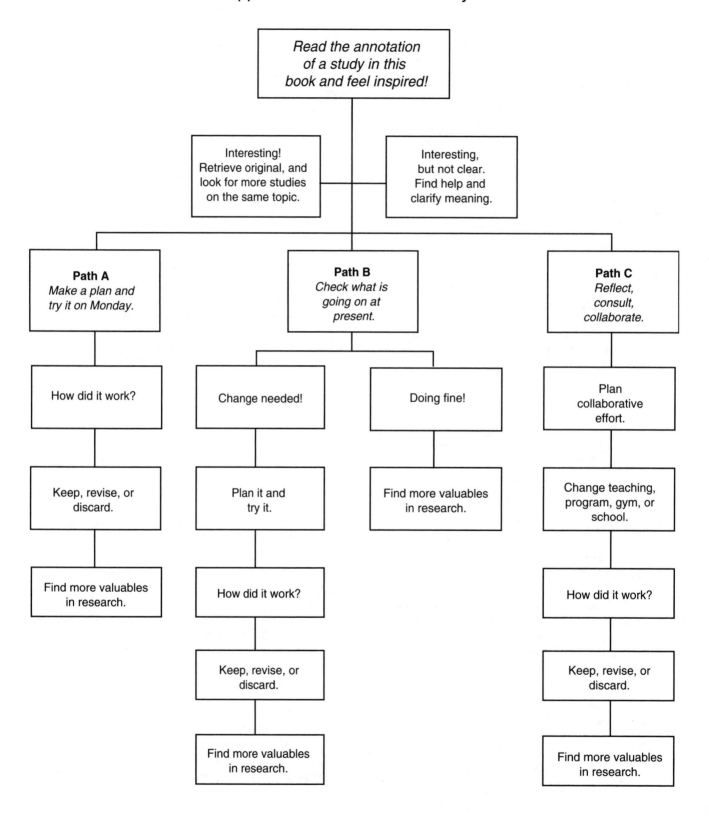

In this text, likely candidates for Path B are chapters 6 ("Active Supervision and Student Learning") and 8 ("Recording and Classifying Teacher Management Behaviors"), as well as 16, 17, and 28, all of which involve listening to what children have to say about various aspects of your teaching or program. All of them require a certain degree of self-inspection before interventions can be considered. One of the common errors is mistaking a topic as appropriate for Path A (immediate action) when it really requires use of the Path B strategy for establishing what is going on at present. In other words, if Path A is "Leap!" then Path B is "Look before you leap." Although it is tempting to yell "Geronimo!" and jump, many circumstances deem that you do a little investigation before diving headfirst into practical application.

Path C

This path is the route of caution, contemplation, consultation, and collaboration. Some studies have implications that are unclear or complicated, and they call for careful reflection. In addition, as we have noted frequently throughout this text, they also call for consultation with colleagues who can help with understanding what the findings really mean and what might be involved in any effort to apply them in your school.

In other instances, the meaning of a study may be perfectly clear, but attempting any sort of application obviously requires an investment of resources, particularly time and energy (although money and political capital may ultimately be demanded as well). Simple prudence dictates that you proceed cautiously in contemplating research applications of that sort.

Finally, other studies simply yield no clear or immediate implication for where to take the findings. Selecting the target for application and devising the exact nature of what has to be done can present difficult problems that call for thought, creativity, and, as always, the sharing of those burdens with others.

In this text, chapters 3 ("More Days per Week Equals More Learning"), 21 ("The Impact of Inclusion on Physical Education Teachers"), 26 through 28 (the three SPARK studies), and all of the chapters dealing with long-term follow-up assessment of student outcomes (such as chapters 29 and 30), are among the logical candidates for treatment as Path C problems in application. This approach has rich potential for growing branches onto the other two paths. For example, some aspects of a study with complicated implications may require a period of self-assessment before serious collaborative planning can begin, while other aspects may permit an immediate trial run as a preliminary test before further investment.

Application As Change

We would be remiss if we did not note that attempts to apply certain research findings can involve a measure of very real professional risk. At the least, the gamble of investing that most scarce commodity—time—is always without any guarantee of a reasonable payoff. Beyond that is the fact that any application of research-stimulated ideas will involve changing what already is happening, and as we all know, tinkering with existing regularities is not always welcome in the school workplace. Nor will every colleague immediately support every proposal for change—even when the idea appears to have a strong basis in research. At such points, application becomes a political problem as well as a pedagogical or curricular one. Resistance, however, is not always a fatal impediment, nor is it always inappropriate. A degree of respect for the feelings of others and a realistic anticipation of objections that might arise can serve to smooth the bumps along any of the three application paths.

The Risks of Unintended Consequences

Finally, you too should be wary of the consequences that flow from change. The process of implementing research-based change in your gymnasium may be exciting, engrossing, empowering, and it can even be successful in producing exactly the desired effect. A particular rule, however, works in the midst of all that positive change, and it always must be observed. *Almost any change you introduce in the way you interact with students (or colleagues, administrators, and parents) will produce at least some unintended consequences.* The world is simply too complicated to allow one change to produce one and only one effect.

Some of those unintended (and thus surprising) outcomes will be negligible or at least neutral; others will be as welcome as an unexpected bonus in your paycheck. A few, however, can be undesirable or in rare instances, dangerous. The appropriate response to the rule of unintended consequences should be obvious. Keep your eyes and ears open; don't get romanced by what you hope will happen; and pay close attention to negative feedback—no matter what the source. With that kind of monitoring, we believe you will find that applications of research yield real benefits and a lot of fun and satisfaction along the path.

APPENDIX A

Annotated Bibliography of Selected References on Reading and Understanding Research

Several decades ago publishers discovered that there was a substantial market for textbooks, guides, and workbooks designed to help students read and comprehend research reports. For readers interested in learning more about research, we have annotated some of the most useful of those texts in this brief bibliography. Some of these appeared briefly in college bookstores only to slip out of print. Others became popular with professors and students, and they persisted through multiple editions with the authors adjusting their content based on the developments in scholarship and feedback from their readerships. We have selected a variety from this genre with emphasis on those particularly directed at the task of reading research in the field of education.

Some of these are now out of print but remain available in libraries and through the used textbook market (many such outlets are available on the Internet). These were included either because they offered unusually sound support for the beginner or because they possessed strength in some particular area of research. Also included in this appendix are several introductory textbooks on research methods and design. These will be useful when you have detailed or technical questions that are not addressed in the general "read and understand" guides. References prepared specifically for physical educators are so noted.

Creswell, J.W. (1994). *Research design: Qualitative and quantitative approaches.* Thousand Oaks, CA: Sage.

We included this book not only because it is a sound introduction to educational research but also because it is particularly well adapted to the needs of readers who are just starting out in the area. While making no assumptions about what the reader already knows, the author starts at the beginning with an overview of the whole process, then moves carefully in step-by-step fashion and breaks the material into short, manageable chapters. All of the latter sections of the book are designed to help readers become more comfortable with the formalities and conventions commonly found in research reports. If you are interested in knowing more about what researchers do and how reports are written but find yourself feeling tentative about diving into strange waters, then this is a good selection.

Gall, M.D., Borg, W.R., & Gall, J.P. (1996). *Educational research: An introduction* (6th ed.). White Plains, NY: Longman.

Easily the most comprehensive text of its kind, this book is a standard in education graduate programs across the nation. Included are full sections on each major type of research—history, case study, and designs from the qualitative tradition. Although explicitly directed at the needs of students who will perform research studies (if not pursue careers in research), the excellent topic index and unusually extensive glossary make it easy to quickly find information about specific questions. Expensive and bulky (no paperbound edition is available), you may find it useful to locate a copy on library reserve as your reference resource for questions about research.

Goodwin, W.L.L., & Goodwin, L. (1996). *Understanding quantitative and qualitative research in early childhood education.* New York: Teachers College Press.

A number of books are now available to assist new research readers in specialized areas of education—of which this is a fine example. Prepared specifically for consumers, the emphasis of this book is on helping readers gain an understanding and an appreciation for research. A particular virtue of this text is the careful explanation of the unique strengths of quantitative and qualitative approaches to inquiry and the degree to which studies performed in those two traditions can have a complementary relationship. Excerpts from recent research on education for young children give a lively tone to the discussion of research procedures. This book offers an opportunity to learn more about programs for children while you improve your skill at reading and digesting research.

Hardyck, C.D., & Petrinovich, L.F. (1975). *Understanding research in the social sciences.* Philadelphia: Saunders.

The oldest in this group (but still held in some university collections), this text was written well before the recent surge of activity in qualitative research. Nevertheless, because it was designed for use by readers studying the social sciences, the book is particularly strong in the areas of field survey and case study. Full reports are reprinted as examples for each chapter, with helpful explanations and comments inserted by the authors.

Leedy, P.D. (1981). *How to read research and understand it.* New York: Macmillan.

Now long out of print, if you can find a tattered copy of this paperbound guide—grab it! The author explicitly directed the text to readers rather than producers of research. It is made unique within this group of books by the fact that it contains a lengthy and thoughtful guide for reading and evaluating historical studies. In addition, the author attends closely to the fact that many new readers struggle with various forms of data presentation, particularly charts, tables, and graphs. The passage of time

may have made some of this venerable text outdated, but the author's sound advice about reading the "lines and columns" is timeless.

Locke, L.F., Silverman, S.J., & Spirduso, W.W. (1998). *Reading and understanding research.* Thousand Oaks, CA: Sage

This textbook is the most comprehensive to be prepared for readers rather than for producers of research. Designed to be used either as a stand-alone tutorial or as a class textbook, this book includes practice exercises and recording forms. It provides support for readers of reports from both qualitative and quantitative designs, in addition to careful attention to preparation for reading reviews of research—that is, reports that include analysis of a group of studies. Although the text is not directed to students from a particular discipline, all three authors are physical educators, who use many examples drawn from their respective field. Presumes no special academic or technical background.

Maxwell, J.A. (1996). *Qualitative research design: An interactive approach.* Thousand Oaks, CA: Sage.

This small and inexpensive paperback is included here for readers who have a particular interest in quickly developing the background necessary to read and appreciate studies that employ qualitative rather than quantitative designs. Intended primarily for educators who are preparing to undertake a qualitative study, the text is brisk, straightforward, and largely devoid of the jargon and dense theory that characterize much writing about this approach to research.

McMillan, J.H. (1999). *Educational research: Fundamentals for the consumer* (3rd ed.). New York: Addison Wesley.

This is not a "how to do research" textbook, and only in a limited sense is it a "how to read research" textbook. Written in a distinctive user-friendly style, it is free of burdensome technical detail and clearly designed for an audience of research users rather than producers. As the title announces, these are the fundamentals of educational research. The author has concluded that what consumers need most is the knowledge required to distinguish correct research procedure from incorrect research procedure. Accordingly, the central focus of this book is "how to evaluate what you read." Although we believe that the author's definition of what consumers need is less than complete, we admit that for those who are concerned about the credibility of a study, this book offers an effective and efficient way to acquire the needed skill. Every chapter contains a list of "tips for consumers," and in a final section, all of these are brought together in expert analyses of specimen studies. The most recent edition (1999) contains an up-to-date chapter on strategies for search and retrieval.

McMillan, J.H., & Wergin, J.F. (1998). *Understanding and evaluating educational research.* Upper Saddle River, NJ: Merrill.

The opening sentence of the preface to this text sums up the authors' intention: "The purpose of this book is to help students become better and more informed consumers of published research articles" (p. iii). They open their effort to accomplish that end by addressing a question that is often neglected by other authors of research consumer guides (perhaps because it seems too obvious), "How do you recognize that a publication is, in fact, research?" (p. 1). They lay out strict criteria for making the distinction between reports of empirical research studies and the many close cousins, such as research reviews, accounts of theory development, and articles that summarize research and current thinking about a topic or problem. All of which signals the reader that this text truly begins at the beginning—and proceeds one measured step at a time.

The main body of the book consists of reprints from 11 published research reports that are used to represent the perspective, design, and methodology that characterize inquiry in four categories of research: (a) quantitative nonexperimental, (b) quantitative experimental, (c) qualitative ethnographic, and (d) action research. All deal with education, and all reached print within the last 5 years. Each report is concluded with the authors' point-by-point evaluation of the study and a series of discussion questions designed to probe the reader's comprehension and to stimulate reflection on the findings. The level of difficulty is low to moderate, and the range of topics included is diverse—curriculum, special education, administration, cooperative learning, middle school science, and so on. Produced in an inexpensive and attractive workbook format, this book is an ideal selection for your library, especially if you are not an advanced graduate student or if this book is going to be your only resource.

Thomas, J.R., & Nelson, J.K. (1996). *Research methods in physical activity* (3rd ed.). Champaign, IL: Human Kinetics.

This comprehensive textbook, used primarily in graduate-level introductory research courses, was included here for readers who may feel more comfortable when learning within a familiar context—in this instance, physical education, physical activity, and sport. For physical educators, this book is the functional equivalent of Gall, Borg, & Gall (1996; see our comments made earlier in this appendix). It is truly a comprehensive reference. Although it was written for producers rather than readers of research, it has several characteristics that may make it attractive when you have special questions about research procedures. It has chapters on historical and philosophical research (the latter is a great rarity among textbooks in this group), authored by guest authors who are expert in those respective fields. This book also is notable for being the only publication of its type in which the authors are not unremittingly serious about the content or themselves. They find honest humor in every aspect of formal inquiry, offering the reader a degree of relief from the grimly serious lectures contained in most books about research.

Tuckman, B.W. (1999). *Conducting educational research* (5th ed.). New York: Harcourt Brace College Publishers.

The latest edition of an old warhorse in education, this guide has the benefit of wide use and long development, and it is primarily intended for students who may actually have to perform research (versus simply "reading" research). The emphasis of the book is on analysis of inquiry procedures, and it includes a strong chapter on evaluating reports ("The Researcher As a Consumer"). All of which makes this book particularly helpful for novices who anticipate making the transition from consumer to producer. Inexpensive copies are usually available in the used book section of the larger Internet sources.

Vierra, A., Pollock, J., & Golez, F. (1998). *Reading educational research* (3rd ed.). Upper Saddle River, NJ: Merrill.

Relatively new within this group, this book is an excellent example of guides prepared with the novice reader in mind. Each chapter includes exercises that allow practice and test the reader's comprehension. In an appendix, the authors provide model responses and commentary for each exercise, a particularly useful feature for novice readers. Among its several virtues are a strong "how to do it" section on the task of evaluating research, as well as extensive attention to the needs of those attempting to read and digest qualitative studies. Three complete studies are reprinted in an appendix, along with critical commentaries by the authors.

Wolpert, E.M. (1981). *Understanding research in education: An introductory guide to critical reading.* Dubuque, IA: Kendall Hunt.

Unfortunately now out of print, this handbook still can be located in the used book marketplace and some college libraries. The book is designed explicitly for consumers of research, with an audience assumed to include students in psychology, sociology, and nursing, as well as education. A particularly lucid and thoughtful rating scheme is applied to examples from several forms of research—an accessory that you might wish to copy for your own use. The book does not, however, include assistance for readers interested in qualitative research.

APPENDIX B

Annotated List of Selected Journals, Indexes, and Research Retrieval Sources

This listing includes resources for retrieving research, research reviews, and discussions of research applications in physical education. It is not intended to be exhaustive; it simply represents a beginning point for readers who may be unfamiliar with what is available. It also may be useful for those who wish to expand the range of physical education research materials that they can retrieve. Not included here are the large number of publications in the area of education that give only limited and occasional attention to research in physical education.

Educational Resources Information Center (ERIC)

The resources and capabilities of ERIC are now so extensive and complex that they make any attempt at brief annotation impossible. Sufficient to say here that this should be your first stop in any attempt to locate research reports, research reviews, or compilations of research-based information on any topic related to teaching and curriculum in physical education. In some form, ERIC is available at almost any library that is large enough to have computer terminals, regardless of whether they have Internet capability or not. This includes many public libraries, as well as academic collections in institutions of higher education.

With the exception of those produced in the United Kingdom, all of the studies annotated in this text are included in the ERIC retrieval system. The three component collections within ERIC include *Current Index to Journals in Education* (CIJE), *Resources in Education* (RIE) and *ERIC Digests* (this latter collection consists of thousands of brief reviews that include highlights from recent research on particular topics in education, including some in physical education). Among the many capabilities that may be available where you use ERIC are online access from your home or office, the capacity to send citations to your own e-mail address, and the wonders of performing searches through the use of a sophisticated keyword system. If you are not familiar with ERIC, we suggest you begin by using the keywords *physical education* as your first search input. The result will be a list of major categories that reveal much about how research on teaching and curriculum has been indexed.

Journal of Sport Pedagogy (Semiannual)

Published in Great Britain, *Journal of Sport Pedagogy* (JSP) is a small but ambitious and often very lively source of studies related to teaching and curriculum. JSP is a relatively recent addition to the list of research journals in the field of physical education, and like most new journals, it shows occasional signs that it still is working to develop strong editorial standards and a cadre of competent reviewers. It already has attracted researchers from both Europe and North America, and it offers promise of becoming a truly international publication. The journal is only infrequently found in college and university serial collections, and it is not yet indexed in any of the major North American retrieval systems. Relatively inexpensive at the present level of $40 per year, individual subscriptions continue to be the best way to access the research in this journal.

Journal of Teaching in Physical Education (Quarterly)

One of the group of journals published by Human Kinetics and now entering its third decade, this journal is the primary North American outlet for research on teaching and curriculum in physical education. What has contributed to a generally high level of quality in the reports published here is a history of careful editorial control and continual efforts to recruit and train a strong team of peer reviewers. The *Journal of Teaching in Physical Education* (JTPE) contains research reports, research reviews, and articles related to the production and use of research-based knowledge. Among the 25 retrieval systems in which JTPE is indexed are *Current Contents/Social and Behavioral Sciences, Current Index to Journals in Education, Education Index, Educational Resources Information Center Database, Physical Education Index,* and *Psychological Abstracts.* With occasional exceptions, this journal will be found only in the serial holdings of larger colleges and universities. Individual subscriptions are presently set at $73 per year.

Physical Education Index (PEI)

Produced by the BenOak Publishing Company since 1977, PEI now is owned and published quarterly by Cambridge Scientific Abstracts. Although it is presently available only in hard copy (paper copy), this retrieval system is widely available in the reference sections of college and university libraries throughout North America. Lacking the speed, flexibility, and search capacities of modern electronic formats for retrieval, PEI clearly is an anachronism in the modern library. Nevertheless, with an exclusive devotion to indexing material from a range of English-language publications (domestic and for-

eign) that deal with dance, health, recreation, sport, sports medicine, physical therapy, and physical education, PEI occupies a special niche among the tools for locating research on teaching and curriculum in physical education. It certainly provides indexing for a far larger list of publication outlets than any other retrieval system. Provided that you have the time needed to become familiar with the system, you can circumvent annoyances that include the lack of a cumulative database and a set of index headings that is both archaic and distinctly quirky.

All of the North American journals abstracted in this text are indexed in PEI, as are many publications that appear in no other system. For example, some of the magazines produced by the state organizations of the American Alliance for Heath, Physical Education, Recreation and Dance are indexed here. Although none of those are research journals—and none provide the same level of quality assurance offered by publications with peer review capabilities—interesting and entirely competent small-scale studies do appear in them with surprising regularity. Other useful inclusions are listings for doctoral dissertations and master's theses in physical education. While both of those are included in other far more user-friendly retrieval systems, those search tools are not always available in the reference section of smaller libraries. Its limitations all aside, if you want to do a truly comprehensive search for research materials on a particular topic in physical education, PEI is an essential tool for your quest.

The Physical Educator (Quarterly)

Sponsored by Phi Epsilon Kappa (a professional fraternity for physical educators), *The Physical Educator* (TPE) has served the profession for more than a half-century. Oriented toward a readership that includes teachers and coaches, as well as scholars, TPE is best characterized as a practitioner's research journal. It contains research reviews and reports from studies of teaching and coaching. Although the quality of individual reports is somewhat uneven, the coverage of interesting research questions is substantially broader than that found in the more highly selective journals. That characteristic makes it valuable as a starting place in any search for studies of particular problems in physical education. Available in the serial collections of most colleges and universities, TPE is indexed in both the *Education Index* and the

Physical Education Index retrieval systems. Individual subscriptions presently are set at $37.50 per year.

Quest (Quarterly)

Published by Human Kinetics, *Quest* is the journal of the National Association for Physical Education in Higher Education. Styled as a professional journal for college teachers and administrators, *Quest* serves primarily as an outlet for articles on theory and opinion rather than research reports, although the latter do appear from time to time. Research reviews, such as those appearing in the annual issue devoted to the *Proceedings of the American Academy for Kinesiology and Physical Education,* offer a valuable resource for locating studies of teaching and curriculum in physical education. Among the 20 retrieval systems in which *Quest* is indexed are the *Education Index, Current Contents/Social and Behavioral Sciences, Current Index to Journals in Education,* and the *Physical Education Index.* This journal can be found in the serial collections of most colleges and universities. Individual subscriptions presently are $45 per year.

Research Quarterly for Exercise and Sport

Sponsored by the American Alliance for Health, Physical Education, Recreation and Dance, this is North America's oldest and most distinguished research journal for sport, exercise, and physical education. The journal itself is divided into sections, each with its own section editor, and one such division, Pedagogy, contains research reports on teaching and curriculum in physical education. Other sections, however, often contain reviews and reports that would be of interest to physical educators, par-

ticularly the divisions for Motor Control and Learning, Measurement and Evaluation, Growth and Motor Development, and Psychology.

Research Quarterly for Exercise and Sport (RQES) employs reviewers who are research specialists in the topical areas of the particular section they serve, and the journal as a whole has a tradition of strong editorial oversight. In consequence, RQES has maintained a generally high standard of quality for the studies it presents. The style of presentation is oriented toward a readership consisting of scholars, researchers, and graduate students. This journal can be found in the serial collections of most college and university libraries. Among the 12 retrieval systems in which it is indexed are *Current Contents/Social and Behavioral Sciences, Current Index to Journals in Education, Education Index, Psychological Abstracts,* and the *Physical Education Index.* Individual subscriptions presently are set at $48 per year.

Sport, Education, and Society (Semiannual)

One of the journals offered by the Carfax Publishing Company, *Sport, Education, and Society* (SES) has editorial headquarters in Great Britain but an editorial board that is international in origin—presently from the United States and the United Kingdom, as well as Australia, Finland, and Germany. Relatively new as a journal in the broad field of physical activity, SES has already acquired a reputation for attracting researchers with special interest in alternative modes of inquiry, including critical theory and qualitative research. With an experienced editorial staff, SES represents a rapidly improving and distinctly cosmopolitan outlet for research on teaching, curriculum, and related public policy. Presently available only in the serial collections of large colleges and universities, individual subscription rates have been set at $56 per year.

APPENDIX C

Learning From Studies of How Teachers Read and Understand Research

How teachers read research is now the topic of a small body of research. The studies include descriptions of their expectations, reading strategies, comprehension, and reactions. The results seem largely congruent across studies although they certainly also contain some surprises that contradict popular wisdom concerning teachers and research. In appendix D, we have placed brief annotations for a representative collection of such studies, as well as for several articles (not themselves research reports) on the topic of reading and using research in physical education. The reports were generally not difficult to read, and as teachers ourselves, we found them both informative and entertaining.

At the time this text was prepared, none of the published studies of teachers' research reading focused explicitly on physical educators—although several included them as part of generic samples of teaching personnel. We have no persuasive reason to expect teachers in our field to differ from classroom teachers or any other special-subject instructors. Accordingly, we will set the stage with some general observations about the place of research and research publications in the lives of educational practitioners.

Research and Educational Practitioners

In varying degrees, each study revealed that at least part of what had been found about reading research could be attributed to the dispositions that participating teachers brought to the reading and respond-

ing tasks they were asked to perform. Central factors in how they approached the reading of research include their conceptions of research as a process, their perception of its potential value as a product, and their expectations for how it might influence or affect their practice. Several of the studies involved direct inquiry in those matters, but even in those that did not, the reports made clear that the investigators had been moved to consider the topic of teachers' assumptions about research.

For instance, several researchers appeared to believe that teachers could be sorted into one of four dispositional categories. These represent states of mind produced by experience and professional development, rather than personality traits. Although the category headings used here were suggested by others (see Zeuli & Tiezzi, 1993), the characterizations are ours.

1. *Nonbelievers.* Some teachers anticipated that research would be irrelevant to their work, purely theoretical, and devoid of practical assistance. Included here would also be teachers who harbored deep suspicions about the political motives and honesty of researchers. Several investigators indicated that the largest number of their participants would fall into this category.

2. *Blind believers.* Some teachers expected research to provide specific instructional techniques and strategies that they could apply immediately. When done properly, research was understood as a process that would generate lists of validated and desirable teacher behaviors. Such research products were expected to specify methods that would solve

problems in the classroom while seeming to be consistent with the teachers' own values—as well as being practical in terms of conditions within their workplace.

3. *Thoughtful consumers.* Some teachers expected research to provide ideas that would illuminate rather than directly alter their practice. These teachers primarily saw research as a means for becoming more aware of the complexities in their work and for identifying alternative ways of thinking about it. There was, however, some indication that only a relatively small number of teachers would be so classified.

4. *Erratic consumers.* Some teachers possessed no consistent definition of research and, in some instances, seemed unable to assimilate one. The distinction between published articles containing authoritative assertions of opinion and actual research reports appeared to be elusive for these teachers. At any point in a study, their performance of reading and response tasks might make them appear to belong in one of the other three categories, but this tendency changed frequently—and not in a logical or predictable manner.

It was clear that investigators had no ready explanation for this latter group. It may be that approaching the reading task in different states of mind leads teachers to make distinctly different interpretations of a research study. Our experience, however, suggests that the roots of tangled responses to research lie in exposures to the distinctly mixed attitudes toward research displayed by significant others—particularly in the context of formal teacher preparation by education professors, as well as during the initial induction to school culture by supervisors, teaching colleagues, and school administrators.

Selected Studies

With that brief introduction, we now turn to the selected studies of how teachers read and understand research that we consulted in preparation for writing this text. Rather than offer a long catalog of results from individual studies, we have compiled a list of summary statements that reflect our own tentative generalizations—all of which are supported by at least several studies and none of which would be directly contradicted by any evidence of which we presently are aware. We have not attempted to impose any particular logic on the sequence of the summary statements. They appear in the order that they came to our attention.

In each study, the critical factors that could influence the results were the procedures used to select participants (sampling), the determination of studies to be read (materials), and the formulation of instructions for reading and response tasks (procedures). In other words, as you contemplate our tentative conclusions, please remember that three dynamic variables—sampling, materials, and procedures—all affect our research-based generalizations. If you see your own experiences reflected in any of these general descriptions, that is a good thing. You should not, however, expect all of our research-based generalizations to provide a comfortable fit. People, of course, are far too complicated for that to be possible.

Tentative Conclusions From Research on How Teachers Read Research

A. The technical difficulty involved in reading did not appear to influence any teacher's perception of the value or the credibility of reports; however, teachers did register considerable annoyance about research jargon and the use of statistics. Those irritations notwithstanding, what they learned from a study and how they evaluated it and its author seemed not to be influenced positively or negatively by the level of reading difficulty involved.

B. Many of the teachers spontaneously employed various study strategies that appeared to assist them in following the main points in a report. Generally, they were quite sophisticated in their use of reading and comprehension skills, such as skimming the entire article before reading it, checking back to previously read sections for clarification, and summarizing either passages individually or the article as a whole.

C. Teachers commonly employed analogies while reading. They made facile connections across subject matter, grade levels, and research questions by recognizing parallel instances in their own work context. Such a skill probably accounts for the fact that when allowed free choice of reports, many teachers would select at least some studies involving variables not represented directly in their own situation.

D. Whether positive or negative, teachers' responses to reading research were frequently quite intense. Whatever the context for their participation, they took the reading task seriously. Evaluations were expressed with vigor, agreements with firm statements, and objections announced with surprising passion. For reasons that are not entirely clear, reading research appears to engage teachers at levels even they find surprising.

E. Comprehension, via self-report or external judgment, improved under certain conditions. As you might suppose, the most accurate understandings were associated with reports selected from practitioner-oriented journals (rather than research outlets intended for scholars), free choice of reports (from a list of options), and ample reading time.

F. Teachers created meanings from what they read in complex and highly personal ways. While their interpretations were not always accurate, they did try to make sense of what they read in terms of their own experience. Teachers did not characteristically hold the content of studies at arm's length. They persistently personalized their responses by asking, What might this mean for my teaching, my workplace, or my understanding of the world? At the same time, and perhaps for the same reason, the way they processed what they read was not always linear and predictable.

G. Whenever study procedures allowed, it was clear that the opportunity to talk with others about what had been read was a valuable adjunct to solitary reading. One suggestion was that the value of such conversations increased as the requisite skills were practiced and improved—for example, the ability to succinctly describe the primary purpose of a study.

H. Teachers did not find any particular type of research—such as experimental, quasi-experimental, case study, survey, classroom ethnography—to be any more persuasive, relevant to their work, or more likely to influence their teaching than any other. Although they certainly could rank individual studies from high to low on those three characteristics, there was no indication that such responses were systematically associated with the kind of research design involved.

I. Studies that addressed the relationship between what the teacher does and what the pupils learn received the highest rankings—irrespective of any other characteristic of the study or the report. This trend applied

whether the relationship was direct, such as studies of instructional methods, or indirect, such as in investigations related to curriculum design. Teachers seemed to value any kind of information that appeared to reduce uncertainty about the consequences of their decisions and actions.

J. So far as we could determine, most of the teachers involved in these studies would hold a single common test for the credibility (truthfulness) of a research finding. That arbiter would be "Will it work that way in my classroom?" Interestingly, relatively few would include reference to the persuasive logic of the research design or the confirmation by other studies (replication) in that final evaluation.

K. Teachers' comments about the reports they had read made it clear that most would not automatically give privilege to research-based knowledge over other sources of wisdom. In fact, most would be inclined to give more credence to the lessons of their own past experience or the voice of their intuition than to formal documentation of any kind.

L. If a researcher were to ask, "Where would you look for help if you had a problem in your teaching?" the answer would be predictable— at least for the teachers described in these reports. Few would turn to research. The majority asserted emphatically that "to get help with a problem in my teaching I would ask someone (working at the same grade level and in the same subject field) who already has solved the problem successfully." Demonstrated success in the classroom was regarded as the most reliable and perhaps the most accessible source of advice about teaching.

M. Paradoxically, among the teachers who were least inclined to invest much time and effort into intensive study of research reports were both those who expected to find little of practical value and those who expected research to find explicit prescriptions for action. Often skeptical about the validity as well as the applicability of findings, the teachers in the former group had little motive to apply intensive study skills. Teachers in the latter group were likely to skim or skip sections dealing with research procedure and to be quite uninterested in how a study supported or failed to support the investigator's conclusions and recommendations. How findings were derived could be treated as irrelevant—only the outcomes mattered. The end result often was that whether skeptics or true believers, these were the teachers who most often settled for an incomplete, idiosyncratic, or simply incorrect understanding of what was in a report.

N. Apparently, many teachers held two beliefs about the nature of research that seemed to cause more difficulty and confusion than any other misunderstanding. First, they held the notion that in performing a study, the researcher is "trying to prove something." In the teachers' minds, the author will therefore be biased in execution of the study or in the interpretation of findings. Second, they also held the belief that if a group of studies examine what appears to be the same question and they produce different results, then either the research is defective or the researchers are dishonest.

O. Few of the studies we reviewed dealt directly with the matter of when, how, and whether teachers transfer ideas that they find in research to create changes in what they do or how they understand their work. Nevertheless, by combining (a) what the investigators reported of the participating teachers' comments about using research findings and (b) our own experience and observations as educators, we found ourselves confident that we could identify the single most common difficulty teachers experience when considering the applicability of research in their own classes. That key problem rests in the expectations held for transferability of findings from the research setting to the actual conditions in the teacher's own work setting. That topic is the subject for our discussion in the following section.

Miscommunication Between Researchers and Teachers

As a slice of the world, research describes how things were or how they worked at some particular time, in some particular place, for some particular set of teachers and students. When teachers read a report or annotation they often assume (sometimes correctly, but more often incorrectly) that the researcher is saying directly, or by implication, "What was found in this study also is true of your work-

place." Because most experienced teachers have an elegantly elaborated sense of the specific physical, social, political, and pedagogical reality of their own classrooms, they immediately recognize why such a claim might be false. They retort (at least mentally), "You don't know a thing about my classroom or school, and if you did, you would know how the situation is completely different here—and why your so-called findings just would not be applicable." As you can imagine, that raises a serious barrier to reading, digesting, and making use of research!

If we may pause a moment to play the role of referee, it seems that what we have here is a serious failure of communication. Most researchers know perfectly well that findings from a study are unlikely to apply in precise detail to any setting other than where the investigation was performed. What they also know, however, is that careful research can reveal regularities in the physical education setting that have at least a moderately high probability of being found in many, if not all, teaching situations.

In that sense, then, research findings in education provide not certainty but clues about the possible location of opportunities to make things better—opportunities that always require adjustment to the particular details of the place where they might be exploited. But most research reports are not written in a manner that makes all of that explicitly clear. The result is that some teachers acquire a much different perception of what researchers assert in their reports. They see researchers as claiming universal truths about places they have never seen and hence do not understand.

A great deal more can be said about that unhappy collision of differing perspectives, but this is not the place for us to take up the topic. If you are interested in exploring what research can teach us about such a difficult issue, one of the readings annotated in appendix D (Huberman, 1993) describes how one group of researchers found a way to deal with the need to bridge the gap between their studies and teachers' sense that the findings did not fit their individual contexts. Among the several strategies the researchers employed, one involved their engaging the teachers at the research site in a full discussion about the findings and the possible implications for making improvements—then they integrated what they learned from the teachers directly into the research report. That process was subsequently associated with a distinctly positive shift in how those teachers and other readers regarded the possibility of transfer from study to practice.

What Practical Value Is to Be Derived From Learning About How Teachers Read and Understand Research?

To close, we feel it is appropriate to pose such a rhetorical question. Our response has two parts. First, the use you make of the information in the preceding pages of this appendix depends on what you learned. If reading about how other teachers encountered research reports helped you to surface and clarify some of your own beliefs and concerns, then such lessons should work to your advantage whenever and wherever you encounter research. For example, you may have less apprehension about being the only educator in the world who has difficulty reading and understanding complex studies, who sometimes feels confused about what benefit should be derived, or who wonders if researchers really appreciate how complicated and context-specific teaching can be. You certainly know now that you are not alone and that none of these difficulties present an insurmountable barrier. You already are on your way to doing what other teachers have done—reading and making use of research.

The second part of our response is to ask you to notice that some of the guidelines we suggested for reading about research (see "Guidelines for Reading Research") had direct connections to what we learned from studies of how teachers read research. For example, research indicates that those teachers who expect all legitimate educational research to provide prescriptions for immediate application are likely to bring a serious handicap to reading and understanding research reports (and to deriving any benefit from doing so). Such a finding provides direct evidence in support of our Guideline Number 6 ("The Main Purpose of Reading Research Is to Help You Understand Your Work") and Guideline Number 8 ("Expect to Find Valuables, Not Easy Answers"). If you insist that every study tell you exactly what to do, you are going to miss half the fun—and much of the profit.

Not to put too fine a point on the matter, but our suggested reading guidelines were not dreamt up out of whole cloth. They were in fact hammered out from a combination of hard experience (ours) and a small but helpful body of research—which certainly does not mean you have to agree with each guideline. What it does mean is that you might be well served by recalling them as suggestions whenever you encounter accounts of research on teaching physical education.

APPENDIX D

Annotated Bibliography of Selected Reports and Articles on How Teachers Read, Understand, and Use Research

For reasons that are obscure, relatively few investigators have pursued questions related to what dispositions teachers have toward research, what studies they read, how they understand them, or what impact the reports have on their practice. Although nearly everyone in education holds (and often expresses) opinions about that matter, surprisingly little data exists to support any description or assertion.

The items annotated below do not represent the products of an exhaustive search, but they do present a reasonable cross section of what is recent and readily available. As background for readers who may be interested, we have included several commentaries written by scholars with particular interest in and familiarity with the topic of teachers and research. In addition, several studies are annotated that attend to the research reading habits of teacher educators, as distinct from teachers and other educational personnel. Items related to physical education are noted.

Gitlin, A., Barlow, L., Burbank, M.D., Kauchak, D., & Stevens, T. (1999). Pre-service teachers' thinking on research: Implications for inquiry oriented teacher education. *Teaching and Teacher Education, 15,* 753-769.

The origins of this study lie in a gradual sea change in teacher preparation that has been taking place in the last decade. In many programs, educational research is no longer used only as a basis for prescribing "right action" for preservice trainees. More frequently, novice teachers are asked to engage in systematic observation projects and data collection activities on which to base their own reflective inquiries about schools, pupils, and instruction. But where do recruits start that process? What do they already believe about research when they enter the door of an undergraduate or master's level professional preparation program: What is research? Who does it? Where do you find it? Does it apply to your problems as a new teacher? How could you use it? Would you try to use it? For one program, the answers are here—and they are not encouraging at all! If these results are generally true of preservice teachers across the nation, teacher educators have a long and difficult task ahead if they truly intend to inculcate the habits of inquiry (or the skills of a critical consumer) in the next generation of teachers.

Hatch, J.A. (1999). What preservice teachers can learn from studies of teachers' work. *Teaching and Teacher Education, 15,* 229-242.

This is not a research report, but it is a thoughtful and detailed proposal for putting research to work in teacher preparation programs. The author's suggestion is that research on teachers' work should be systematically included in teacher education curricula. In support of his proposal, he summarizes recent research in three areas: characteristics of teaching as work, characteristics of the teacher's workplace, and teaching as coping and adapting to those characteristics. He argues that teachers need to have a more active role in their own socialization into the vocational role. They will be better prepared to survive and grow during their initial years of teaching when they know more in advance about the nature of the job, when that information is more vivid and credible, and when what they learn is more closely fitted to their other preparation experiences. An evaluation of such an effort in a physical education preparation program would make a splendid thesis or dissertation—and perhaps a valuable contribution to what we know about how teachers can profit from research.

Huberman, M. (1993). Changing minds: The dissemination of research and its effects on practice and theory. In C. Day, J. Calderhead, & P. Denicolo (Eds.), *Research on teacher thinking: Understanding professional development.* Washington, DC: Falmer.

Imagine this: A large, federally funded investigation of teaching that is designed from the outset to move its findings from the researchers and their reports to the minds and practices of the teachers and administrators who had been involved. Further, imagine that before completion of the study, the findings were negotiated through a dialogue in which the teachers could provide input in ways that accurately contextualized the data and that shaped the meanings assigned to the research results. Do you think research conducted in that manner might be more likely to exert a positive influence on both school policies and teachers' classroom actions?

To answer that question, the evidence presented by the author is overwhelming. The study reported here consists not just of one such investigation but of 11 research efforts, each involving the topic of *negotiated findings.* Although the degree of success differed across the 11 component studies, one outcome was underscored by the experience of all. With careful planning and patient interactions, research findings can be moved from investigators to teachers, and the meanings of those findings can be added to the worlds of policy and practice as well as to the more restricted domain of academic theory.

This combination review and report is completely without technical or conceptual impediments to understanding. To appreciate the analysis requires nothing more than careful reading. The message is written large—particular steps must be attended and they are not always simple or easy. If everyone is committed to each step's execution, then teachers can understand and implement research. Further, an interesting surprise waits at the end of such successful efforts. Teachers are not the only people who can be changed by this kind of dissemination. How researchers conceptualize their own findings and, in some instances, how they understand the process of inquiry may not be left untouched.

Johnson, M.E.B. (1966). Teachers' attitudes to educational research. *Educational Research, 9*(1), 74-79.

We had a particular reason for including this rather elderly study, which is also a bit of an anomaly in this book because its participants were teachers in Great Britain. The study is a model of simplicity: 270 elementary and secondary teachers filled out a carefully constructed 36-item questionnaire concerning their attitudes toward research and its possible applications in their work. Hidden among the attitude items, however, were 10 questions that could only be answered correctly if the respondent was familiar with findings from recent research. The results provided many clues that would help you think about your own beliefs and dispositions toward research and teaching in physical education. For example, as you would suspect, positive attitudes are associated with much higher familiarity with recent research. But, are you sure you know which comes first—familiarity or positive attitude? Why was there a large gender difference showing males to be more positive about research and much more optimistic about its applications? Would any or all of these findings be true for physical education teachers in North America? We would love to know the answers to questions such as those as they would add wonderful complications to our puzzling about how and whether research works in the lives of teachers.

Kelley, E.J., & Lindsay, C.A. (1977). Knowledge obsolescence in physical educators. *Research Quarterly, 48,* 463-474.

A large part of this study involved the creation of an inventory of recent research-based knowledge in physical education. The resulting instrument, in fact, was a written examination to be used in assessing what teachers knew about selected aspects of their work—instructional methods, curriculum, adapted programs, physical conditioning, and exercise physiology. A sample of 1,024 male secondary school physical education teachers completed the inventory. Despite being relatively young (40% were under 30) and still engaged in professional development activity (90% had taken graduate credits in physical education), the participants demonstrated that they were severely out of date with regard to current knowledge. Results showed that 99% scored below what experts considered reasonable for teachers in each of the areas previously noted. There are endless questions about the meaning of those results (the study never was replicated), not least of which is, "So what?" A partial answer to that question lies in the details of the study, but we confess that it is difficult for us to know how to apply the concept of *knowledge obsolescence* to our own definition of a good teacher. If you decide to look at this very interesting and provocative study, we would like to hear what you think.

Kennedy, M.M. (1999). A test of some common contentions about educational research. *American Educational Research Journal, 36,* 511-541.

Despite the fact that it is a complicated study with a large number and variety of findings, this report is a relatively easy read—testimony to the fact that good writing is a key element in the research process. When reading this study as preparation for writing this book, we focused our attention on the central question that shaped the investigation, "Do teachers respond differently to different kinds of research (experiments, surveys, case studies, and so on)?" Answering that question involved a set of four subquestions about what the participating group of teachers found credible, understandable, relevant, and likely to be influential among a set of nine studies they read, rated, and discussed with the researcher. The results were clear and unambiguous—the answer was no. For most of the teachers in this investigation, the type of research did not determine their reactions. Their ratings of each study did differ, but those differences appeared to have been driven by something else, specifically by how clearly studies related teaching actions to student learning. That finding and others from this report had a direct influence on which studies we selected for you to read in this book. In the same sense, the present text reflects our belief that under the right conditions research can serve the people who must make professional decisions.

Lawson, H.A. (1992). Why don't practitioners use research? Explanations and selected implications. *Journal of Physical Education, Recreation, and Dance, 63*(9), 36, 53-57.

The title of this article tells it all. This report is a survey of all the commonly encountered explanations for the lack of connection between the assertion that a teacher of physical education is a professional and what many physical education teachers actually do in the course of their careers. Professions demand that practice primarily be shaped and continually revised in terms of research-based knowledge. If this maxim is true in physical education, it is only valid in very limited ways and unevenly so at best. Before you sound the objection that your favorite explanation is not given, please read the entire article first.

Lawson certainly had heard and cataloged all of our own preferred explanations, including the most fundamental ones: failures of teacher preparation, restrictive workplace conditions, and the simple fact that a great deal of excellent physical education is delivered every day without any clear connection to research whatever! The author's conclusion—if there truly is a problem, it lies in the system itself rather than in the behavior of individuals or groups—may ring true for you after hearing him out. But we wonder what you would do with that understanding? We are not entirely sure ourselves and would welcome your comments. This special thematic issue of the *Journal of Physical Education, Recreation, and Dance* contains other articles on the same topic.

Lawson, H.A. (1993). Teachers' use of research in practice: A literature review. *Journal of Teaching in Physical Education, 12,* 366-374.

As indicated in the title, this is a review of investigations related to teachers' use of research in their daily practice (see the previously annotated item). The review is quite comprehensive for what was available at the time in physical education, and it selectively uses research on classroom teachers. At the close of the review, the author describes a small, unpublished pilot study undertaken with his colleagues. The findings serve to tie together and illuminate many of the points that were highlighted in the review. Although you would have to bring the review up to the present date, this place is an excellent one to begin if you are curious about this topic.

Littman, C.B., & Stodolsky, S.S. (1998). The professional reading of high school academic teachers. *Journal of Educational Research, 92*(2), 75-84.

Despite the fact that this report deals neither with elementary school practitioners nor the subject of physical education, it comes as close to anything we have found that confirms the extent to which public school teachers read research from journal publications concerning their professional work. For all practical purposes, it appears that they simply do not do so. Using a national sample of 666 teachers of mathematics, English, science, and social studies, the authors found that slightly more than half reported any reading at all in professional journals over the previous year. Of that number, only 7% had examined articles in a journal dealing with general education, such as *Phi Delta Kappan, Educational Leadership, Education Week.* The rest had limited their reading to subject-specific journals, such as *The Mathematics Teacher, The English Journal, Social Education*—a publication type within which information based on educational research is only rarely found and actual reports almost never found. Thus, the only point of contact for the teachers in this carefully selected sample would be through the occasional research-based article in one of the general education journals, publications read by fewer than 10% of the participants. Using a combination of our experience and the opinion of experts in this field of inquiry, we would expect the reading rates for elementary teachers, including physical educators, to be even lower.

Locke, L.F. (1987). Research and the improvement of teaching: The professor as the problem. In G.T. Barrette, R.S. Feingold, C.R. Rees, & M. Pieron (Eds.), *Myths, models, and methods in sport pedagogy* (pp. 1-26). Champaign, IL: Human Kinetics.

This article is both an extended essay on the topic named in the title, "Research and the Improvement of Teaching," and a review of research related to that topic. The focus here, however, is not on teaching in school programs but on the role of research in the design and operation of programs preparing physical education teachers. As suggested by the subtitle, "The Professor as the Problem," the author finds evidence that research-based knowledge is more honored by its neglect than by its use in professional preparation. In more direct terms, teacher educators are portrayed as, at best, ambivalent about research, whether in regard to teacher education itself or pedagogy in the wider context of physical education. If one searches for the origins of disinterest among teachers concerning the alleged benefits of research for their daily work, one needs to look no further than the professorial models they encountered when preparing for their careers. The reference list for the article is now out of date, but there is no reason to believe that the analysis would be much changed if it were to be repeated today.

Metzler, M.W., & Freedman, M.S. (1985). Here's looking at you PETE: A profile of physical education teacher education faculty. *Journal of Teaching in Physical Education, 4,* 123-133.

We include this report here not because it is unambiguous in its findings or current in its coverage (18 years can be a significant interval in studies of this kind). It is here because it provides just about the only real data we have on the subject of how teacher education professors read and use research, which is a question that might (and probably should) interest you. It will not spoil your fun if we reveal what the 171 participants reported. First, they did little research, averaging about four publications over their entire career. Second, they spent little time doing research, about 3% of their total schedule. Third, they subscribed to few research journals; fewer than half of this sample did so. Finally, they did not often cite research as a personal preference among their responsibilities—only 16% put it in the top three activities. While we may be fortunate to have even these sketchy findings (professors do not do very well at investigating their own behaviors), an enormous number of unanswered questions about teacher educators still remain, not least of which are (a) how do they understand the research they do read, (b) how does that knowledge influence their daily work, and (c) why are they not more deeply engaged in the production and consumption of research?

Mitchell, M.F. (1993). Linking teacher educators, knowledge, and the quality of practice in schools. *Journal of Teaching in Physical Education, 12,* 399-412.

This was a review of the research literature available in 1993 that dealt with the three questions with which we closed the previous annotation. The author does not arrive at definitive conclusions, but he is able to construct some modestly persuasive assertions about the physical-education/teacher-education professor by making cautious use of the research on teacher educators outside the subject field of physical education. What most intrigued us, however, was his observations about the linkages among professors, teacher preparation programs, teachers, and school programs. The proposition that we can understand the relationship between teachers and research only if we consider it in the context of an interlinked system (of which teachers are only one part) seems intuitively correct. This point is one that may not be far from your own direct experience. How did professors and professional training shape or not shape your encounters with research, and in turn, how have those influenced or not influenced the quality of your work? Mitchell has his responses and we have our own, but what are yours—and in what ways might they be products of a system rather than just individual dispositions?

Shearer, B.A., & Lundeberg, M.A. (1996). Do models of expert reading strategies facilitate graduate students' reading of research? In D.J. Leu, C.K. Kinzer, & K.A. Hinchman (Eds.), *Forty-fifth Yearbook of National Reading Conference* (pp. 430-436). Chicago: National Reading Conference.

The purposes of this small study were clearly to explore (rather than resolve) several of the problematic aspects of teachers' encounters with research. One of those goals was achieved when following a brief period of instruction, a group of teachers significantly increased the number of strategies they employed in reading research reports. Further, it was clear that even simple forms of assistance can be useful in sensitizing teachers to the differences among types of studies and the corresponding need for matching reading strategies to the demands of each report. Also of interest here, the instructional treatment employed was based on a set of skills displayed by teachers who had been successful readers in a previous study of research reports. All of this suggests that adults who are competent learners (certainly the case with teachers) can improve their research reading skills with less difficulty than is commonly anticipated.

Shearer, B.A., Lundeberg, M.A., & Coballes-Vega, C. (1997). Making the connection between research and reality: Strategies teachers use to read and evaluate journal articles. *Journal of Educational Psychology, 89,* 592-598.

It is important to understand that the elementary, middle, and high school teachers participating in this study were selected because there was evidence that they were professionally active, which included participating in organizations and conferences, as well as subscribing to journals. That having been said, the picture of how they made connections between research and the realities of their lives is both fascinating and revealing. All participants read an article that each had selected based on personal interest, and while doing so, they talked aloud about what they were doing and thinking. The audiotapes of those commentaries were transcribed and analyzed, and those data have the quality of live, real-time descriptions that both illuminate the nature of the reading process and contradict some of the conventional wisdom about teachers' ability

to read and understand research. We leave the details for you to discover, but we are pleased to note here that teachers who remain professionally active can develop sophisticated reading strategies and impressive skills as research consumers.

Tiezzi, L.J., & Zeuli, J.S. (1995). *Supporting teachers' understanding of educational research in a master's level research course* (Research Report No. 95-5). East Lansing, MI: Michigan State University, National Center for Research on Teacher Learning. (ERIC Document Reproduction Service No. ED395916)

This report begins with a reprise of the findings from the study annotated after this one (Zeuli, 1994). The authors used those data, in addition to information from related studies, as a starting place to construct a master's-level course for experienced teachers. The class emphasized understanding research as one tool for asking questions about classroom practice, called here a *professional approach,* rather than using research just to receive answers and prescriptions, called here a *consumer approach.* Seminar activities, assignments, and materials are described in detail.

The authors then focus on the responses of the four teachers who entered the course with strongly established consumer orientations toward research. Data from an analysis of completed assignments and a series of interviews revealed modest shifts away from those narrow expectations toward the more professional approach to research. Progress, however, was slow, uneven, and difficult. A follow-up interview conducted a year after completion of the course revealed that the participants had found in the schools where they worked little or no opportunity or encouragement to practice or extend what they had learned about research.

Zeuli, J.S. (1994). How do teachers understand research when they read it? *Teaching and Teacher Education, 10*(1), 39-55.

This study provides a description and an analysis of how teachers read research in the light of their prior beliefs about what research is and how it should influence their teaching. Two groups of veteran teachers, roughly equivalent in terms of professional experience and training, were interviewed about their beliefs, expectations, and past experiences concerning research. Teachers in one group had at least one year of experience as teacher collaborators in public school research projects. The other group had no direct experience with formal inquiry. All were asked to read three research reports, then to describe that experience in written and oral formats, and finally to respond to questions that allowed assessment of how well they understood what they had read.

Analysis of the resulting data revealed great variation in the participants' responses to the required readings. Those who had the greatest difficulty understanding what they read, however, shared certain beliefs about research—beliefs that clearly were different from those held by teachers with experience in research activity. When the participants read research with a sole focus on finding prescriptions for how they should teach, they started with a burden that appeared to severely limit what they could learn. Additional data from this study are reported in Zeuli and Tiezzi (1993) in the following annotation.

Zeuli, J.S., & Tiezzi, L.J. (1993). *Creating contexts to change teachers' beliefs about the influence of research* (NCRTL-Research Report No. 93-1). East Lansing, MI: Michigan State University, National Center for Research on Teacher Learning. (ERIC Document Reproduction Service No. ED364540)

This report begins with presentation of an instrument designed to identify teachers' beliefs and dispositions about research. Vignettes were constructed in which three fictional teachers described what they believed about research and how they expected it to influence their classroom practice. The three were designed to express broad clusters of interrelated beliefs as either (a) generally irrelevant to practice, (b) the source of answers to questions and instructions for correct practice, or (c) the source of complicating ideas and new questions about practice. The remainder of the report describes how and why each teacher selected the vignette that was "most like me," what background factors seemed to be associated with that selection, and what consequences it had for their subsequent performance in reading research.

The resulting picture is complicated and often shows deep inconsistencies in what teachers believe; nevertheless, several firm conclusions were possible. For these participants, educational credentials in the form of undergraduate and graduate study (including courses in research) appeared to have no predictable impact on their beliefs about research. Opportunities for direct experience with research projects had a much more powerful and generally liberating impact on their dispositions. In reading this report, we found that frequent use of quotations from participating teachers' interview transcripts contributed both credibility to the authors' assertions and a sense of lively personalization to what might otherwise have been a dense and heavily theoretical analysis.

193

APPENDIX E

Annotated Bibliography of Selected Books Presenting Models of Teaching or Curriculum That Are Grounded on Research-Based Knowledge

The purpose of this brief annotated list of textbooks is to provide specimen models of instruction and curriculum that were inspired and shaped by the direct use of research-based knowledge. By the word *model* in this context, we mean a complete system (more or less), presented with the parts and the relationships among the parts, all of which are described and justified. In that sense, the word does not denote *ideal* or *exemplary,* but rather *archetype.*

As physical educators, we become aware of such systems when they are presented in publications, workshops, or conferences. An example of a curriculum model would be the SPARK program that was used in the studies presented in chapters 26, 27, and 28. An example of a teaching model would be the system presented by Graham, Holt-Hale, and Parker (1998).

Some models were not only based initially on research, but they were also examined in actual use through evaluative research. They produced additional research-based knowledge that can validate the teaching method or curriculum and expand our understanding of what happens when its underlying concepts are applied in practice. An example of such a model would be the cooperative learning model (see Vermette, 1998, in this appendix).

In the subject field of physical education, truly research-based models for teaching and curriculum are relatively rare. For the most part, the popular systems that have dominated public elementary school physical education have drawn primarily upon blends of creative inspiration, the craft wisdom accumulated by the creators of models, the traditions that have accumulated around school practice, and the impulses provided by social and political ideology. All of those can be valuable resources in making decisions about how to teach, but they do not make direct use of research-based knowledge. An example of such a data-free model would be Muska Mosston's Spectrum of Teaching Styles (Mosston & Ashworth, 1994).

A difficult and time-consuming task is grounding the models for pedagogy or a curriculum in a body of knowledge that has been explored (if not validated) by systematic inquiry. It is not the sort of work that easily recruits the passionate enthusiasm of potential textbook writers (a primary outlet for new models in physical education). It is also true that in the final analysis, even authors who make the greatest use of research-based knowledge must have some recourse to their own subjective sense of what makes for sound teaching or an effective curriculum. That point will be perfectly obvious if you look closely at any of the physical education books included in this appendix. In each case, however, we would argue that research-based knowledge was at least the starting place for the individual or group who designed the model.

Among the books that came most readily to our minds were several that dealt with the world of classroom teaching (see Bloom, 1981; Vermette, 1998). Those have been included here because they represent the clearest instances of fully explored linkage between research and practice. The best of that genre rely not only on basic research in the related academic disciplines, but they also make subsequent use of field evaluations of the pedagogical models that were created. When such tests include an initial round of exploratory classroom and laboratory experiments, in addition to subsequent large-scale longitudinal studies in field settings, they serve to define an educational utility that has been truly validated by research-based knowledge.

Many textbooks are, of course, generic in nature, rather than being filled with explications of a single model of teaching or curriculum. In some of those, the authors do attempt to make careful use of research in documenting, explaining, and supporting their recommendations for sound educational practice. Such books primarily are designed for use in preservice teacher preparation programs (see Rink, 1998; Saphier & Gower, 1997; Siedentop & Tannehill, 2000).

The great variety of topics that must be included in such generic texts makes it impossible to evaluate their content in the same way that researchers have investigated singular models—such as cooperative learning, phonics, and instruction based on learning styles—or, in physical education, the spectrum of styles, games for understanding, and sport education. Nevertheless, it seemed reasonable to include several of them as examples of texts that are grounded in research-based knowledge.

Finally, we have included one text (Ellis & Fouts, 1997) that offers descriptions of the extent to which a wide range of current innovations in education were initially shaped and later validated by research-based knowledge. We think you will find it a useful resource in considering the different ways in which research can be used in the process of developing models for instruction and curriculum.

Bloom, B.S. (1981). *All our children learning: A primer for parents, teachers and other educators.* New York: McGraw-Hill.

This book is not a "how to do it" manual of methods for a particular model of instruction or a particular design for curriculum content. Instead, it presents the basic formulation from which an endless variety of instructional and curricular alternatives can be constructed—all formulated with the research-based assertions of the design called *mastery learning.*

The text here is a collection of selected publications from the work of Benjamin Bloom. Among the articles reprinted is a set of four in which he established the tenets of mastery learning. The theoretical basis for Bloom's formulation can be traced directly to the work of educational psychologist John Carroll (1963), and from Carroll, back to the vast reaches of behavioral research on human learning.

Using that body of knowledge and theory about human behavior, Bloom proposed redefinitions for some of the fundamental elements in the instructional process. For example, in mastery learning, a student's aptitude is not regarded as an intangible intellectual capacity somehow resident in the brain but rather as "how long it takes a learner to master a given unit of learning." In this case, "less time" serves as the functional equivalent of higher aptitude. That may sound like a minor distinction, but its implications for teaching are enormous. Not the least of those consequences is the logical corollary that nearly all children can (and should) learn anything that we deem of sufficient importance to include in the school curriculum. All we need do is provide sound instruction and give the learners enough time.

The mastery model for teaching integrates the elements of time, opportunity for success, and task analysis to produce a guide for instruction. It starts with the theoretical propositions that (a) all children can learn, (b) anything that is to be learned must be broken down into its component parts, and (c) the parts must then be correctly sequenced. The model is comprehensive in that it gives direction to planning, instructing, and evaluating as they occur in any school subject matter. For example, some aspects of mastery learning would be familiar to physical education teachers who have employed traditional forms of skill progression in their classes.

What gives pause to some educators is the use of the reductionist approach in mastery learning—the breaking of a content down into constituent parts. If you are willing, however, to use the strategies of direct instruction and you are particularly interested in outcomes such as raising scores on standard achievement tests, then the evidence fully supports what this text asserts concerning effective teaching.

Often used as the primary instructional tool in outcomes-based curricula, mastery learning has been refined and implemented for more than 3 decades, during which time it has produced an impressive and persistently positive collection of evaluation studies. That level of success can be attributed in large measure to the research-based knowledge that served as the basis for the original design of mastery learning.

Ellis, A.K., & Fouts, J.T. (1997). *Research on educational innovations* (2nd ed.). Larchmont, NY: Eye on Education.

The authors of this book discuss and document the research basis for each of 12 theories that qualify as the basis for a current educational innovation. Written entirely in nontechnical prose, this lively text examines each theory and its resulting educational program at three levels: (a) basic research, the roots of a theory in the academic disciplines; (b) exploratory educational research on outcomes through classroom and laboratory experiments; and (c) program evaluations at school and district levels of implementation.

Even against the criteria established for adequate evidence at all three levels, some currently popular school initiatives fare surprisingly well—for example, programs based on the theoretical models for cooperative learning, mastery learning, and direct instruction. In other cases, some programs fail utterly—for example, the Hunter Model, most educational programs based on brain research, and curricula that make use of various theories of self-esteem. Finally, some innovations in teaching and curriculum currently lack sufficient study at one or several levels of examination; thus, we must await a final verdict. Examples include efforts to build programs based on research-based theories about thinking skills, learning styles, and authentic assessment.

The authors are careful to point out that research support is not the only consideration in selecting a teaching method or curriculum. A reading of any of their analyses, though, is likely to convince you that an examination of the relevant research is a wise place to begin! If you want to gain a better sense of how research-based knowledge inspires, shapes, and (in some instances) confirms new ideas in education, this book is an ideal introduction and guide.

Pangrazi, R.P., & Corbin, C.B. (1994). *Teaching strategies for improving youth fitness* (2nd ed.). Reston, VA: American Alliance for Health, Physical Education, Recreation and Dance.

As documented by the recent publication of *Physical Activity and Behavioral Medicine* by Sallis and Owen (1999), the several research fields concerned with human physical activity—motor learning, exercise physiology, biomechanics, public health, exercise epidemiology—have produced a body of research-based knowledge that is large, diverse, of exceptionally high quality, and theoretically rich. Accordingly, one might expect to find a plethora of models for instruction and curriculum in physical education that make direct use of that knowledge as the foundation for their design.

It is a peculiarity of the publishing business that such is not the case. Most textbooks dealing with teaching physical fitness, promoting active lifestyles, and encouraging wellness behaviors through school physical education have been produced for students, often with accompanying manuals for teachers. Within that genre, we have been unable to locate any texts that directly and comprehensively explicate the source of their assertions about instruction for teachers or content for teachers or students. Aside from short reference lists and an occasional footnote, such books do little to describe the research sources that support what they endorse.

Of course, there may be valid reasons for that omission, it sometimes being assumed that teachers and students are simply uninterested in such technicalities. Whatever the case, with joint sponsorship by a professional organization (the American Alliance) and a research and development organization (the Cooper Institute for Aerobics Research), this book comes close to representing what might be done to make the research basis for fitness instruction and programs apparent to any reader.

Here the reference list includes carefully selected studies with emphasis on accessibility to a wide reading audience in the categories of public health, physiology of exercise, epidemiology of physical activity, test development, adoption and adherence, and heredity. Footnotes in the main text lead directly to this listing. In addition, the text was reviewed before publication by prominent leaders in the research community associated with the areas of wellness and fitness.

Close inspection revealed that the links between research and recommendations for instruction were not as fully developed as the ties between research and the authors' assertions about appropriate curriculum content. Overall, however, it was not difficult to discern how research-based knowledge shaped most of the recommendations for improving youth fitness, including the concept of a community-based program. We suggest that you inspect any of the current crop of wellness or fitness publications designed for adoption as school textbooks and do so with an eye for how carefully the book's research foundations are explained to student readers.

Rink, J.E. (1998). *Teaching physical education for learning* (3rd ed.). Boston: WCB/McGraw-Hill.

As with the following annotation of the text by Siedentop and Tannehill (2000), this is a book deeply rooted in findings from three decades of research on effective teaching in the classroom. Further, the two texts are also linked by their reliance on findings from a series of doctoral dissertations at The Ohio State University and the many publications that ensued. Utilizing systematic observation and recording of behaviors of teachers and students in physical education classes, those studies provided the ground for Rink's ideas concerning class management, task presentations, and use of time.

A salient difference between the two texts, however, rests in the considerable extent to which Rink's book attends to content development as a component of instructional design. Over the course of three editions, it has in fact been content development—described by the keywords *informing, refining, extending,* and *applying*—that provided the most distinctive elements in this textbook, elements that became a part of the technical culture (language and concepts) shared by physical education teachers and teacher educators throughout North America.

Rink proposed arranging sequences of practice tasks that would match the learner's progressive development of a motor skill. The sequence therefore bridged the stages from initial acquisition, through refinement of execution and control, to final application of the skill in a natural setting. The notion of content development driven by skill development was in turn based on her reading of research and theory in the areas of instructional design and motor skill acquisition, most notably that provided by Gentile (1972) and Schmidt (1987). Although not yet evaluated by large-scale empirical tests in school settings, what Rink asserts about teaching physical education was inspired and shaped by research in both the academic disciplines and in the applied field of education.

Saphier, J., & Gower, R. (1997). *The skillful teacher* (5th ed.). Acton, MA: Research for Better Teaching.

Now in its fifth edition and entering its third decade of use in teacher education, one might expect a textbook produced by a publisher called "Research for Better Teaching" to make careful use of research-based knowledge in describing sound edu-

cational practice. Across each of 20 broad topic areas—such as discipline, attention, time, teaching styles, and classroom climate—the authors have attempted to support what they assert about good teaching with reference to findings from educational research. For example, when the authors address the treatment of time as a factor in teaching, they not only cite and quote from many of the classic studies and reviews of time allocation in the classroom, but they also employ language and constructs drawn directly from that literature.

The development of some topics must make use of a fairly narrow research base. Unlike the treatment of time, the explanation of teaching momentum draws upon only four sources, and two of them (Kounin, 1970; Doyle, 1979) include most of what we have learned about that subject. The recommendations for teaching practice, however, do seem reasonable as extensions of the knowledge base.

In contrast to the research base for teacher momentum, the authors used 50 reports, reviews, and other research-based publications to examine the topic of discipline, which truly reflected the relative size of such research literature. The complexity of the subject, as well as the controversy that attends it, demanded that the authors explain their recommendations with more than ordinary attention to empirical evidence. Whether the base is narrow or broad, it would be rare for a reader to ask, Why do it that way? without a research-based response from Saphier and Gower located somewhere nearby.

Siedentop, D., & Tannehill, D. (2000). *Developing teaching skills in physical education* (4th ed.). Mountain View, CA: Mayfield.

To fully appreciate the complex ways through which bodies of research-based knowledge have influenced this textbook, you would find it necessary to inspect all four of the editions. Nevertheless, although the book has evolved over time (most notably with the recent edition) and drawn upon several research traditions in its 25-year history, its deepest roots have remained both constant and visible.

At any point in the 16 chapters, it is possible to trace what is being espoused for physical education teachers back to the opening section of the book, where the authors lay out a series of assertions about teaching that were derived from inspection of the research literature. Further, the models for teaching and curriculum in this textbook have been closely associated with a large and cohesive graduate program at The Ohio State University. They therefore benefit from the fact that doctoral students, faculty, and graduates have returned again and again to the task of understanding the nature of teaching—further extending the network of ideas about what constitutes effective physical education.

The primary source of knowledge for this text was drawn from the 35-year tradition of research on effective teaching. That extensive group of studies was later supplemented by a smaller but growing research literature focusing on questions about effective teaching in physical education. Much of the latter was enriched with studies employing the tools of behavioral science, particularly those that involved observation of student behavior during the learning process. More recently, the empirical work of Walter Doyle (1986), who examined the classroom as an ecological system, has been used to analyze the transactions of physical education classes as a series of student tasks. Each of those streams of inquiry played a distinctive part in shaping the content of this book.

It might be expected that a text so thoroughly influenced by a particular set of research traditions would espouse a single best method of instruction. The eclectic tone of the book therefore may come as a surprise to many readers. The authors appear to be completely comfortable with the notion that there may be alternative means to achieve the same educational objective. What they do insist, however, is that not all choices are equal for all purposes—or for all teachers, students, and schools. They assert that how and what we choose to teach in physical education has consequences for learners and teachers that are observable and substantially predictable, on the basis of what we have learned from research, that is.

Vermette, P.J. (1998). *Making cooperative learning work: Student teams in K-12 classrooms.* Upper Saddle River, NJ: Merrill.

We selected this particular text from among a number of candidates because it employs a set of research annotations much like those used in the present book. They demonstrate how research-based knowledge has initially shaped cooperative learning as a model for instruction and how it later confirmed its efficacy in educational settings. As a sort of how-to manual for teachers, this text not only draws upon a extensive body of research and theory, but it also describes and juxtaposes five well-developed instructional variations on the central format of cooperative learning.

More than a half-century ago, in the then new discipline of social psychology, investigators such as Kurt Lewin and Morton Deutsch made important discoveries concerning the power of group dynamics and social interaction to influence what people can do and learn. Theories of social interdependence were promptly erected on that empirical base, and in turn, those attracted the attention of educational researchers such as the brothers David and Roger Johnson (1999) at the University of Minnesota and Robert Slavin (1985, 1990) at Johns Hopkins University. They and others produced a large body of research concerning the effects of student cooperation as compared with conditions of isolation or individual competition in the school classroom.

Small-scale studies of single classrooms have expanded across 50 years to include massive investigations in which entire schools and school districts were the unit of analysis. The more than 300 published research reports lead to a simple conclusion. Given well-trained teachers and adequate contextual supports, instruction through the model of cooperative learning produces learning outcomes that are superior to many other models. That finding applies across subject matters, student characteristics—such as age, ability, and gender—and, most importantly, many alternative kinds of outcome measures. Whether the educational objective is academic achievement in the form of problem-solving skills or retention of simple factual information or whether the objective is development of desirable attitudes toward learning, school, subject matter content, and fellow students, the evidence from research is uniform and overwhelmingly positive.

Cooperative learning as a format for group instruction appears in many physical education textbooks (including Rink, 1998; and Siedentop & Tannehill, 2000), and it is at the very least an implicit component of several models for teaching sports that have a substantial research base—for example, see Siedentop's textbook *Sport Education: Quality PE Through Positive Sport Experiences* (1994). Further, Grineski's book *Cooperative Learning in Physical Education* (1996) offers a useful first step in explicating the potential uses of cooperative learning as a format for teaching and organizing curriculum in the gymnasium.

Cooperative learning represents a clear case in which research-based knowledge served first to inspire, then to shape and define, and ultimately to confirm the effectiveness of an instructional method. In the best sense of the words, cooperative learning represents a new and refined educational technology in the classroom or gymnasium. In many respects, its origins, development, testing, and refinement make it comparable to the newest computer. At this time, cooperative learning may even have the advantage over hardware-based technologies. Lower initial cost, minimal maintenance, and benefits that have unequivocal support from research are powerful considerations.

REFERENCES

Anderson, A., Vogel, P., & Albrecht, R. (1999). The effect of instructional self-talk on the overhand throw. *The Physical Educator, 56,* 215-221.

Ashy, M., & Humphries, C.A. (2000). "Don't use balloons on windy days": Elementary education majors' perceptions of teaching physical education. *Action in Teacher Education, 22*(1), 59-71.

Berliner, D.C., & Casanova, U. (1996). *Putting research to work in your school* (2nd ed.). Arlington Heights, IL: SkyLight.

Bloom, B.S. (1981). *All our children learning: A primer for parents, teachers and other educators.* New York: McGraw-Hill.

Carroll, J.B. (1963). A model of school learning. *Teachers College Record, 64,* 723-733.

Chase, M.A., Ewing, M.E., Lirgg, C.D., & George, T.R. (1994). The effects of equipment modification on children's self-efficacy and basketball shooting performance. *Research Quarterly for Exercise and Sport, 65,* 159-168.

Commission for Fair Play. (1990). *Fair Play for Kids.* Ottawa, Canada: Author.

Creswell, J.W. (1994). *Research design: Qualitative and quantitative approaches.* Thousand Oaks, CA: Sage.

Crouch, D.W., Ward, P., & Patrick, C.A. (1997). The effects of peer-mediated accountability on task accomplishment during volleyball drills in elementary physical education. *Journal of Teaching in Physical Education, 17,* 26-39.

DeLine, J. (1991). Why can't they get along? Developing cooperative skills through physical education. *Journal of Physical Education, Recreation, and Dance, 62*(1), 21-26.

DeVoe, D.E. (1991). Teacher behavior directed toward individual students in elementary physical education. *Journal of Classroom Interaction, 26*(1), 9-14.

Doyle, W. (1979). Making managerial decisions in classrooms. In D.L. Duke (Ed.), *78th Yearbook of the National Society for the Study of Education* (pp. 75-115). Chicago: University of Chicago.

Doyle, W. (1986). Classroom organization and management. In M.C. Wittrock (Ed.), *Handbook of research on teaching* (3rd ed., pp. 392-431). New York: Macmillan.

Ellis, A.K., & Fouts, J.T. (1997). *Research on educational innovations* (2nd ed.). Larchmont, NY: Eye on Education.

Gall, M.D., Borg, W.R., & Gall, J.P. (1996). *Educational research: An introduction* (6th ed.). White Plains, NY: Longman.

Gentile, A.M. (1972). A working model of skill acquisition with application to teaching. *Quest, 27,* 3-23.

Gibbons, S.L., Ebbeck, V., & Weiss, M.R. (1995). *Fair play for kids:* Effects on the moral development of children in physical education. *Research Quarterly for Exercise and Sport, 66,* 247-255.

Gitlin, A., Barlow, L., Burbank, M.D., Kauchak, D., & Stevens, T. (1999). Pre-service teachers' thinking on research: Implications for inquiry oriented teacher education. *Teaching and Teacher Education, 15,* 753-769.

Goodwin, W.L.L., & Goodwin, L. (1996). *Understanding quantitative and qualitative research in early childhood education.* New York: Teachers College Press.

Graham, G., Holt-Hale, S., & Parker, M. (1998). *Children moving: A reflective approach to teaching physical education.* Mountain View, CA: Mayfield Publishing.

Griffey, D.C., & Housner, L.D. (1991). Differences between experienced and inexperienced teachers' planning decisions, interactions, student engagement, and instructional climate. *Research Quarterly for Exercise and Sport, 62,* 196-204.

Grineski, S. (1996). *Cooperative learning in physical education.* Champaign, IL: Human Kinetics.

Hardyck, C.D., & Petrinovich, L.F. (1975). *Understanding research in the social sciences: A practical guide to understanding social and behavioral research.* Philadelphia: Saunders.

Hastie, P.A., Sanders, S.W., & Rowland, R.S. (1999). Where good intentions meet harsh realities: Teaching large classes in physical education. *Journal of Teaching in Physical Education, 18,* 277-289.

Hastie, P.A., & Saunders, J.E. (1991). Effects of class size and equipment availability on student involvement in physical education. *Journal of Experimental Education, 59,* 212-224.

Hatch, J.A. (1999). What preservice teachers can learn from studies of teachers' work. *Teaching and Teacher Education, 15,* 229-242.

Hellison, D. (1995). *Teaching responsibility through physical activity.* Champaign, IL: Human Kinetics.

Henkel, S.A. (1991). Teachers' conceptualization of pupil control in elementary school physical education. *Research Quarterly for Exercise and Sport, 62,* 52-60.

Hill, G.M., & Miller, T.A. (1997). A comparison of peer and teacher assessment of students' physical fitness performance. *The Physical Educator, 54,* 40-46.

Hopple, C., & Graham, G. (1995). What children think, feel, and know about physical fitness testing. *Journal of Teaching in Physical Education, 14,* 408-417.

Houston-Wilson, C., Dunn, J.M., van der Mars, H., & McCubbin, J. (1997). The effect of peer tutors on motor performance in integrated physical education classes. *Adapted Physical Activity Quarterly, 14,* 298-313.

Huberman, M. (1990). Linkage between researchers and practitioners: A qualitative study. *American Educational Research Journal, 27,* 363-391.

Huberman, M. (1993). Changing minds: The dissemination of research and its effects on practice and theory. In C. Day, J. Calderhead, & P. Denicolo (Eds.), *Research on teacher thinking: Understanding professional development.* Washington, DC: Falmer.

James, W. (1983). *Talks to teachers on psychology and to students on some of life's ideals.* Cambridge, MA: Harvard University Press.

Johnson, D.W., & Johnson, R.T. (1999). *Learning together and alone: Cooperative, competitive, and individualistic learning* (5th ed.). Boston: Allyn and Bacon.

Johnson, M.E.B. (1966). Teachers' attitudes to educational research. *Educational Research, 9*(1), 74-79.

Kelley, E.J., & Lindsay, C.A. (1977). Knowledge obsolescence in physical educators. *Research Quarterly, 48,* 463-474.

Kelly, L.E., Dagger, J., & Walkley, J. (1989). The effects of an assessment-based physical education program on motor skill development in preschool children. *Education and the Treatment of Children, 12,* 152-164.

Kennedy, M.M. (1999). A test of some common contentions about educational research. *American Educational Research Journal, 36,* 511-541.

Kounin, J. (1970). *Discipline and group management in classrooms.* New York: Holt, Rinehart & Winston.

LaMaster, K., Gall, K., Kinchin, G., & Siedentop, D. (1998). Inclusion practices of effective elementary specialists. *Adapted Physical Activity Quarterly, 15,* 64-81.

Lawson, H.A. (1992). Why don't practitioners use research? Explanations and selected implications. *Journal of Physical Education, Recreation, and Dance, 63*(9), 36, 53-57.

Lawson, H.A. (1993). Teachers' uses of research in practice: A literature review. *Journal of Teaching in Physical Education, 12,* 366-374.

Leedy, P.D. (1981). *How to read research and understand it.* New York: Macmillan.

Littman, C.B., & Stodolsky, S.S. (1998). The professional reading of high school academic teachers. *Journal of Educational Research, 92*(2), 75-84.

Locke, L.F. (1987). Research and the improvement of teaching: The professor as the problem. In G.T. Barrette, R.S. Feingold, C.R. Rees, & M. Pieron (Eds.), *Myths, models, and methods in sport pedagogy* (pp. 1-26). Champaign, IL: Human Kinetics.

Locke, L.F., Silverman, S.J., & Spirduso, W.W. (1998). *Reading and understanding research.* Thousand Oaks, CA: Sage.

Maxwell, J.A. (1996). *Qualitative research design: An interactive approach.* Thousand Oaks, CA: Sage.

McKenzie, T.L., Alcaraz, J.E., & Sallis, J.F. (1994). Assessing children's liking for activity units in an elementary school physical education curriculum. *Journal of Teaching in Physical Education, 13,* 206-215.

McKenzie, T.L., Alcaraz, J.E., Sallis, J.F., & Faucette, F.N. (1998). Effects of a physical education program on children's manipulative skills. *Journal of Teaching in Physical Education, 17,* 327-341.

McMillan, J.H. (1999). *Educational research: Fundamentals for the consumer.* New York: Addison Wesley.

McMillan, J.H., & Wergin, J.F. (1998). *Understanding and evaluating educational research.* Upper Saddle River, NJ: Merrill.

Metzler, M.W., & Freedman, M.S. (1985). Here's looking at you, PETE: A profile of physical education teacher education faculty. *Journal of Teaching in Physical Education, 4,* 123-133.

Mitchell, M.F. (1993). Linking teacher educators, knowledge, and the quality of practice in schools. *Journal of Teaching in Physical Education, 12,* 399-412.

Mosston, M., & Ashworth, S. (1994). *Teaching physical education* (4th ed.). New York: Macmillan.

Pangrazi, R.P., & Corbin, C.B. (1994). *Teaching strategies for improving youth fitness* (2nd ed.). Reston, VA: American Alliance for Health, Physical Education, Recreation and Dance.

Patrick, C.A., Ward, P., & Crouch, D.W. (1998). Effects of holding students accountable for social behaviors during volleyball games in elementary physical education. *Journal of Teaching in Physical Education, 17,* 143-156.

Pissanos, B.W., & Allison, P.C. (1993). Students' constructs of elementary school physical education. *Research Quarterly for Exercise and Sport, 64,* 425-435.

Ratliffe, T., Imwold, C., & Conkell, C. (1994). Children's views of their third grade physical education class. *The Physical Educator, 51,* 106-111.

Rink, J.E. (1998). *Teaching physical education for learning* (3rd ed.). Boston: WCB/McGraw-Hill.

Sallis, J.F., Condon, S.A., Goggin, K.J., Roby, J.J., Kolody, B., & Alcaraz, J.E. (1993). The development of self-administered physical activity surveys for 4th grade students. *Research Quarterly for Exercise and Sport, 64,* 25-31.

Sallis, J.F., McKenzie, T.L., Alcaraz, J.E., Kolody, B., Faucette, N., & Hovell, M.F. (1997). The effects of a 2-year physical education program (SPARK) on physical activity and physical fitness in elementary school students. *American Journal of Public Health, 87,* 1328-1334.

Sallis, J.F., & Owen, N. (1999). *Physical activity & behavioral medicine.* Thousand Oaks, CA: Sage.

Sanders, S., & Graham, G. (1995). Kindergarten children's initial experiences in physical education: The relentless persistence for play clashes with the zone of acceptable responses. *Journal of Teaching in Physical Education, 14,* 372-383.

Saphier, J., & Gower, R. (1997). *The skillful teacher* (5th ed.). Acton, MA: Research for Better Teaching.

Schmidt, R.A. (1987). *Motor control and learning: A behavioral emphasis* (2nd ed.). Champaign, IL: Human Kinetics.

Shearer, B.A., & Lundeberg, M.A. (1996). Do models of expert reading strategies facilitate graduate students' reading of research? In D.J. Leu, C.K. Kinzer, & K.A. Hinchman (Eds.), *Forty-fifth Yearbook of the National Reading Conference* (pp. 430-436). Chicago: National Reading Conference.

Shearer, B.A., Lundeberg, M.A., & Coballes-Vega, C. (1997). Making the connection between research and reality: Strategies teachers use to read and evaluate journal articles. *Journal of Educational Psychology, 89,* 592-598.

Shephard, R.J., & Trudeau, F. (2000). The legacy of physical education: Influences on adult lifestyle. *Pediatric Exercise Science, 12,* 34-50.

Siedentop, D. (Ed.). (1994). *Sport education: Quality PE through positive sport experiences.* Champaign, IL: Human Kinetics.

Siedentop, D. (Ed.). (1989). The effective elementary specialist study [Monograph]. *Journal of Teaching in Physical Education, 8,* 187-270.

Siedentop, D., & Tannehill, D. (2000). *Developing teaching skills in physical education* (4th ed.). Mountain View, CA: Mayfield.

Slavin, R.E. (1990). *Cooperative learning: Theory, research, and practice.* Englewood Cliffs, NJ: Prentice Hall.

Slavin, R.E., Sharan, S., Kagan, S., Hertz-Lazarowitz, R., Webb, C., & Schmuck, R. (Eds.). (1985). *Learning to cooperate, cooperating to learn.* New York: Plenum Press.

Solmon, M.A., & Carter, J.A. (1995). Kindergarten and first-grade students' perceptions of physical education in one teacher's classes. *The Elementary School Journal, 95,* 355-365.

Sweeting, T., & Rink, J.E. (1999). Effects of direct instruction and environmentally designed instruction on the process and product characteristics of a fundamental skill. *Journal of Teaching in Physical Education, 18,* 216-233.

Thomas, J.R., & Nelson, J.K. (1996). *Research methods in physical activity* (3rd ed.). Champaign, IL: Human Kinetics.

Tiezzi, L.J., & Zeuli, J.S. (1995). *Supporting teachers' understanding of educational research in a master's level research course* (Research Report No. 95-5). East Lansing, MI: National Center for Research on Teacher Learning. (ERIC Document Reproduction Service No. ED395916)

Treanor, L.J., Vanin, S.K., Nolan, C., Housner, L.D., Wiegand, R.L., & Hawkins, A. (1997). The effects of 3-day-a-week and 1-day-a-week physical education on the development of children's motor skills and knowledge in the United States. *Pedagogy in Practice, 3*(2), 3-18.

Trudeau, F., Laurencelle, L., Tremblay, J., Rajic, M., & Shephard, R.J. (1998). A long-term follow-up of participants in the Trois-Rivières semi-longitudinal study of growth and development. *Pediatric Exercise Science, 10*, 366-377.

Trudeau, F., Laurencelle, L., Tremblay, J., Rajic, M., & Shephard, R.J. (1999). Daily primary school physical education: Effects on physical activity during adult life. *Medicine and Science in Sports & Exercise, 31*, 111-117.

Trudeau, F., Espindola, R., Laurencelle, L., Dulac, F., Rajic, M., & Shephard, R.J. (2000). Follow-up of participants in the Trois-Rivières growth and development study: Examining their health-related fitness and risk factors as adults. *American Journal of Human Biology, 12*, 207-213.

Tuckman, B.W. (1999). *Conducting educational research* (5th ed.). New York: Harcourt Brace College Publishers.

van der Mars, H., Vogler, B., Darst, P., & Cusimano, B. (1994). Active supervision patterns of physical education teachers and their relationship with student behaviors. *Journal of Teaching in Physical Education, 14*, 99-112.

Vermette, P.J. (1998). *Making cooperative learning work: Student teams in K-12 classrooms.* Upper Saddle River, NJ: Merrill.

Vierra, A., Pollock, J., & Golez, F. (1998). *Reading educational research* (3rd ed.). Upper Saddle River, NJ: Merrill.

Ward, P., & O'Sullivan, M. (1998). Similarities and differences in pedagogy and content: 5 years later. *Journal of Teaching in Physical Education, 17*, 195-213.

White, A.G., & Bailey, J.S. (1990). Reducing disruptive behaviors of elementary physical education students with sit and watch. *Journal of Applied Behavior Analysis, 23*, 353-359.

Wolpert, E.M. (1981). *Understanding research in education: An introductory guide to critical reading.* Dubuque, IA: Kendall Hunt.

Zeuli, J.S. (1994). How do teachers understand research when they read it? *Teaching and Teacher Education, 10*(1), 39-55.

Zeuli, J.S., & Tiezzi, L.J. (1993). *Creating contexts to change teachers' beliefs about the influence of research* (Report No. NCRTL-93-1). East Lansing, MI: National Center for Research on Teacher Learning. (ERIC Document Reproduction Service No. ED364540)

INDEX

A

Academic Learning Time—Physical Education (ALT-PE) 4
accountability. *See* student accountability
Albrecht, R. 61-64
Alcaraz, J.E. 143-146, 147-150, 151-154
Allison, P.C. 94-98
Anderson, A. 61-64
Ashworth, S. 194
Ashy, M. 101-105
assessment 131-134
  by adults 135-139
  in lesson planning 131-134
  of long-term results 94-98, 157-163, 167-171
  by peers 135-139
  of skill acquisition 131-134

B

Bailey, J.S. 23-27
Barlow, L. 188
basic skills 11-14, 131-134, 147-150
basketball 15-19
behavior analysis 23-27, 32-36, 53-57
  contingencies in 32
  delayed multiple baseline design 49-50
  interventions in 32
  multiple baseline design 33
  withdrawal design 53
Berliner, D.C. xii
Bloom, B.S. 195
Borg, W.R. 176
Burbank, M.D. 188

C

Carroll, J.B. 195
Carter, J.A. 89-93
Casanova, U. xii
Chase, M.A. 15-19
children's fitness 143-146
class schedule 11-14
class size 3-6, 106-110
class management 23-27, 28-31, 37-41
classroom teachers. *See* in-service teacher development
Coballes-Vega, C. 192
Commission for Fair Play 32, 42
Condon, S.A. 146
Conkell, C. 79-83
constructivism 94-95
cooperative learning 198-199
Corbin, C.B. 196
Creswell, J.W. 176
Crouch, D.W. 32-36, 53-57
Cusimano, B. 28-31

D

Dagger, J. 131-134
daily physical education 106-110
Darst, P. 28-31
DeLine, J. 36

developing teaching skills 197-198. *See also* teacher education
DeVoe, D.E. 7-10
direct instruction 65-69
disruptive students 23-27, 79-83
Doyle, W. 197-198
Dulac, ,F. 167-171
Dunn, J.M. 49-52

E

Ebbeck, V. 42-46
Educational Resources Information Center (ERIC) 180
effects of physical education
  experimental studies 143-146, 147-150, 157-163
  review of studies 157-163
  studies of long-term benefits 157-163, 167-171
  studies of short-term benefits 157-163
  tracking studies 157-163
  Trois-Rivières Growth and Development Study 157-163, 167-171
Ellis, A.K. 195-196
equipment
  amount of 3-6
  modification of 15-19
Espindola, R. 167-171
Ewing, M.E. 15-19
experimental studies 160, 167-168
  interventions 32
  treatments 32
explicit teaching. *See* instruction

F

fair play 42-46
Faucette, F.N. 143-146, 147-150
fitness instruction 196-197
fitness testing 84-88, 135-139, 143-146
follow-up studies. *See* assessment of long-term results
Fouts, J.T. 195-196
Freedman, M.S. 191

G

Gall, J.P. 176-177
Gall, K. 111-117
Gall, W.R. 176
gender differences 7, 16-19, 89-93, 96-97, 144-146, 149-150
generalizability of results. *See* research application
Gentile, A.M. 197
George, T.R. 15-19
Gibbons, S.L. 42-46
Gitlin, A. 188
Goggin, K.J. 146
Golez, F. 178
Goodwin, L. 177
Goodwin, W.L.L. 177
Gower, R. 195, 197

Graham, G. 73-78, 84-88, 127, 194
Griffey, D.C. 124-128
Grineski, S. 198

H

Hardyck, C.D. 177
Hastie, P.A. 3-6, 106-110
Hatch, J.A. 188
Hawkins, A. 11-14
Hellison, D. 32
Henkel, S.A. 37-41
Hertz-Lazarowitz, R. 198
Hill, G.M. 135-139
Holt-Hale, S. 127
Hopple, C. 84-88
Housner, L.D. 11-14, 124-128
Houston-Wilson, C. 49-52
Hovell, M.F. 143-146
Huberman, M. 189
Humphries, C.A. 101-105

I

Imwold, C. 79-83
inclusion 111-117. *See also* students with special needs
Individual Teacher Behavior and Analysis System (ITBAS) 8
in-service teacher development 143-146, 147-150
instruction
  direct 65-69
  with environmental cues 65-69
  explicit 82
  individualized 116
instructional tasks 53-54
integrated classes 49-52. *See also* inclusion; students with special needs

J

James, W. 172
Johnson, D.W. 198
Johnson, M.E.B. 189
Johnson, R.T. 198
Journal of Sport Pedagogy 180-181
Journal of Teaching in Physical Education 181

K

Kagan, S. 202
Kauchak, D. 188
Kelly, E.J. 189
Kelly, L.E. 131-134
Kennedy, M.M. 190
Kinchin, G. 111-117
kindergarten and first-grade children 73-78
knowledge obsolescence 189-190
Kolody, B. 143-146
Kounin, J. 197

L

LaMaster, K. 111-117
Laurencelle, L. 167-171

ABOUT THE AUTHORS

Lawrence F. Locke, PhD, is professor emeritus of education and physical education at the University of Massachusetts at Amherst. He has written extensively on the application of research to teaching and teacher education, and he has authored several books about how to plan and fund educational inquiry as well as how to understand research reports.

As a teacher, graduate advisor, and consultant, Locke has supervised many studies of physical education. Much of his work has focused on the use of the qualitative research paradigm in the study of teachers, teaching, and teacher development. He recently received the Clark Hetherington Award for lifetime achievement in scholarship and service from the American Academy of Kinesiology and Physical Education. He also was honored when the American Educational Research Association's annual selection of the outstanding doctoral dissertation in physical education was designated as the Lawrence F. Locke Award. His numerous awards include the NAPEHE Dudley Allen Sargent Scholar Award, the NASPE Curriculum and Instruction Academy Honor Award, the NAPEHE Distinguished Scholar Award, and the AAHPERD Presidential Citation Award.

A native of Connecticut, Locke received his bachelor's and master's degrees from Springfield College and a PhD from Stanford University. He makes his home in Sunderland, Massachusetts with his wife, Professor Lorraine Goyette; he spends part of each year writing, running, and exploring the Beartooth Mountains at Sky Ranch in Reedpoint, Montana. He can be contacted at lflocke@hotmail.com.

Dolly Lambdin, EdD, knows firsthand what physical education teachers face, having taught for 16 years at the elementary school level and for 24 years at the university level. During much of this time, she taught simultaneously at both levels, a situation that required her to spend part of each day meeting the teaching and research demands of academia while tackling the daily adventure of teaching 5- to 12-year-olds.

Lambdin began her conversations with Lawrence Locke during her undergraduate years at the University of Massachusetts at Amherst, where he was her mentor. She received her master's degree at Columbia University and her doctorate at the University of Massachusetts. Lambdin has served on numerous local, state, and national committees, including the writing teams for the Texas Essential Knowledge and Skills in Physical Education, the NASPE Beginning Teacher Standards, and the NASPE Cabinet. Lambdin has recently been named the Texas AHPERD Outstanding College and University Physical Educator of the Year. Lambdin is a senior lecturer in the Department of Kinesiology and Health Education at the University of Texas at Austin, where she teaches courses in children's movement, methods of teaching, and issues and trends and has supervised more than 60 student teachers.

Her passions are playing with her family and friends, camping, canoeing, and spending summers in a cabin by a lake in Maine. She lives in Austin with her husband, Larry Abraham, and their two children, Andrew and Becca. She can be contacted at lambdin@mail.utexas.edu.